POLITICAL IDEAS OF SARDAR VALLABHBHAI PATEL

POLITICAL IDEAS OF SARDAR VALLABHBHAI PATEL

Sikata Panda

KALPAZ

ISBN: 978-81-7835-999-1

Price : ₹ 960

First Published 2014

Published by

Kalpaz Publications
C-30, Satyawati Nagar,
Delhi - 110052
E-mail: kalpaz@hotmail.com Ph.: 9212142040

Laser Typesetting : Rajender Vashist, Delhi

Printed at : G. Print Process, Delhi

Cataloging in Publication Data--DK
Courtesy: D.K. Agencies (P) Ltd. <docinfo@dkagencies.com>

Panda, Sikata.

Political ideas of Sardar Vallabhbhai Patel / Sikata Panda.
p. cm.
Includes bibliographical references.
ISBN 9788178359991

1. Patel, Vallabhbhai, 1875-1950–Political and social views. 2. India–Politics and government–20th century. I. Title.

DDC 954.035 23

Dedicated to

My Dear Father

Contents

Preface

The present study entitled "Political Ideas of Sardar Vallabhbhai Patel" is a research work that pertains to the academic realm of Political Thought. The relevance of the study of Political Thought derives from the fact that it contains alternative models of state and state-individual relationships from which mankind may select, emulate and approximate for realising the goal of best Political Existence. It, thus contains political visions and ideas of intellectuals and scholars and constitutes a store-house of wisdom and knowledge on the model state and the Political Society. This academic enterprise has been and is being upgraded by the intellectual contributions of both Western and Eastern Thinkers over a period of time. Indian scholars, intellectuals, leaders, and statesmen have also immensely contributed to enrich it and their contributions may be captioned as 'Indian Political Thought'.

Among modern Indian Political Thinkers and men of ideas, Vallabhbhai Patel stands out as a bold and towering figure. The importance of Vallabhbhai derives from the fact that he was a great leader and statesman in both the pre-independence and post-independence periods and above all, he was an astute architect of the modern Indian Nation–State. He was not a visionary, but a man of pragmatic ideas. He sought to synthesise Western political ideas and principles with Indian socio-political values and traditions for realising the goal of best political existence for the people of India in contemporary time. Hence, this academic endeavour has been undertaken to delineate and portray the pattern of his political ideas in a coherent way as an alternative model for appraisal and appreciation.

The present work spreads over six chapters. Chapter 1 is the introductory chapter which highlights the relevance of the research work, provides an overview of relevant literature, outlines the major objectives of the study, and spells out the methodology adopted for the purpose of this work. Chapter 2 deals with the life sketch of Vallabhbhai, with an aim to find out the impact of various personalities and events upon him in the context of formation of his political orientations. Chapter 3 delineates the pattern of Vallabhbhai's political values concerning Rights, Liberty, Equality and Justice. Chapter 4 focuses on Vallabhbhai's ideas on the Nation–State. Chapter 5 analyses the contributions of Vallabhbhai as a Nation builder. Chapter 6 contains concluding remarks which outline the pattern of political ideas of Vallabhbhai.

The research work has been prepared under the guidance of Dr S.P. Guru, Professor in the Post-Graduate Department of Political Science and Public Administration, Sambalpur University (Odisha). I would like to express my profound sense of gratitude to him for his constant support, encouragement and guidance at all stages in preparation of this work.

This work would not have been possible without the kind gesture of the University Grants Commission, New Delhi. It sanctioned a Minor Research Project and provided me financial support to undertake the research work.

I am grateful to the staff members of libraries of Nehru Memorial Museum, National Archives of India, Jawaharlal Nehru University, Delhi University, Indian Institute of Public Administration, Indian Council of World Affairs, Central Secretariat and that of Parliament for the academic cooperation I have received from them during my research work. I acknowledge the help and cooperation of the staff of the libraries of Sambalpur University, Gangadhar Meher College, Sambalpur, Utkal University, Harekrushna Mahatab Library and State Archive, Bhubaneswar.

I express my gratitude to my parents and parents-in-law for their consistent support and moral encouragement and for extending every possible help to carry out this research work. I am thankful to my son Nippon who suffered the most during the research work but extended full cooperation. I am in dearth of words to express my heartfelt thanks to my husband Dr Manas Ranjan Pujari for being a constant source of inspiration to me all these years.

Sikata Panda

1

Introduction

1.1 The Research Problem

The present topic on which an in-depth, descriptive and analytical research work is intended to be undertaken is "Political Ideas of Sardar Vallabhbhai Patel." It is a research work that pertains to the realm of Modern Indian Political Thought, and its relevance is derived from the fact that it seeks to enquire into, and delineate the pattern of political ideas of Vallabhbhai Patel who was a great political leader of modern India and also an architect of the Indian Nation–state.

1.1.1 Nature of Political Thought

In the most general sense of the term, "Political Thought is Thought about Politics".[1] It may be defined as: "A system of political ideas in its most complete sense."[2] Since politics pertains to the affairs of the state, and the state is the highest political organisation of the society, Political Thought relates to thought about the state. It connotes an inherent conceptual scheme, designed on state and state-individual relationship for attainment of the goal of the Best Political Life. In this context, focussing on the nature and themes of Political Thought, William Archibald Dunning emphatically points out: "...it contains a set of well-defined ideas...in reference to the origin, nature and scope of state and authority through which the relations of members of the community to one another are determined."[3] C.L. Wayper succinctly points out: "Political Thought is thought about the state, its nature, its structure and its purpose. Its concern is nothing less than the moral phenomena of human behaviour in society. It seeks not so much an explanation of the existence of the state as a justification of its continuation. What is the state and why should I obey it? What are the proper limits of its authority and whom may I refer to obey it? How is the authority of the state with which I cannot dispense to be made compatible with the liberty without which I am less than a man? These are the questions which Political Thought is forever striving to answer."[4] It, therefore, contains ideas concerning the origin and nature of the state, its structures and functions, and its ends and purposes which are sought to be realised through the functioning of its agent called the Government[5]. It also contains ideas concerning the relationship between the state and individual, the rulers and the ruled, the Government and the governed, the extent of the state-authority, and ideas such as individual rights, liberty, equality and justice and the bases of political obligation[6]. All these political ideas constitute a coherent conceptual scheme that focuses on the best state or the best political society and contains prescriptions and recommendations for realising the goal of the best political life. As such, it is concerned with, points out Andrew Hacker: "the search for the principles of the good state and the good society"[7]. It is also concerned with, opines William T. Bluhm: "Search for meaning in society and politics."[8] Political Thought, thus, is the outcome of intellectual exercises and it manifests the vision and values of the thinkers on state and politics.

The political thinker, in course of explaining the political phenomena of his time, carves out the blueprint of the model state on the basis of his vision of man. It is then the concept of human nature that constitutes the foundation of his model state and his intended pattern of state-individual relationship for realising the goal of the Best Political Life.[9] Of course, the basic assumptions of fundamental postulates on human nature may be formed on the employment of either the Deductive or Inductive method.[10] Both the methods are reasoning processes, and the basic difference between them is that the Deductive method is intuitive and speculative whereas the Inductive method is factual and realistic.[11] In case of the Deductive method, concept of human nature is formed through intuition, speculation and reflection, and reasoning proceeds from the general to the particular, whereas in case of the Inductive method, concept of human nature is formed through observation and experience, and reasoning proceeds from the particular to the general.[12] Either the deductive method, focussing on idealism or the inductive method, relying upon realism, may be employed in forming basic assumptions on human nature, for which the blueprint of the model state in terms of the nature and goal, state-individual relationship is conceptualised and designed. Accordingly, Political Thought may be classified into two types such as the Idealist Political Thought and Empirical Political Thought.[13]

Concepts on the nature and structure of the state and state-individual relationship may also be formed in two different perspectives such as the organic perspective and mechanistic perspective[14]. In case of the organic perspective, the state is envisioned as a natural organism of which the individuals are merely parts. Hence, the state is considered as an end in itself and the individuals are thought of as means for subserving the state and attainment of its goal. The individual is required to identify his interest with the interests and goals of the state and to become duty-conscious and duty-bound, to render unquestioning obedience to the authority of the state as manifested in its directions, laws and policies. As distinguished from it, the Mechanistic perspective portrays the state as an artificial mechanism, deliberately created by individuals for their own good. Hence, the state is considered as an instrument, as a means to the goal or end of the individuals, who have formed it. Thus, these two perspectives portray the nature of the state and the state-individual relationship in different directions. Whereas the organic view makes the state authoritarian in its relationship with the individuals, the mechanistic perspective presents the blueprint of the liberal state that champions and upholds the rights and liberty of its people and makes them the decision-makers of their own good and welfare. Thus, Political Thought may also be classified into two types such as the Authoritarian Political Thought and Liberal Political Thought.

Moreover, ideas and concepts of the model state and state-individual relationship as formed by the thinkers, tend to bear and reflect the impact of the prevailing socio-economic and political conditions of the society. The thinker, being a member of the society, cannot remain immune and indifferent to such influences. As an intellectual, he subjects the contemporary societal conditions to scrutiny and tends to form his vision and views either for justifying or for transforming it so as to realise the goal of the Best Political Life. Thus, Political Thought is "secreted....in the interstices of political and social crises"[15] and "it is designed for solving socio-political crises and turmoil."[16] In the context of the intellectual enterprise, "if the model of state as designed by the Thinkers justifies the prevailing pattern of political existence and favours socio-political customs and traditions, including the status of the individual and his right to private property, his Political Thought may be classified as Conservative Political Thought."[17] On the contrary, Political Thought may be classified as Critical or Radical Political thought,[18] if it provides for a new model of political society which is antagonistic to the conventional political order and hostile to the individual privilege and private property.

Thus, Political Thought may be classified into various types and kinds, particularly based on methods of study, vision about the genesis and goals of the state, and views on individual-state relationship, involving issues such as rights, liberty, equality, justice and political obligation. Accordingly, it may be classified as Inductive or deductive Political Thought, idealist or empirical Political Thought, Authoritarian or Liberal Political Thought and conservative or radical Political Thought.

Thus, there are various kinds and types of Political Thought, presenting models of state and state-individual relationship. These intellectual enterprises endeavour not only to classify political terms and to give them precision and definitions,[19] but also they provide alternative models of political society for realising the goal of the Best Political Life. Theories of state as conceptualised and formed by Political Thinkers, therefore, provide intellectual insights to mankind to choose from these political alternatives, and to structure their political life and existence accordingly. Without Political Thought containing the theory of the state, mankind would grapple in dilemma in search of the best political Life. On this tremendous importance and relevance of Political Thought, Arnold Brecht emphatically points out: "It is the function of the political theorist to see sooner than others and to analyse more profoundly than others, the immediate and the potential problems of the political life of the society; to supply the practical politicians, well in advance, with alternative courses of action, the foreseeable consequences of which have been fully thought through; and to supply him not only with brilliant guides but also with a solid block of knowledge on which to build. When political theory performs its functions well, it is one of the most important weapons in our struggle for advance of humanity. To imbue people with correct theories may make them choose their goals and means wisely so as to avoid the roads that end in terrific disappointment."[20] As Political Thought in course of offering solutions for the contemporary problems, illuminates principles of political actions for any civilised society, it is of relevance for the posterity, too. David Thomson argues: "Political Thought, like any other kind of thought is fully understood only by relating it to the context of time, place and personality in which it occurred. But, the ideas of a great thinker are not necessarily or even probably, 'representative' of the thought of his time. They are more likely to be heretical and unrepresentative.... The great political thinkers deserve to be read carefully because they are men of genius who concerned themselves with complex human problems which cannot escape from in our own lives."[21] Hence, the study of Political Thought seems to be a worthy and highly deserving academic enterprise.

1.1.2 Nature and Themes of Indian Political Thought

In view of the relevance of Political Thought for the mankind, it is quite pertinent to analyse the socio-political ideas of Indian intellectuals, leaders and statesmen, and to bring to light the distinguishing attributes and themes of Indian Political Thought. It has become, therefore, necessary to highlight the contributions of Indian Political Thinkers to the realm of Political Thought as a whole.

Indian Political Thought, beginning from the Classical Hindu interpretation down to the Modern thinking has managed to retain a remarkable continuity.[22] Though the portrayal of human nature from a spiritual perspective blurs the distinction between philosophy and politics, yet such an analysis seems to have provided it with a more or less consistent thinking on the best political life, or the desired pattern of individual-state relationship involving issues like the extent of Rights, Liberty, equality, justice and the grounds of political obligation. Thus, in India, the whole edifice of politics revolves round the spiritual nature of man which reflects upon the purposes of social organisations and nature of political authority.

The Hindu Political Thinkers believe that the universe is characterised by '*Rta*', the inviolable cosmic order which is regulated by the operation of laws, representing the divine intelligence. The individual is viewed as an integral part of the cosmic order. He is known to have the element of eternal Absolute Consciousness in him, and hence is endowed with a sense of dignity. He has a spark of divinity which motivates him to undertake his assigned duty or *Dharma*, an element governing the cosmic order.[23] Both God and the Absolute Consciousness in individual being above experience, are equated as divine. It has been rightly observed: "God as the material and instrumental efficient cause of the world cannot be regarded as wholly different from the Absolute."[24] Thus, as in case of the West, in India the individual has not been portrayed as the materialistic vitalistic agglomeration of physical and chemical elements with a distinct self identity.[25] Rather, as an essential part of the cosmic order, he is expected to know himself and internalise true freedom through 'salvation'. In the Hindu philosophy, the goal refers to a pre-determined process of realisation of spiritual freedom. The ultimate objective of freedom entails within itself the scope for equality which ensures a sense of fraternity and paves the way for holding the universe together. It urges each and everyone to become fearless of the internal and external barriers and realise himself. But, this does not imply an independent life for him. As man has to undertake the responsibilities depicted by *Dharma*, he has to rise above narrow self-interest and lead a moral and virtuous life. No doubt, he needs freedom of thought, expression and action but as an integral part of the universe, his freedom is far from absolute. He needs to suppress his lower self and become altruistic and humanistic both in his thinking and action. The objective of salvation depersonalises a man to a large extent, and motivates him to play such a role. Thus, human nature becomes instrumental in creating a just order.

The moral nature of man encourages him to be rational to become part of the prescribed rightful means for the end of the exploration of the divine self. Here, rationality does not refer to a self-seeking attitude, as depicted by the western political thinkers for a man in the market society. In fact, it implies giving honour to the divine dispensation through rightful means. The whole process appears to be in tune with the individual's nature that has been depersonalised for the goal of salvation. But, prior to the attainment of the final objective in life, he is expected to strive for other goals like *kama* (physical sustenance and procreation), *Artha* (economic utilitarian goals) and *Dharma* (moral obligations). Any how, all these goals are complimentary to the ultimate desire for salvation. The individual, given his responsibility towards others, is supposed to pursue after them within certain limits. Thus, the strive for materialism has been made secondary to the objective of spiritualism. Endowed with different qualities like *Sattva* (brightness), *Raja* (commitment for duty) and *Tama* (inclination for worldly desires), man pursues these goals in different phases of his life like *Brahmacharya* (stage of learning), *Garhastha* (stage of householder), *Vanaprastha* (stage of relative withdrawal) and *Sanyasa* (stage of complete withdrawal). Such a pre-determined scheme is devoid of any personal decision. Betty Heimann rightly observes: "For the Indian personification in this or another form is but a momentary appearance which in the following moments may be cast off, or exchanged for another form in the cosmic course of events. 'Person', thus interpreted, never gains the value of constancy or finality."[26] Hence, in each station, an individual is expected to perform his *karma* or follow the right means. Indian political philosophy links the concept of '*Dharma*' and '*Karma*' inextricably. If *Dharma* assigns the station and goal of life, *Karma* defines the rightful means to realise it.

The sense of righteousness in man and his rational mindset teach him to be conscious and tolerant towards other's existence. In India, the hold of *Dharma* upon the individual in general and inter-personal relationship in particular is much more comprehensive than mere religion. If religion refers to a faith in certain theology, sacrament and institutionalised ecclesiastical hierarchy, *Dharma* implies a way of life where the individual is supposed to perform his assigned duties, quite in conformity with his true-self, which is the 'divine-self' or moral self. Thus, *Dharma* makes man a secular being and ensures peaceful coexistence. It is mostly derived from the world outside the religion. Having its root in the *Vyavahara* (tradition and custom), *caritam* (conduct of good man) and *raja sasana* (royal edict), *Dharma* helps in the realisation of the cosmic order.[27]

Given the nature of human being, 'integral humanism' becomes the central theme of the Indian Political Thought. Even though guided by a pre-determined universal order, man endowed with a moral vision, rational mindset and secular attitude, becomes a key player in the realisation of expected inter-personal relationship in the society and the perfect ruler-ruled equation in the polity so as to reproduce the universal order.

For the Hindu Political Thinkers, the society represents the order of the universe, created to enable the individual to attain spiritual freedom. It is held together by the principle of *Dharma* and is an ordered whole. The very principle becomes the basis of personal and social life. Hence, the society is not a collection of individuals but a community of communities where each one is expected to perform his *Karma* (Role) in accordance with his *Dharma* (Duty). Such a pluralistic basis of the society bound by *Dharma*, has been perceived by Betty Heimann as: "Types instead of single individuals, series of times instead of single events are India's *foci* of research and investigation. India seeks for the combining and unifying factor within diversity and individuality. Her series and types are based on the dogma of an underlying unity beyond the accidental appearances of individuals and specific instances."[28] Thus, group becomes the basis of all societal relations. The representation of the society, through a network of groups, termed as 'caste' is an essential attribute of analysing the role of an individual. Hence, "Caste is seen as the foundation and core of Indian civilisation; it is responsible for the transmission and reproduction of the society in India."[29] But, the caste groups such as the *Brahmans*, *Kshatriya*, *Vaishya* and *Shudra* are hierarchically organised either in terms of function, or status which makes the Indian society highly inegalitarian. In fact, religion plays a crucial role in legitimising social inequality. Weber argues: "caste is and remains essentially social rank and the central position of the Brahmanas in Hinduism rests primarily upon the fact that social rank is determined with reference to Brahmanas."[30] The permanence of the unequal order restricts to a large extent the scope for any sectional interest which may violate the principle of *Dharma* and lead to anarchy. Thus, the Indian society appears to be highly conservative. It revolves round the prescribed moral order and rules out the possibility of social conflict. Karl Marx believed such representation of the society had given rise to 'oriental despotism'. To him, it seems to have restricted the human mind within the smallest possible compass, making it the unresisting tool of superstition, enslaving it beneath traditional rules, depriving it of all grandeur and historical energies[31]. But the assessment seems to be too sweeping. The successive foreign invasions, emergence of heretical groups within the fold of Hinduism and growth of trade and commerce provided ample scope for individual initiatives like inter-marriages.[32] The deeply held moral principles of respect for each others strengthened the pluralist social base within the broadly defined hierarchical set-up. Rajni Kothari rightly concludes: "Steeped in the tradition of pluralism... (as distinct from the mere political pluralism as found in Western democracies) and in a conception of unity based on dispersed identities and shared value, endowed with a non-theological religious pedigree, without a fixed doctrine or an official clergy and given its high tolerance of ambiguity and deeply ingrained tradition of skepticism, India may be better placed than most societies to carve out a niche for itself in a world undergoing great transformation."[33]

Indian Political Thinkers favour a political authority to take care of the deviants of the moral order. Human beings can fall victim to illusions and temptations and deviate from his *Dharma*. Hence, the polity has been created to regulate such people through *Danda* or punishment in order to ensure *Dharma* and restore the cosmic order. Thus, *Dharma* and *Danda* are considered to be the essence of Indian Political Philosophy. Hindu political writings can be broadly divided into two categories. While the works on *Dharmashastras* tend to philosophise the role of the individual and appear to be moralistic, the advocates of *Dandaniti* emphasise upon the ruler-ruled relationship and seem to be realistic. Nevertheless, politics has been perceived by both to cover the whole range of social activity, affecting the relationship between the ruler and the ruled. It has been rightly observed: "The theory of *Shanti Parva* in the *Mahabharata* makes the sphere of activity of politics co-terminus with the state itself. The state should ceaselessly foster righteousness, guide, control and correct the moral life of the people, make the world habitable and comfortable for men."[34] Here, political authority, as a means, is supposed to facilitate the study of the Vedas and philosophy, encourage the development of industry and commerce, maintain inter-caste relationship and ensure the observance of *Dharma* in different stages of individual's life. The king as the head of the polity has been empowered to enforce *Danda* for the maintenance of *Dharma*. But, in no stage he has been allowed to be a despot. Palmer argues: "Such a philosophy sustains a conception of the state not as a Leviathan or as the '*terminus ad quem* of man's whole development', but as a means to the attainment by man his self-realisation."[35] The limited nature of authority is revealed from its elective and contractual character. Obligation to the authority is linked with the ability to ensure *Dharma*. Here, the elaborate process of king's coronation reflects the respect given to the office than the person in power. The king's position appears to be conditional as "Sovereignty is established as a result of a compact by which in return for protection, the people consented to obey and to pay taxes to the sovereign."[36] Very often, the comparison of the king with various divine entities reminds him of his moral responsibilities towards the people. The attempt to regulate the authority through *Dharma*, customs, various deliberative bodies like Sabha and Samiti and other autonomous socio-economic groups reflects the restricted jurisdiction of the political authority. Kautalya's view of the ruler as an organism consisting of 'seven limbs' reveals the spirit of division of power[37]. In fact, the very argument that kingship in India has never involved in Plenary Sovereignty,[38] substantiates the role of the king as a means for the restoration of the order where the divine self of the individual can fulfill himself.

With the advent of the British traders in India in the Sixteenth Century and the subsequent establishment of the British Colonial Regime, the Indian socio-political arena became open to influences of Western ideas, ethos and traditions. Moreover, the introduction of English education contributed tremendously in reinforcing and fostering the impact of Western socio-political ideas upon the Indian intellectuals, elites and leaders in the context of formation of their vision and views on society and polity, and helped in the process of evolution of Indian political thinking. The Renaissance in Indian political thinking commenced because of the influence of Western ideas and education. As the process coincided with the colonial exploitative policies, revivalism became equally dominant in Indian Renaissance.[39] The aspiration of the people to have an independent Nation–State had a deep impact upon the evolution of Modern Indian Political Thought. In course of seeking to synthesise the basic socio-political values of both India and the West, it has evolved over the years. Thus viewed, Modern Indian Political Thought can be divided into three categories. The first one makes more or less an imitative reproduction of the West; the second advocates the revival of the classical tradition and the third and the most numerical one makes a creative blending of both the paradigms of politics.[40]

Modern Indian political thinking began with the first group of thinkers who were advocates of the British administration in India. Such an articulation was initiated in the mid-nineteenth century by Rammohun Roy. He was inspired by the Western rational spirit and wanted to reform the Indian society accordingly to restore the dignity of the individual. His favourable attitude towards the British rule was due to its ability to ensure security and civil liberty and bring economic development through the introduction of the capitalist mode of production[41]. This view was reiterated a few years after by a section of Congress leaders like Surendranath Banerjee, Dadabhai Naoroji, Gopalkrishna Gokhle and others. Given the constraint of the period, these thinkers supported the British rule despite its loopholes as the best possible alternative. Gokhale declared: "The Western type of administrative machinery has been substituted in place of what once we had. The country enjoys new uninterrupted peace and order, justice though costly, is fairly dispensed . . . . Then, you have introduced Western education with freedom of speech and freedom of writing. These are all things that stand to your credit."[42] Though, this group argued that sustenance of the British link was possible on the basis of fulfillment of mutual obligations by both the ruler and ruled, such as protection of rights and liberty and payment of tax, yet it could hardly visualise any alternative to the British regime in the given period. On the whole, it introduced the essence of Western democracy like personal rights, individual freedom, conditional political obligations etc. and reposed full confidence upon the alien power to associate the people of India in the administration gradually to ensure all such privileges for them.

In contrast to the first group, the second one put tremendous faith in the moral foundation of Indian Political Thought which was inclusive enough to regulate human nature, inter- personal relationship and the nature of polity itself. It emerged as a defence mechanism against the impact of the alien political power and contributed a lot for the growth of Indian nationalism. A new humanist and cosmopolitan interpretation was made upon the old writings. Hence, it criticised the first group: "the last generation merely attempted to initiate and reproduce with a servile fidelity the ideas and forms of the West."[43] This group was inspired by people like Dayananda Saraswati, Vivekananda, Aurobindo and others. It highlighted the superiority of spiritual (inner) domain of India over the material (outer) domain of the West. Such conceptualisation emphasised upon the inherent goodness of man and creation of a conducive atmosphere for the realisation of the divine self. Vivekananda reminded the people about the concept of spiritual equality and realisation of spiritual freedom[44]. In tune with his predecessor, Aurobindo argued: "The master idea that has governed the life, culture, social ideals of the Indian people has been the seeking of man for his true spiritual self and the use of life."[45] Hence, in pursuance of Dayananda's earlier emphasis upon the religious scriptures to reform the society,[46] he urged to restore the dignity of individual by reviving the old values. In fact, the emphasis upon the past conveyed the message of national superiority and led to the birth of Indian nationalism. Aurobindo claimed: "Foreign rule is unnatural and fatal to a Nation precisely because by its very nature it throws itself upon these activities and capacities and crushes them down in the interests of its own continued existence. Even when it does not crush them down violently, it obstructs their growth passively by its very presence. The subject nation becomes dependent, disorganised and loses its powers by atrophy. For this reason, national independence is necessary for national growth."[47] Thus, demand for political liberty became a means for the realisation of spiritual freedom. In fact, this group believed that the society should be a pluralistic set-up, meant more for private rather than the political sphere of human conduct. Hence, to restore the dignity of individual, if people like Dayananda restricted the political sphere by elevating the status of the ruled as the 'king of the kings,'[48] Vivekananda criticised the excessive thrust upon the growth of political structures.[49] In the same vein Aurobindo argued: "Indian polity never arrived at that unwholesome substitution of the mechanical for the natural order of the life of the people which has been the disease of the European civilisation, now culminating in the monstrous artificial organisation or the bureaucratic and industrial state."[50] Thus, protection of individual dignity with the help of an indigenous and regulated political set-up was the essence of the second category of advocates of Modern Political Thinking.

The last group made a synthesis of the old values with that of Western concepts, and presented it in a new format. Viewed from this perspective Indian Political Thought can be termed as 'modern' from a chronological sense as there is much in it that was traditional.[51] The originality of this group lay in being able to adopt the Western concepts into the experiences of a non-Western society. It was best represented by Ranade, Tilak, Gandhi, and Nehru. The inherited old values, Appadorai points out, relate to consent as the basis of exercise of power, dependence of ends upon the means, regulation of wants to ensure the well-being of all, self-government to provide good governance, decentralisation as a means to limit the authority and personal suffering as a technique of persuasion.[52] At the same time, the last group incorporated many Western concepts such as nationalism, republicanism, constitutionalism and concepts of personal rights and liberty. Exposure to such Western liberal political values created a fertile ground for further growth of Indian nationalism. If the British exploitative policies were responsible for the growth of revivalism in the past, the Western rational outlook deeply influenced the Indian mind which subsequently prepared the ground work for the demand of 'self-determination' status. Ranade was inspired by the growth of regulated capitalism in Germany, Italy, and France, and raised voice against British exploitation. Subsequently, Tilak was influenced by the ideas of Mazzini, Mill and Burke, and his ideas shaped the growth of Indian nationalism. Gandhi's idea of Sarvodaya was invoked, to a large extent, by the Western anarchist tradition, and his views on Sarvodaya echoed the spirit of participatory democracy. Last but not the least, the intellectual and social influence of the West appeared to have largely moulded the liberal democratic ideas of Nehru. He confessed: "my roots are still perhaps partly in the Nineteenth century and I have been too much influenced by the humanist, liberal tradition to get out of it completely.[53] In fact, he succeeded in redefining the role of the state to ensure the political, economic and social justice for the individual. All these factors provided opportunities for synthesising the socio-political ideas of India with that of the West. Hence, it has been rightly observed: "The modern Indian intellectuals no longer accept a doctrine, secular or religious, merely because it is the result of European civilisation. They search for new standards of their own outside Europe and its ways . . . . Despite their Western preoccupations, it is towards their own traditions that their loving gaze is turned. Their study of Shakespeare, Milton, Bacon and Locke does not in the least diminish their reverent allegiance to the Asiatic heroes, poets, saints and law-givers of old."[54]

Thus, the Indian Political Thought, characterised by a moral foundation, non-dualistic epistemology and metaphysics, appears to be quite distinct from that of the West. V.R. Mehta points out: "While Western Thought works in terms of antagonism, dichotomies and antimonies between spirit and matter, the individual and society, bread and culture, necessity and freedom, Indian Thought has always considered such dichotomies as artificial and unreal."[55] With a distinct continuity maintained over a period of time, the Modern Indian Political Thought reiterates the old value of 'integral humanism' in course of incorporating new Western values of liberal democracy, welfarism, and political nationalism.

1.1.3 Importance of Vallabhbhai Patel

Modern Indian Political Thought has been enriched by the intellectual contributions of many scholars, leaders and statesmen among whom Vallabhbhai occupies a place of special importance. As a great political leader of modern India, he dominated the Indian political scene from 1917 to 1950. He served the country in various capacities. During the pre-independence period, he dedicated his life to the freedom struggle. He then played a decisive role in reorganising the Indian National Congress, the most prominent political party of the period, into a disciplined, mass-based organisation. He provided an effective leadership to it during its struggle for independence. As India became independent of the British rule on 15th August 1947, Vallabhbhai was entrusted with the most important and sensitive portfolios like the home and states. He also served as the country's first Deputy Prime Minister. When, in the days following the partition, the country was strife torn, he strove hard to establish order and discipline. He was instrumental in taking measures to restructure the Bureaucracy and infusing in it a new spirit of vigour. Also, as the Minister of States, he played a key role in convincing the rulers of the Princely States to become part of the Indian Union and succeeded in maintaining the unity of India. Last but not the least, he contributed significantly in laying down the foundation of political democracy in India by playing a significant role in the drafting of the Constitution of India. Thus, he appeared to be an astute leader and a sagacious statesman. He is, therefore, acknowledged by many as the 'Iron Man' and builder of modern India. Hence, an in-depth study and analysis of his socio-political ideas seem to be a highly deserving academic enterprise.

1.2 Overview of Literature

The whole range of available literature on Vallabhbhai Patel can be divided into two segments. The first one covers the works by Vallabhbhai himself. It includes mostly his letters and speeches, made available in various private papers, newspapers and collected works. Unlike most of his contemporaries, Vallabhbhai had little faith in writing his ideas and experiences for the purpose of records.[56] Hence, whatever letters and speeches written and delivered by him in different contexts have become an important source of literature on him. As regard the second category of source-materials, it includes works on Vallabhbhai by both Indian and foreign scholars, and these are mostly biographical and issue based works.

1.2.1 Letters and Speeches of Vallabhbhai Patel

A collection of important speeches delivered by Vallabhbhai in between 1947-49 has been published by the Publication Division, Government of India, under the title '*On Indian Problems*.'[57] Subsequently, an enlarged version of it has been published by the same publication and is entitled '*For a United India*.'[58] These books reveal Vallabhbhai's ideas on the integration of states, communal harmony, economic and defence policies.

Another volume of Vallabhbhai's speeches has been compiled by Narahari Dwarikadas Parikh and Uttamchand Deepchand Shah under the title '*Sardar Patel Ke Bhashan*.'[59] The book covers the views of Vallabhbhai on various issues beginning from his public career in 1918 up to independence of the country in 1947. It gives special thrust on the events in the early part of his life, his role in the Ahmedabad civic body and the Non-Cooperation Movement.

The Official Report of the Constituent Assembly Debates[60] also reveals the ideas of Vallabhbhai particularly on the issues of Fundamental Rights, Provincial Constitution and Minorities.

Many private papers of great statesman like Gandhi,[61] Nehru,[62] Rajendra Prasad,[63] N.B. Khare,[64] Govind Vallabh Pant,[65] and B.G. Khare[66] throw light on Vallabhbhai. These people record the views of the leader as they came in contact with him in various capacities. Of all these people, Gandhi and Nehru Papers appear to be more exhaustive on Vallabhbhai. In subsequent period, the exchange of letters between Gandhi and Vallabhbhai has been published as '*Letters to Sardar Vallabhbhai Patel.*'[67] In his own private paper,[68] Vallabhbhai records many exclusive events of his life. Besides covering his role in the Ahmedabad Municipality, Borsad, Nagpur and Bordoli *Satyagrahas*, Patel Papers give a vivid account of his experience in the provincial administrative set-up of the 1930's and that of the National Administration in the post-independence period. Various files of the Congress Party, particularly in relation to Elections, Provincial Administration etc. refer widely to the comments of Vallabhbhai Patel.[69] Many Government records on the policies of the then British Government towards freedom struggle also throw light on Vallabhbhai.[70]

Vallabhbhai's letters written in between 1945-1950 have been edited by Durgadas in his ten volumes of work '*Sardar Patel's Correspondence.*'[71] The series covers the correspondences of the leader, made particularly in the capacity of the Minister of Home both in the Interim Government and the First Cabinet of the country. These books highlight his role in the context of Kashmir, central and provincial elections of 1946, supervision over provincial ministries, partition, integration of states, Hyderabad police action, refugee rehabilitation and in the formulation of the foreign and defence policies of the country. The sixth and tenth volumes refer extensively to his differences with the Prime Minister Nehru.

Two volumes of letters of Vallabhbhai Patel have been compiled by his Private Secretary V. Shankar. The books titled 'Sardar Patel: Select Correspondence,'[72] too, cover the same period from 1945-50. While the first volume relates to the 1946 election, negotiation with the Cabinet Mission, integration of Kashmir, communal uprisings etc., the second one focuses upon the working of the Interim Government.

G.M. Nandurkar has edited extensively the letters of Vallabhbhai Patel both in English and Gujarati. The English edition includes five Birth-Centenary volumes[73] and three Post-Centenary volumes.[74] The Birth-Centenary Series comprises of works such as '*This was Sardar: The Commemorative Volume*', '*Sardar Patel: In Tune with the Millions*' (I and II) and '*Sardar's Letters Mostly Unknown*' (I and II). The three volumes of Post-Centenary works have been published as '*Sardar's Letters Mostly Unknown*' (I, II and III). All these books except the commemorative one reflect views of Vallabhbhai on issues such as integration of states, bureaucracy, judiciary, press, party reorganisation, refugee rehabilitation, education, planning, provincial administration, communal harmony and labour organisations. Other series by the author such as '*Sardarshri Na Patro*' (5 Vols)[75] and '*Sardarshri Ke Patro*' (2 Vols)[76] are in Gujarati and depict views of the leader on various socio-economic problems.

P.N. Chopra in his fifteen volumes of compilation titled 'The Collected Works of Sardar Vallabhbhai Patel'[77] covers the whole public career of the leader from 1917-50. The collected letters highlight Vallabhbhai's various roles such as the leader of the grassroot mobilisations and various National Movements, President of the Congress Party, Chairman of the Congress Parliamentary Board, Member of the Constituent Assembly and that of his contributions as the Minister of Home and States. Besides the views of the leader, the whole series too includes various Government reports and newspapers comments made on Vallabhbhai. It translates many of his writings from Gujarati to English. Later on, the author has edited another volume of letters titled '*The Thematic Volume on Vallabhbhai* Patel: Kashmir and

Hyderabad'[78] which throws light on the leader's role in connection with the annexation of both the provinces.

1.2.2 Works on Vallabhbhai Patel

The works on Vallabhbhai Patel are basically of two types. The early writings on the leader are mostly biographical and narrative. Most of them analyse and explain the course of events through which the leader passed through during his lifetime. Hence, all these works not only unveil important aspects of his personalities and his ideas but also unfolds the history of the nation. The second category of writings is analytic and focuses upon any of the issues advocated and addressed by the leader.

Biographical Works

The first two biographical works on Vallabhbhai Patel have been published prior to independence. The books entitled '*The Iron Dictator: A Biographical Study of Gandhi's General*'[79] by Hiralal Sheth and '*The Leader by Merit*'[80] by Abdul Majid Khan highlight his role in the context of the reorganisation of the Congress especially during the freedom struggle. Abdul Majid Khan appreciates Vallabhbhai's effort in the late 1930's for his effort to infuse democratic spirit within the party against several odds.

The first exhaustive biographical work on Vallabhbhai has been done by Narahari D. Parikh. The two volumes of work titled '*Sardar Vallabhbhai Patel*'[81] give a detail account of his life and contributions. The first volume provides a deep insight into his upbringing and delineates his traits at the childhood stage which finally enabled him to become a successful leader. It also traces his association with Gandhi. The second volume concentrates on the developments of the Indian political scenario especially after the 1930's. It highlights his effort in redefining the position of the Congress particularly in relation to Gandhi, the socialists and the native princes. Though, the author covers the role of Vallabhbhai only up to the Quit India Movement, yet the work appears to be noteworthy for the minute analysis he has made after interaction with persons with whom the leader is known to have shared a close relation. The background information provides sufficient insight to assess Vallabhbhai in connection with the subsequent developments.

K.L. Panjabi in his book '*The Indomitable Sardar*'[82] presents a political biography of Vallabhbhai Patel. His work basically relates to the role of the leader as the party organiser, negotiator with the outgoing British authority, maker of the Constitution of India and as a ruthless administrator. In fact, he tries to assess his contribution as the builder of modern India. He compares the leader with Chanakya, the Prime Minister of Chandragupta Maurya for having the same sense of realism, decisiveness, and single-minded pursuit of his objective. He counters the allegations levelled against Vallabhbhai, holding him responsible for the partition of the country.

P.U. Patel's work '*Sardar Patel: India's Man of Destiny*'[83] traces the important personality traits of Vallabhbhai which supported him to play the role of a politician and statesman. He argues that his inherent qualities like independence, fearlessness, realism, toleration, and decision-making and organising abilities helped him to control the provincial Congress units and influence the British authority. The author also finds that the consistent approach of Vallabhbhai enabled him to cope with the differences with Azad and Nehru which emerged in course of carrying out the agenda of the nation building activities.

'*The Indian Triumvirate*'[84] by V.B. Kulkarni depicts the role of Vallabhbhai Patel as a patriot, provincial leader, disciplinarian and a statesman. It highlights the independent mindset of the leader which has provided him strength to differ from Gandhi both prior to and after independence and to play multifaceted role. The author too gives an account of the influence of the elder brother Vithalbhai upon the leader. He also makes a comparative assessment of the leadership of Gandhi, Nehru and Vallabhbhai.

D.V. Tahamankar in his work '*Sardar Patel*'[85] presents an exhaustive and analytical political biography of the leader. In course of his analysis, the author has consistently tried to link the national and international developments of the given period to grasp perfectly the motivations behind the various roles of the leader. Though, he has made a chronological analysis of the life events of Vallabhbhai, yet he puts more thrust upon his role played during the Second World War, leading to the initiation of the constitutional developments in the country. He makes a minute analysis of his contribution as the builder of modern India. He differentiates Vallabhbhai from Nehru and Gandhi and compares him with the Greek Statesman Pericles, known for not being loved but for commanding respect by virtue of his achievements.

The book of Susane Heredia titled '*A Patriot for Me*'[86] finds out the nationalistic orientation of Vallabhbhai in course of analysing his character and achievements. The author argues that such a mindset seems to have developed in him due to the influence of his family and community. Subsequently, she observes that Vallabhbhai's association with Gandhi appears to have strengthened it. Thus, the author finds it quite natural on the part of Vallabhbhai to have contributed to the articulation of the Foreign and Defence Policies of the country to strengthen the base of India.

Another political biography titled '*Sardar Patel*'[87] by L.N. Sarin summarises the achievements of Vallabhbhai as a statesman. He argues that unlike Gandhi's spiritualism and Nehru's idealism, it is Vallabhbhai's realism which enabled him to search for permanent solution for any given problem and distinguished him from the rest. Sarin believes such a trait helped him to understand the true meaning of Swaraj and convinced him to agree for partition, harmonise the relation between the capitalists and labour, introduce 'privy purse' for the native princes, reorganise the bureaucracy and be careful of aggressive neighbours.

B.K. Ahluwalia in his book '*Sardar Patel: A Life*'[88] presents the life sketch of the leader. The author in another book titled '*Facets of Sardar Patel*'[89], compiles several articles including that of Maniben, the daughter of Vallabhbhai, which unveil many significant aspects of his personality. The book highlights the role of Vallabhbhai as a freedom fighter, consolidator of India, maker of the Indian Constitution, Parliamentarian and supporter of minorities. B.K. Ahluwalia and Sashi Ahluwalia in their book titled '*Sardar Patel: Rebel and Ruler,*'[90] observe traits of flexibility in Vallabhbhai. His use of resistance and support to the authority depended on expediency. They argue that harmonisation of such traits enabled him to challenge the British authority effectively and take up the nation-building responsibilities subsequently.

S.R. Bakshi's book, '*The Bordoli Satyagraha*'[91] has been subsequently enlarged and published under the title '*Sardar Patel: His Political Ideology.*'[92] Here, the author finds that the concern for the nation to be the sole motivating factor behind all the actions of Vallabhbhai.

The work of Rajmohan Gandhi, '*Patel: A Life*'[93] is an exhaustive and analytical political biography. While giving an account of the life sketch of the leader, the author unveils the history of freedom struggle in India. It tries to clear many of the misgivings levelled against Vallabhbhai and thereby compares him with other leaders of his time. He argues that it is the leader's pragmatism which enabled him to rise above other contemporary leaders. The book throws new light on the Congress' acceptance of office in the thirties, Azad's portrayal of Vallabhbhai as communal, Gandhi's apparent partiality towards Nehru and the Socialists' irreconcilable differences with the leader.

P.N. Chopra's '*The Sardar of India*'[94] narrates the life and achievements of Vallabhbhai. It counters the allegations levelled against him that he was a reactionary and communal leader. Given Vallabhbhai's liberal economic thinking, grip over the provinces and ability to counter Pakistan, the author finds him relevant for the present Indian leadership, grappling with the challenges of globalisation, political instability and parochialism. He argues that Vallabhbhai's patriotism, practical knowledge and humane approach can still be of immense help in finding solutions to many of the current problems.

B. Krishna's '*Sardar Vallabhbhai Patel: India's Iron Man*'[95] depicts Vallabhbhai's hold over the party, influence upon the native Princes and command over the Bureaucracy. The author finds that such a grip over vital sectors seems to be the key to his success both during the freedom struggle and after the liberation of the country. He compares Vallabhbhai with Kautalya, the prominent kingmaker in the Maurya dynasty for his statesmanship and rates him more capable than Bismarck for integrating the country with the least use of force. He believes that without the practical approach of Vallabhbhai both Gandhi and Nehru would have hardly succeeded.

The book '*Inside Story of Sardar Patel: The Story of Maniben Patel (1936-50)*'[96] by P.N. Chopra and Prabha Chopra is based on the personal diary of Maniben, the daughter of Vallabhbhai Patel. It discloses many rare interviews and correspondences of Vallabhbhai during his stint as the Chairman of the Congress Parliamentary Sub-Committee. It also throws light on the differences between Nehru and Patel. Interestingly, Maniben claims these differences to have been blown out of proportion.

1.3 Issue-Based Works

The second category of writings analyses critically particular aspects of Vallabhbhai's achievements. A few of them focus directly on him and many others refer to him either in the context of partition or peasant mobilisation or that of party reorganisation. Mahadev Desai's '*The Story of Bordoli*'[97] is the first issue-based writing on him. Here, the author reflects upon the command of Vallabhbhai over the rural society of Gujarat which helped him to organise people during the Bordoli *Satyagraha* and to counter the British authority. In subsequent period, Ishwarlal I. Desai covers the same issue, almost with the same approach under the title '*Bordoli Satyagraha.*'[98]

Asoka Mehta's '*Economic Consequences of Sardar Patel*'[99] critically reviews the economic vision of Vallabhbhai. The author compares Vallabhbhai with Churchill and observes that his apparently liberal orientation emphasising upon the protection of personal endeavour, seems to have several adverse fallouts such as unemployment, labour retrenchment, imbalance trade ratio, inflation, etc.

V.P. Menon's '*The Story of the Integration of the Indian States*',[100] reveals the strategy of Vallabhbhai as the Minister of States, adopted to foil the British plan of balkanising India through the Cabinet Mission Plan. The book gives a detail account of Vallabhbhai's policy of integration designed to create the Union of India by bringing several constitutional, administrative and financial changes. The author, known to have played a key role in the integration process, gives a vivid description of the problems and prospects faced by Vallabhbhai in course of implementation of the task. He appears to be more elaborative for problematic states like Kashmir, Hyderabad and Junagarh.

'*The End of An Era*'[101] by K.M. Munshi reflects particularly upon the integration of Hyderabad with India. The author reveals the firmness of Vallabhbhai in pursuing the military operation in the state to counter the malafide intention of the Nizam and the fissiparous activities of the Razakars.

The work of Arya Ramchandra G. Tiwari titled '*Making of the Leader: Sardar Vallabhbhai Patel*,'[102] reveals the evolution of his leadership. He gives credit to Vallabhbhai's association with the Ahmedabad civic body which appears to have transformed him into a national leader.

N.V. Gadgil's book '*Government from Inside*'[103] discusses in detail the challenges experienced by the first Cabinet of the country. He gives sole credit to Vallabhbhai who seems to have played a significant role in maintaining the efficiency of the Government by infusing the democratic spirit of collective responsibility.

K.M. Munshi's two volumes of '*Indian Constitutional Documents*'[104] unfold the role of Vallabhbhai as the maker of the Indian Constitution. The book of B.S. Rao entitled '*The Framing of India's Constitution: A Study*'[105] too describes the contributions of Vallabhbhai in the making of the Constitution of India. The author analyses the leader's articulation made in the capacity of the Chairman of sub-committees on Fundamental Rights, Minorities and Provincial Constitution. Frank Anthony's book, 'Britain's Betrayal in India'[106] narrates Vallabhbhai's role as the Chairman of the Minority Sub-committee, particularly in the context of protecting the interests of the Anglo-Indian community.

The two volumes by V. Shankar, titled '*My Reminiscence of Sardar Patel*'[107] present a vivid account of Vallabhbhai's role both in the Interim government and the first cabinet of the country. The author reveals in detail the dissensions affecting the political set-up, characterised by a heterogeneous composition. He puts more thrust upon the Nehru-Patel differences especially on issues such as integration, communal organisations and formulation of economic and foreign policies. He narrates the attempts of both the leaders to influence the elections of the Congress Party President to have a grip over the political organisation and create a support base for the implementation of their vision of nation-building.

R.K. Murthi in his book '*The Man and his Contemporaries*'[108] finds out the essential traits of Vallabhbhai's personality. He believes that the leader's essential attributes like firmness, farsightedness, humane approach, pragmatism, patriotism etc. helped him in taking decisions at the crucial hour and made him more successful than any other leaders of his time.

The work of Devavrat Pathak and Pravin Sheth titled, '*Sardar Vallabhbhai Patel: From Civic to National Leadership*'[109] reveals a unique aspect of leadership of Vallabhbhai. The authors confine their work to his association in the civic body of Ahmedabad and believe that the leader's civic and national leadership developed therein simultaneously. They find that Vallabhbhai's innovation of '*linkage politics*' which had the potential to connect Ahmedabad-Gujarat-India through the Gandhian technique, seems to have brought success to the civic body and created enough political consciousness to lead any all India struggle. The authors conclude that this unique leadership ability transformed

Vallabhbhai from a provincial to national leader and distinguished him from the other contemporary leaders.

Rabindra Nath Kumar's book '*Role of Sardar Patel in the Integration of States*'[110] reflects upon Vallabhbhai's policies of integration. He appreciates the leader's innovative techniques like conciliation, good office, diplomacy from the position of strength and bargaining etc. He hails the leader for using minimum amount of force in all the stages of merger such as accession, reconstitution and centralisation.

Rani Dhavan Shankardass' book '*Vallabhbhai Patel: Power and Organisation in Indian Politics*'[111] reveals Vallabhbhai's faith in power structure to bring socio-economic changes. She finds that because of this conviction the leader with a high sense of realism, successfully managed to change his strategy from agitation to electoral participation and from horizontal to vertical mobilisations of people. She observes that in pursuance of his goal, he not only accepted the social hierarchy but also reorganised the political party as a ruthless disciplinarian. The book unfolds his strategy in building up the Congress as an alternative to the British power by sidelining successfully the Socialists and the Muslim League and grabbing skillfully all opportunities of negotiation.

Varinder Grover's '*Political Thinkers of Modern India: Sardar Vallabhbhai Patel*'[112] is a compilation of several articles by prominent personalities. All of them try to focus upon various aspects of his contributions.

'*The Last Days of Sardar Patel*'[113] by Vijaya Tendulkar depicts Vallabhbhai's difference of opinion with many other leaders on various issues of nation-building activities. The author appears to be more particular about the leader's relation with Azad and Nehru which exposed their different visions on the issue of partition and integration of Kashmir respectively.

Michael Lyon's book '*Sardar Patel and Indian Independence*'[114] reveals the attempt of Vallabhbhai to create a broad based Indian nationalism as a pre-requisite of a stable nation-state. The author believes that in this regard he had been helped by the comprehensiveness of the Hindu culture and the long duration of the freedom struggle to synthesise successfully the Western liberal values and transform his initial Anglophile outlook into anti-colonial mindset. The organised peasant base in Gujarat seems to have provided him with a fertile ground to spearhead Indian nationalism. Lyon argues that Vallabhbhai's strategy of horizontal and vertical mobilisation of the mass through various socio-economic groups and political party became successful due to his command over the rural social hierarchies and hold over the Princely States.

Rafiq Zakaria in his book '*Sardar Patel and Indian Muslims*'[115] tries to find out the veracity of the allegation levelled against Vallabhbhai that he was a man with communal leanings. The book has essentially two parts, dealing with his attitude towards the Muslims in India prior to partition and after partition. He finds Vallabhbhai to have a balanced approach towards all communities at least up to the forties and argues that the change in him seems to be due to the rise of the Muslim League and its agenda to create Pakistan and subsequently its nefarious designs to destablise the country. The author justifies his firm stand which became essential for the unity, integrity and the peaceful co-existence of the country. He tries to show the secular attitude of Vallabhbhai through his audacious agenda to reform the Hindu religion and keenness to show sympathy towards the minorities.

Rajula Jain's book '*Vallabhbhai Patel and the Indian National Congress (A Study 1934-1939)*'[116] reflects upon the role of Vallabhbhai in building the Congress party as an alternative to the British authority. The book highlights the sense of independence which motivated Vallabhbhai to deviate from Gandhi to monitor the Council-entry programme. It also depicts his grip as the Chairman of the Congress Parliamentary Sub-committee over the provinces.

The work of S.R. Maheswari titled '*Administrative Thinkers*'[117] describes the contribution of Vallabhbhai in reviving the Indian

Bureaucracy. The author compares his innovations with that of the rational-legal authority of Weber. He appreciates Vallabhbhai's effort to grant constitutional protection to the civil service to enable it to cope with the challenges of disintegration.

There has been another category of issue-based writings which examine Vallabhbhai indirectly either in the context of peasant mobilisations or party reorganisation or the partition of the country. Some of these works adopt a sociological perspective and examine the *Patidar* background of Vallabhbhai in the context of peasant uprisings in Gujarat. David Pocock's '*Kanbi and Patidar*,'[118] David Hardiman's 'Peasant Nationalists of Gujarat Kheda District (1917-34)'[119], Jan Berman's '*Peasant Migrants and Paupers: Rural and Labour Circulation and Capitalist Production in West India*,'[120] Shirin Mehta's, '*The Peasantry and Nationalism: A Study of the Bordoli Satyagraha*'[121] and D.N. Dhanangare's '*Peasant Movement in India: 1920-1950*'[122] refer widely to the solidarity-seeking trait, independent mindset and practical outlook of the *Patidar* community of Vallabhbhai which seems to have helped the leader to lead the peasant struggle. All of them argue that Vallabhbhai managed to play the role of a linkman on behalf of the community and linked the province with the freedom struggle. In this regard, David Hardiman, Shirin Mehta and D.N. Dhangare have exhaustively highlighted Vallabhbhai's ability to utilise caste, religion etc. as effective techniques of the freedom struggle.

Writings on partition of India too narrate the role played by Vallabhbhai during the period. Some of the important works are V.P. Menon's '*The Transfer of Power in India*'[123], Abul Kalam Azad's '*India Wins Freedom*'[124], Ram Manohar Lohia's '*Guiltymen of India's Partition*,'[125] H.W. Hodson's '*The Great Divide*,'[126] Alan Campbell Johnson's '*Mission with Mountbatten*,'[127] Larry Collins and Dominique Lapierre's '*Freedom At Midnight*'[128] *Manmathnath Das*' '*Partition and Independence of India*,'[129] Sucheta Mahajan's, '*Independence and Partition*'[130] and Rafiq Zakaria's, '*The Man who Divided India*.'[131] Azad and Lohia hold Vallabhbhai responsible to a large extent for the partition of the country while V.P. Menon considers it to be an unavoidable reality and Zakaria claims the partition happened because of the changed personality of Jinnah, the Leader of the Muslim League.

Vallabhbhai has also been referred in the context of the growth and organisation of the Indian National Congress. Some such works are Pattabhi Sitaramayya's '*The History of the Indian National Congress*,'[132] S.A. Kochanek's '*The Congress Party of India*'[133] and B.R. Tomlinson's '*The Indian National Congress and the Raj*.'[134] All these works highlight the role of Vallabhbhai as a disciplinarian who reorganised successfully the party machinery.

1.4 Objectives of the Study

The major objectives of the present study entitled '*Political Ideas of Sardar Vallabhbhai Patel*' are as follows:

(i) To enquire into the life process of Vallabhbhai, and to trace the impact of major events and important personalities on him in the process of formation of his socio-political ideas.

(ii) To enquire into, and analyse Vallabhbhai's ideas on Rights, Liberty, Equality and Justice, and to delineate the pattern of his political values.

(iii) To enquire into Vallabhbhai's ideas on Nation–State and state–individual relationship.

(iv) To enquire into Vallabhbhai's roles as a Nation-builder.

(v) To assess Vallabhbhai's contributions to Modern Indian Political Thought by examining his socio-political ideas as a whole, and to evaluate his position as a political thinker of India.

1.5 Methodology

For the purpose of this research work the method of study that has been employed is the normative method.[135] Data concerning Vallabhbhai's socio-political ideas and values have been discerned from various speeches as well as statements issued by him, and observations made by him on varieties of local and national incidents. Inferences have also been drawn on by enquiring into and analysing his role as a political activist, as a party organiser and also as '*the Iron Man*' in the Union Government. For this purpose, a number of authoritative works including letters of Vallabhbhai compiled by many scholars have been taken into account. Moreover, official documents and records have been collected, perused and scanned. Besides, works authored on him by scholars have been consulted and analysed. These information and data have been subjected to normative scrutiny and analysis and accordingly Vallabhbhai's pattern of political values, his concept of Nation–State, and his role as a Nation-builder of modern India have been discerned and evaluated.

Notes and References

1 E.J. Meehan, *Contemporary Political Thought: A Critical Study* (Homewood, Illinois: The Dorsey Press, 1967, p. 2).

2. Mulford O. Sibley, *Political Ideas and Ideologies: A History of Political Thought* (Delhi: Surjeet Publications, Indian Reprint 1981, p. 4).

3. William Archibald Dunning, *A History of Political Theories: Ancient and Medieval* (Allahabad: Central Book Depot, 1970, Indian Reprint, pp. xvi-xvii).

4. C.L. Wayper, *Political Thought* (New Delhi: B.I. Publications, Indian Edition, 1984, p. vii).

5. William T. Bluthm, *Theories of Political System* (Englewood Cliff, N.J.: Prentice Hall, 1965, p. 9).

6. Mulford O. Sibley, *Political Ideas and Ideologies: A History of Political Thought, op. cit.*, pp. 592-4. D.D. Raphael, *Problems of Political Philosophy* (London: Pall-Mall Press, 1970).

7. Andrew Hacker, *Political Theory: Philosophy, Ideology, Science* (New York: Macmillan, 1961, p. 5).

8. William T. Bluhm, *Theories of Political System, op. cit.*, p. 2.

9. *Ibid.*, p. 13.

10. *Ibid.*, p. 13.

11. Vermon Van Dyke, *Political Science: A Philosophical Analysis* (Stanford, California: Stanford University Press, 1960, p.184).

12. Thomas, P. Jenkin, *The Study of Political Theory* (Garden City: Double Day, 1955, pp. 15-21). Moris R. Cohen and Ernest Nagel, *An Introduction to Logic and Scientific Method* (New York: Harcourt Brace, 1934, pp. 279-99). Hans Reichenback, *The Rise of Scientific Philosophy* (Berkeley University: California Press, 1951, pp. 215-49). Max Black, *Critical Thinking* (New York: Prentice Hall, 1952, 2nd Edition, p. 5).
13. William T. Bluhm, *Theories of Political System. op. cit.*, p. 13.
14. C.L. Wayper, *Political Thought. op. cit.*, p. x.
15. G.H. Sabine, "What is Political Theory", *Journal of Politics*, 1939, p. 3
16. William T. Bluhm, *Theories of Political System. op. cit.*, p. 2.
17. Lawrence C. Wanlacs, *Gettle's History of Political Thought* (London: George Allen and Unwin, 1953, pp. 10-12).
18. *Ibid.*, pp. 10-12.
19. *Ibid.*, p. 14.
20. Arnold Brecht, *Political Theory, The Foundations of Twentieth Century Political Thought* (Bombay: *The Times of India Press,* 1970, Indian Reprint, pp. 20-21). Originally published by the Princeton University Press, USA, 1959.
21. David Thomson (ed.), *Political Ideas* (London: Pelican Books, 1965, pp. 18-9).
22. Bhikhu Parekh, "Some Reflections on the Hindu Tradition of Political Thought" in Thomas Pantham and Karl Deutsch (ed.), *Political Thought in Modern India* (New Delhi: Sage Publication, 1986, p. 17).
23. V.P. Varma, *Ancient and Medieval Indian Political Thought* (Agra: 1961, p. 588).
24. A.N. Whitehead in V.P. Varma, *ibid*, p. 284.
25. Badrinath Chaturvedi, "The Place of Individual in Indian Thought and Polity", in Imtiaz Ahmed, Partha Ghosh and Helmut Reifeld (ed.), *Pluralism and Equality: Values in Indian Society and Politics* (New Delhi: Sage Publications, 2000, p. 34).
26. Beity Heimann, *Facets of Indian Thought* (London: George Allen and Unwin, 1964, pp. 174-75).
27. Bhikhu, Parekh, "Some Reflections on the Hindu Tradition of Political Thought", *op. cit.*, p. 22.

28. Betty Heimann, *Facets of Indian Thoughts. op. cit.*, p. 67.
29. Nicholas Dirks, "The Study of State and Society in India", in Sudipta Kaviraj (ed.), *Politics in India* (New Delhi: Oxford, 1997, p. 160).
30. *Ibid.*, p.160.
31. *Ibid.*, p.159.
32. Bhikhu, Parekh, "Some Reflections on the Hindu Tradition of Political Thought", *op. cit.*, pp. 21-22.
33. Rajni Kothari, "The Crisis of Moderate State and the Decline of Democracy" in Peter Lyon and James Monor (ed.). *Transfer and Transformation: Political Institutions in the New Commonwealth* (Leicester: Leicester Press, 1983, p. 45).
34. Beni Prasad, *State in Ancient India* (Allahabad: 1929, p. 98).
35. Norman, D. Palmer, "Indian and Western Political Thought: Coalescence and Clash", *American Political Science Review*. Vol. 9, No. 3, September, 1955, p. 761.
36. K.M. Pannikar, The Idea of Sovereignty of State in *Indian Political Thought* (Bombay: Bharatiya Vidya Bhavan, 1963, p. 19).
37. *Ibid.*, p. 100.
38. *Ibid.*, p. 9.
39. V.P. Varma, *Modern Indian Political Thought* (Agra: 1961, p. 4).
40. W.H. Morris-Jones, "Parochialism in Political Thought", *Political Studies*. Vol. 20, No.4, 1972, pp. 475-77.
41. Thomas Pantham, "The Socio-Religious and Political Thought of Rammohan Roy" in Thomas Pantham and Karl Deutsch (ed.), *op. cit.*, p. 43.
42. A. Appadorai, *Indian Political Thinking in the Twentieth Century* (New Delhi: South Asia Publishers, 1987, p. 17).
43. Sri Aurobindo, *The Spirit and Forms of Indian Polity* (Calcutta: Arya Publishing House, 1947, pp. 11-14).
44. Dennis Dalton, "The Ideology of Sarvodaya: Concepts of Politics and Power in Indian Political Thought" in Thomas Pantham and Karl Deutsch (ed.), *op. cit.*, p. 279.
45. *Ibid.*, p. 280.
46. B.R. Purohit, "The Social and Political Ideas of Swami Dayananda Saraswati in Thomas Pantham and Karl Deutsch (ed.), *op. cit.*, p. 50.

47. Haridas Mukherjee and Uma Mukherjee, *Sir Aurobindo and New Thought in Indian Politics* (Calcutta: 1964, pp. 22-27).
48. *Ibid.*, p. 62.
49. Dennis Dalton, "The Ideology of Sarvoday: Concepts of Politics and Power" in *Indian Political Thought, op. cit.*, p. 278.
50. *Ibid.*, p. 280.
51. S.P. Aiyar, "Some Aspects of the Study of Modern Indian Political Thought", *The Indian Journal of Political Science*. Vol. xxxiii, No. 4, Oct.-Dec. 1972, New Delhi, p. 404.
52. A. Appadorai, *Indian Political Thinking in the Twentieth Century. op. cit.,* p. 145.
53. Jawaharlal Nehru, *An Autobiography* (London: 1955, p. 541).
54. Sir Richard Temple, "Man and Society of any time in India" in L.S.S.O.' Malley, *Modern India and the West* (London: Oxford 1968, p. 92).
55. V.R. Mehta, *Ideology, Modernisation and Politics in India* (New Delhi: Manohar, 1983, p. 74).
56. P.N. Chopra and Prabha Chopra,(ed.), *Inside Story of Sardar Patel: The Dairy of Maniben Patel: 1936-50* (New Delhi: Vision Books, 2001, p. 27). Narahari, D. Parikh, *Sardar Vallabhbhai Patel.* Vol. I (Ahmedabad: Navajivan, 1953, p. 9).
57. Publication Division, *On Indian Problems* (New Delhi: 1949).
58. Publication Division, *For a United India: Speeches of Sardar Vallabhbhai Patel, 1947-50* (New Delhi: 1967).
59. Narahari, D. Parikh and Uttamchand and Dwarikadas Shah, *Sardar Patel Ke Bhashan, 1918-1947* (Ahmedabad: Navajivan, 1950).
60. *Constituent Assembly Debates*, Official Report, Vol. 1 to 12. (New Delhi: Lok Sabha Secretariat, 1966).
61. *Mahatma Gandhi Papers,* Gandhi Smarak Nidhi Sangrahalaya, New Delhi.
62. *Jawaharlal Nehru Papers*. National Memorial Museum and Library (NMML), New Delhi.
63. *Dr. Rajendra Prasad Papers,* National Archives of India (NAI), New Delhi.

64. *Dr. N.B. Khare Papers*, National Archives of India (NAI), New Delhi.
65. *Govind Vallabh Pant Papers*, National Memorial Museum and Library (NMML), New Delhi.
66. *G.B. Kher Papers*, National Memorial Museum and Library (NMML), New Delhi.
67. *M.K. Gandhi Letters to Sardar Vallabhbhai Patel* (Ahmedabad: Navajivan, 1957).
68. *Vallabhbhai Patel Papers*, Navajivan Trust, Ahmedabad.
69. *All India Congress Committee Papers*. Nehru Meorial Museum and Library (NMML), New Delhi.
70. Government Records, Home Department (Political) National Archives of India (NAI), New Delhi.
71. Durgadas, (ed.), *Sardar Patel's Correspondence*. 10 Vols, (Ahmedabad: Navajivan, 1971). New Lights on Kashmir (Vol. I). Election to Central and Provincial Legislatures – Direction of Congress Campaign (Vol. II). Guidance to Ministries, Constituent Assembly Problems – Interim Government Deadlock – Reforms in Indian States (Vol. III). Transfer of Power: Communal Holocaust and Partition – Administration and Stability (Vol. IV). Control over Congress Ministries – Indian States Accession (Vol. V). Patel-Nehru Differences – Assassination of Gandhi, Services Reorganised, Refugee Rehabilitation (Vol. VI). Integrating Indian States – Police Action in Hyderabad (Vol. VII). Foreign Policy in Evolution – Constitution Making – Political and Administrative Problems (Vol. VIII). Political Controversies – Refugee from East Bengal, Territorial Integration of Princely States (Vol. IX). Acute Power-Struggle – Triumph of Mutual Accommodation – Warning Against China (Vol. X).
72. V. Shankar,(ed.), *Sardar Patel Select Correspondence (1945-50)*, 2 Vols. (Ahmedabad: Navajivan, 1976-77).
73. G.M. Nandurkar (ed.), *Sardar Patel Centenary Volumes*, 5 Vols. (Ahmedabad: Sardar Patel Smarak Bhawan, 1974-8). This was Şardar –Commemorative Volume, Volume – I, Ahmedabad, 1974. Sardar Patel – *In Tune with the Millions*, Volume-II, Ahmedabad, 1975. Sardar Patel – *In Tune with the Millions*, Volume-III, Ahmedabad, 1976. *Sardar's Letters Mostly Unknown*, Volume-IV, Ahmedabad, 1977. *Sardar's Letters Mostly Unknown*, Volume-V, Ahmedabad, 1978.

74. G.M. Nandurkar (ed.), *Sardar's Letters: Post Centenary Series,* 3 Vols. (Ahmedabad: Sardar Patel Smarak Bhawan, 1980-3). *Sardar's Letters Mostly Unknown*, Post-Centenary Series, Vol.-I, Ahmedabad, 1980. *Sardar's Letters Mostly Unknown*, Post-Centenary Series, Vol.-II, Ahmedabad, 1981. *Sardar's Letters Mostly Unknown*, Post-Centenary Series, Vol.-III, Ahmedabad, 1983.

75. G.M. Nandurkar (ed.), *Sardarshri Na Patro*, 5 Vols. (Ahmedabad: 1925-8).

76. G.M. Nandurkar (ed.), *Sardarshri Ke Patro*, 2 Vols. (Ahmedabad, 1981).

77. P.N. Chopra,(ed.) *The Collected Works of Sardar Vallabhbhai Patel,* 15 Vols. (New Delhi: Konark Pvt. Ltd., 1990-9). The Kheda, Non-Cooperation Movement, Nagpur Flag agitation and Borsad *Satyagraha*, (Vol. I), New Delhi, 1990. Flood Relief in Gujarat and the Bordoli *Satyagraha*, (Vol. II), New Delhi, 1991. The Salt *Satyagraha*, Jail Diary, President of the Indian National Congress (Vol. III), New Delhi, 1993. The Civil Disobedience Movement (Vol. IV), New Delhi, 1994. Chairman of the Congress Parliamentary Board and the Plague Relief work in Gujarat (Vol. V), New Delhi, 1994. The Provincial Assembly Election (Vol. VI), New Delhi, 1995. Supervision of the Congress Ministries (Vol. VII), New Delhi, 1996. Difference with Subash Bose, (Vol. VIII), New Delhi, 1996. The Quit India Movement, (Vol. IX), New Delhi, 1997. Negotiation with the Cabinet Mission, (Vol. X), New Delhi, 1997. Sardar Patel as the Constitution Maker, (Vol. XI), New Delhi, 1997. Rehabilitation of Refugee and Difference with Nehru, (Vol. XII), New Delhi, 1998. Support for Partition: Integration of States: Accession of Kashmir, (Vol. XIII), New Delhi, 1998. Support for Membership in the Commonwealth Guarantee Provision for Privy Purse and Protection of Services, Views on Economic Policy, (Vol. XIV), New Delhi, 1999. Support for a Strong India: Hindu-Muslim Unity: Big Army, Prophetic Observation on Chinese Aggression, (Vol. XV), New Delhi, 1999.

78. P.N. Chopra (ed.), *Thematic Volumes on Sardar Vallabhbhai Patel: Kashmir and Hyderabad* (New Delhi: Konark Pvt. Ltd., 2002).

79. Hiralal Sheth, *The Iron Dictator: A Biographical Study of Gandhi's Greatest General Sardar Vallabhbhai Patel* (Lahore: Hero Publication, 1945).

80. Abdul Majid Khan, *Leader By Merit* (Lahore: Indian Printing Works, 1946).

81. Narahari D. Parikh, *Sardar Vallabhbhai Patel.* 2 Vols. (Ahmedabad: Navajivan, 1955-6).

82. K.L. Panjabi, *The Indomitable Sardar* (Bombay: Bharatiya Vidya Bhavan, 1962).

83. P.U. Patel, *Sardar Patel: India's Man of Destiny* (Bombay: 1964).

84. V.B. Kulkarni, *The Indian Triumvirate: A Political Biography of Gandhi, Patel, Nehru* (Bombay: Bharatiya Vidya Bhavan, 1969).

85. D.V. Tahamankar, *Sardar Patel* (London: George Allen and Unwin, 1970).

86. Susane Heredia, *A Patriot for Me* (Bombay: Orient Longman, 1972).

87. L.N. Sarin, *Sardar Patel* (New Delhi: S. Chand & Co. Pvt. Ltd., 1972).

88. B.K. Ahluwalia, *Sardar Patel: A Life* (New Delhi: Sagar Publications, 1974).

89. B.K. Ahluwalia, (ed.), *Facets of Sardar Patel* (New Delhi: Kalyani, 1974).

90. B.K. Ahluwalia and Sashi Ahluwalia, *Sardar Patel: Rebel and Ruler* (New Delhi: Akbe Group, 1981).

91. S.R. Bakshi, *The Bordoli Satyagraha* (Delhi: Akashdeep Publishing House, 1988).

92. S.R. Bakshi, *Sardar Patel: His Political Ideology* (New Delhi: Anmol, 1990).

93. Rajmohan Gandhi, *Patel: A Life* (Ahmedabad: Sardar Vallabhbhai Patel Memorial Society and Navajivan, 1991).

94. P.N. Chopra, *The Sardar of India: A Biography of Vallabhbhai Patel* (New Delhi: Allied Publishers Ltd., 1995).

95. B. Krishna, *Sardar Vallabhbhai Patel: India's Iron Man* (New Delhi: Indus, 1995).

96. P.N. Chopra and Prabha Chopra (ed.), *Inside Story of Sardar Patel, The Diary of Maniben Patel: 1936-50* (New Delhi: Vision Books, 2001).

97. Mahadev Desai, *The Story of Bordoli* (Ahmedabad: Navajivan, 1929).

98. Ishwarlal I. Desai, *Bordoli Satyagraha* (Surat: 1970).

99. Asoka Mehta, *Economic Consequences of Sardar Patel* (Hyderabad: Chetna, 1949).

100. V.P. Menon, *The Story of the Integration of the Indian States* (Calcutta: Orient Longman, 1956).

101. K.M. Munshi, *The End of an Era* (Bombay: Bharatiya Vidya Bhavan, 1957).

102. Arya Ramchandra Tiwari, *Making of the Leader: Sardar Vallabhbhai Patel* (Vallabh Vidyanagar: Sardar Patel University, 1967).

103. N.V. Gadgil, *Government from Inside* (Meerut: Meenakshi Prakashan, 1968).

104. K.M. Munshi, *India Constitutional Documents*. 2 Vols. (Bombay: Bharatiya Vidya Bhavan, 1967).

105. B.S. Rao, *The Framing of India's Constitution: A Study* (Nasik: Government of India Pres., 1968).

106. Frank Anthony, *Britain's Betrayal in India* (New Delhi: Allied Publishers, 1969).

107. V. Shankar, *My Reminiscences of Sardar Patel,* 2 Vols. (New Delhi: Macmillan, 1974-75).

108. R.K. Murthi, *The Man and his Contemporaries* (New Delhi: Sterling Publishers Pvt. Ltd., 1976).

109. Devabrat Pathak and Pravin Sheth, Sardar Vallabhbhai Patel:*From Civic to National Leadership* (Ahmedabad: Navajivan, 1980).

110. Rabindra Nath Kumar, *Role of Sardar Patel in the Integration of India* (Muzaffarpur: Prabha Publications, 1987).

111. Rani Dhavan Shankardass, *Vallabhbhai Patel: Power and Organisation in Indian Politics* (New Delhi: Orient Longman, 1988).

112. Verinder Grover (ed.), *Political Thinkers of Modern India: Vallabhbhai Patel,* Vol. 18, (New Delhi: Deep and Deep Publications, 1992).

113. Vijaya Tendulkar, *The Last Days of Sardar Patel* (Bombay: Popular Prakashan, 1993).

114. Michael H. Lyon, *Sardar Patel and Indian Independence* (New Delhi: Konark Pvt. Ltd., 1996).

115. Rafiq Zakaria, *Sardar Patel and Indian Muslims* (Mumbai: Bharatiya Vidya Bhavan, 1996).

116. Rajula Jain, *Vallabhbhai Patel and the Indian National Congress: A Study 1934-39* (New Delhi: Gyan Sagar Publication, 1997).
117. S.R. Maheswari, *Administrative Thinkers* (New Delhi: Macmillan, 1998).
118. David F. Pocock, *Kanbi and Patidar: A Study of the Patidar Community of Gujarat* (London: Oxford, 1972).
119. David Hardiman, *Peasant Nationalists in Gujarat: Kheda District (1917-24)* (New Delhi, Oxford, 1981).
120. Jan Berman, *Peasant Migrants and Paupers: Rural Labour Circulation and Capitalist Production in West India* (Delhi: 1985).
121. Shirin Mehta, *The Peasantry and Nationalism: A Study of the Bordoli Satyagraha* (New Delhi: Manohar, 1984).
122. D.N. Dhangare, *Peasant Movements in India (1920-50)* (New Delhi: Oxford, 1991).
123. V.P. Menon, *The Transfer of Power in India* (New Delhi: Orient Longman, 1957).
124. Abul Kalam Azad, *India Wins Freedom* (Calcutta: Orient Longman, 1959).
125. Ram Manohar Lohia, *Guilty Men of India's Partition* (Allahabad: 1960).
126. H.W. Hodson, *The Great Divide* (London: Huchinson, 1969).
127. Alan, Campbell Johnson, *Mission with Mountbatten* (London: Robert Hale, 1972).
128. Lary Collins and Dominique Lapierre, *Freedom at Midnight* (New Delhi: Vikash Publishing House, 1976).
129. Manmathnath Das, *Partition and Independence of India* (New Delhi: Vision, 1982).
130. Sucheta Mahajan, *Independence and Partition* (New Delhi: Sage Publication, 2000).
131. Rafiq Zakaria, *The Man Who Divided India* (Mumbai: Popular Prakashan, 2001).
132. Pattabhi Sitaramayya. *The History of Indian National Congress* (New Delhi: S. Chand & Co., 1969).
133. S.A. Kochanek, *The Congress Party of India* (Princeton University Press: 1968).

134. B.R. Tomlinson, *The Indian National Congress and the Raj (1929-42).* The Penultimate Phase (London: Macmillan, 1976).

135. Vernon Van Dyke, *Political Science: A Philosophical Analysis*, *op. cit.*, pp. 181-84. William T. Bluhm, *Theories of the Political System*, *op. cit.*, p. 13.

2

Vallabhbhai Patel: A Life Sketch

Political ideas of a leader are inextricably linked with his socio-economic and cultural moorings. His thinking process is deeply associated with his political socialisation experiences gained by him throughout the whole span of life as he gradually matures from childhood to adulthood. Because, the very process involves "all political learnings formal and informal, deliberate or unplanned at every stage of the life cycle, including not only explicitly political learning but also nominally non-political learning of politically relevant personality characteristics."[1] All these learnings and experiences tend to condition and shape his mindset, ideas, attitudes and pattern of his socio-political culture. Therefore, for understanding and appreciating his political ideas, a study and analysis of his socialisation experiences and the impact of the socio-economic and political environment upon him at different stages of his life becomes imperative. With this assumption, some major events and milestones in the life of Vallabhbhai, pertaining to his childhood, adolescence and adulthood have been depicted, portrayed and analysed.

2.1 Pre-adulthood

Vallabhbhai was born in an age reverberating with the after-effects of the cataclysmic Sepoy Mutiny (1857). In the given circumstances, the subtle way of colonial penetration paved the way for the germination of Indian nationalism. Amidst such surcharged atmosphere, Vallabhbhai was born on 31st October

1875 in the influential *Patidar* community as the fourth child of Ladba and Jhaverbhai of Karamsad, in the Kheda district of Central Gujarat. His father Jhaverbhai was a petty farmer with moderate means. He belonged to a community known for its upward mobilisation from a low migrant status to a well-entrenched powerful and independent community by virtue of its perseverance, pragmatism and agricultural know-how.[2] His ancestors, considered to be the founders of the Karamsad village were subsequently divided over the years.[3] As a result, by the end of the nineteenth century, Jhaverbhai was left with a meagre ten acres of land to manage a family of eight with six little children. As substantiated by the Administrative Report (1875), such division was quite natural in the given period, anticipating which the *Patidars* used to have separate *khadkis* (gates) at the time of the construction of houses for the coming generations to live as independent units under one roof.[4] Jhaverbhai's difficulty was not for the small amount of land in the Charotar tract. Given the fertile character of the land it should have been sufficient to manage a family[5]. In fact, it was due to his deep association with the prevailing Swami Narayana Cult of the *Vaishnava* sect,[6] he became less concerned of the regular household affairs. Jhaverbhai took to the cult with such devotion that he persuaded the family members to observe rituals like fastings and started spending more and more time in the temples as his sons grew up to manage the land. His stoic nature was revealed from his attitude towards materialistic possession. As he said: "What is the sense of making money? You cannot take it with you when you die and can not eat when you are alive. Why should I bother about it so long as my family has enough to eat and I do not have to borrow from my friends? I am quite happy with what God has given me"[7]. Jhaverbhai used to command a lot of respect in the village as the 'Motakaka' (great uncle). He was part of the superior *Patidar* clan, which established the Karamsad village as one of the Chhagam villages (six settlements).[8] His command over the village people was in tune with the

Patidar ethics which relied upon the ability and seniority of the leadership.[9] True to the *Patidar* spirit, he was also known for his sense of independence, bluntness and leadership quality.

Given the preoccupation of Jhaverbhai, the role of Ladba had become indispensable for the family. It was strengthened by her affluent maternal background. She belonged to a well-off *Patidar* clan of Nadiad, another Chhagam village of the Charotar tract. The connection was of great use to Jhaverbhai, especially at the time of the confinement of his wife and providing education to some of his children at Nadiad. Besides her ability to manage the house, Ladba was known to be a lady with great devotion to duty, religious inclination and communitarian attitude. It was revealed from her keenness to play the role of a mid-wife in the village.[10] Her sense of independence was reflected from her attempt to have self-sufficiency through *khadi.*[11]

Jhaverbhai had six children. True to his temperament, he gave them names bearing religious connotation. They were Somabhai (meaning the Sun God), Narshibhai (after the Narsingh God), Vithalbhai (representing Vithalnathji), Vallabhbhai (after Vallabhacharya) and Kashibhai (coined after Kashi or Varanasi). In between Vallabhbhai and Kashibhai, he had a daughter called Dahiba. As parental hopes were centered on Soma and Narshi as the eldest two and affection was primarily on Dahiba and Kashibhai as the youngest two, Vallabhbhai very often complained of being ignored as the middle child.[12] The typical *Patidar* patriarchal joint family system, characterised by the longevity of the father and the wide age gap between the eldest and the youngest one,[13] provided scope to the eldest one in the family to manage the house after the father. Jhaverbhai's preoccupation and Somabhai's early death made Narshibhai the '*Motakaka*' of the family soon. In subsequent periods, such hierarchy influenced Vallabhbhai to be in constant touch with the eldest brother.[14] The family compulsions compelled the siblings to have a tough childhood. It not only forced the family to incur debt but also left the children with little option but to compromise with study and work in the land.[15]

In the given situation, when Somabhai and Narshibhai had to discontinue their studies early to take care of the Karamsad land and the homestead, Vithalbhai and Vallabhbhai were fortunate enough to get scope for education. But the process was not a smooth one especially for Vallabhbhai because of the poor financial condition of the family. Unlike Vithalbhai, who was supported by the maternal uncle and could begin his studies at five, for him it was almost seven. It got further delayed as in the absence of the facility for English education in Karamsad, he had to repeat the initial study first in Gujarati then in English. The prevailing craze for the foreign language and the example of Vithalbhai inspired him to take the risk of repetition. At this stage too, the family condition demanded him to manage the school and land simultaneously. Hence, he could have a broader horizon than the children of his age. Tahamankar observes: "when Vallabhbhai was a student in the primary school at Karamsad, he had a better knowledge of the neighbouring fields and villages than he had of his school books."[16] He was inspired by the teaching of the village school teacher who insisted upon 'learn by yourself'. He finished his primary education at the age of seventeen and decided to leave for Petland for further studies. The ambition of becoming a great man[17] which happened to be the privilege of lawyers or barristers, encouraged him to look beyond the teaching profession visualised for him by the village school Headmaster Kahandas Patel and maternal uncle Doongerbhai Desai.[18] Hence, he became less conscious of his age and pursued his studies. At Petland, he managed himself independently in a mess, shared by six other schoolmates. Subsequently like Vithalbhai, he left for his maternal uncle's house at Nadiad to complete his school education. He passed his matriculation from Nadiad in 1897, at an advanced age of 22.

As a student, Vallabhbhai had no interest to read or write beyond what was required for practical purposes.[19] But he was very much keen in games like *gilli danda*, *hututu*, *kho*, *gedi dada* etc. Besides the conventional team events, he was highly inclined towards wrestling to 'develop body and mind together without being cruel and bloody'[20]. During his school days, he claimed to have shown his 'captaincy of mischief' for good cause.[21] If in Petland, he resisted teachers like Chhaganlal Kansara for giving undue physical punishment, in Baroda he challenged both the teacher Chhotalal and the Principal Narvane for showing inhuman attitude towards the students and following defective teaching methods. While raising voice against the double punishment imposed by the teacher for a single offence, he said: "I accepted without demur the punishment given to me for rudeness and stood on the bench. But the extra punishment of writing table was unjust. Besides, I am a student of the sixth standard. It is an unjust to me if I am asked to write tables which is what boys of six or seven are asked to do."[22] It has also been found that in order to ensure punctuality among teachers like Mr Agrawala he resorted to leg pulling in the form of singing song in his class. He organised a boycott against the Parsee teacher who used physical punishment to compel the students to purchase drawing equipment from his own shop. Besides having frequent rows with the teachers on the ground of deviation of school discipline and dereliction of duty, he also advocated in favour of a teacher such as Mr Bhatt, who decided to contest the Municipal election against a high profile candidate, Tatya Saheb. All these developments provided him enough scope to organise the students and to gain their confidence.

Vallabhbhai was married at the age of seventeen while he was still in school. In fact, child marriages used to be quite common in the *Patidar* community. Vithalbhai had to face it at the age of nine. But unlike his elder brother and father who got married in higher *Patidar* clans of the Chhagam villages, Vallabhbhai had the typical hypergamous marriage, arranged in between the superior Patidars of any of the Chhagam villages and an inferior *Patidar* family lying outside the cluster of such villages. Such marriages proved to be beneficial for both the sides as the former used to get huge dowry in lieu of providing scope for upward mobility to the latter. It was believed: "In giving away his daughter with a large chunk of his wealth, a *Patidar* father was among other things purchasing a share in an increasingly profitable corporate enterprise, one which may be thought of as an agrarian banking system."[23] Hence, Vallabhbhai's marriage to Jhaverba in the family of Desaibhai Punjabhai Patel of Gana, might be for the straitened circumstance of Jhaverbhai and longing for better status by the girl's father.[24]

Vallabhbhai was able to pursue his higher studies as such a marriage prevented the girl from coming to her in-laws house immediately after marriage. After matriculation, he decided to follow the footsteps of Vithalbhai and appear the District Pleader's examination, in order to be a lawyer. Given his late education and financial condition, he found it to be the easiest and cheapest way to become independent with sufficient scope for making himself a barrister. He said: "I came from a middle class family. My father lived a humble and pious life and died in the temple he loved. He had no means to enable me to fulfil my ambitions... I realised finally that if I wanted to go to England, I had to earn money myself. I, therefore, studied very earnestly for the Law Examination and resolved firmly to save sufficient money for a visit to England."[25] Finally, after toiling for three years, he managed to clear the examination in 1900 and became a lawyer at the age of twenty five. The gruelling struggle made during the period was evident from his experience at Bakrol, where in the absence of medical facilities, he risked removing a boil from his armpit with the help of a barber. In the long run, such experiences sharpened his perseverance and determination.

2.2 Adulthood

After becoming a lawyer, Vallabhbhai started his legal practice in the same year in 1900 in Godhra. Subsequently he shifted to Borsad. Very soon, he established himself as a successful criminal lawyer because of his commonsense, extraordinary skill in cross-examination and ability to analyse evidence. It was proved not only from the amount of money he earned, but also from the fact that the established lawyers of the area became so panicked that they shifted the base of the resident magistrate from Borsad to Anand. But his method of working was different from Vithalbhai, who was also engaged in legal practice simultaneously with him. It was found that while the latter's personal relations with prominent people were cordial and his influence with the police was immense,[26] the younger brother preferred to keep away from police officers and magistrates except when he found it necessary in open courts to tackle their insulting and intimidating behaviour towards the lawyer."[27] This attitude enabled Vallabhbhai to fight against injustice at each and every level and earned him an enviable image. It helped him to save even Vithalbhai from the vindictive attitude, adopted by some of the local judicial officers at Borsad. During this period, he got ample scope to learn legal procedures and peculiarities of interpersonal relationship which sharpened his ability to make quick judgement and turn the table against the opponent. The earning from the legal practice was used to support his own family as by 1905 he had become a father of two children, Maniben and Dayabhai. He also managed to look after the family at Karamsad. It was evident from the way he felt guilty for sending back home during the plague in Godhra, the youngest brother Kashibhai whose responsibility he had taken up. Explaining his inability to the elder brother Narshibhai, he wrote, "Night and day I think of you to assist you. Just now I am helpless, but you will be able to count on me when the situation improves."[28]

Despite all his obligations, Vallabhbhai for his middleclass spendthrift habit,[29] managed to save around 10,000 rupees to realise the goal of becoming a barrister. He found people holding institutional authority, were held in high awe in the society. As a true *Patidar* who was never accustomed to servility, he felt humiliated for being an ordinary pleader and was determined to become a barrister. It encouraged him to go to England for higher studies, the goal he had nourished since long. In fact, desire to visit a far-off place especially in search of better opportunities was very much in the blood of a *Patidar*, who was known to be least hesitant of migrating to East Africa in the late nineteenth century. Vallabhbhai was hardly an exception. It was further influenced by his exposure to Western education. He admitted: "I was anxious to go overseas to see the people of England, who living 7000 miles away, were able to rule us for so for long."[30] The subsequent humiliation of being a pleader in the local court made him so determined that by 1905 he had made up his mind to utilise the saved money for a trip to England. But it was shattered as Vithalbhai, a typical *Patidar* elder brother expressed his desire to avail the opportunity first.[31] Subsequently the early death of Jhaverba, his own wife and Diwaliba, the wife of Vithalbhai in 1909 and 1910 respectively, delayed his trip to England. Finally, he could make his way to England in 1910. He left his two kids in the custody of Queen Mary's Boarding School in Bombay. He had no option but to leave early as the upcoming new law was going to restrict the Indian students without the degree of L.L.B., admission into the Bar-at-Law.

Vallabhbhai was admitted into the Middle Temple, one of the Law colleges in England. During his sojourn, due to his mature age and responsibilities back at home, he had hardly any other interest beyond his studies. Hence, he was least interested towards the ongoing political developments even in relation to India.[32] His hard labour paid off as he topped the examination in Roman Law within six months of time. By June 1912, he managed to secure the same position in the final examination and secured an exemption of two terms. Amidst a lot of adversities he qualified the Bar-at-Law within two and half years, almost six months earlier than the stipulated schedule. The extraordinary achievements enhanced his inherent self-confidence, which had been on the ascendance since the beginning of his professional career. The period he spent in England, provided him the opportunity to acquaint himself with the operations of the British judicial system. He was attracted by the deep sense of discipline and democratic orientation of the English people.

Vallabhbhai returned to India in early 1913, with a lot of confidence, cynical attitude and a rational mindset. His westernised attire, chain-smoking habit and fluency in English were indicative of his elevated status. Indulal Yagnik, one of his associates observed: "He seemed to be 125 per cent Europeans"[33]. Another friend Mavalankar noted: "A smart young man, dressed in well-cut clothes with a felt, had worn slightly at an angle, stern and reserved, his eyes piercing and bright, not given to many words, receiving visitors with just a simple greetings, but not entering into any conversation and of a firm and pensive expression as if he looked down upon the world with a sort of superiority complex, talking with an air of confidence and superiority whenever he opened his lips."[34] He shared a close relationship with a selected few like Mavalankar and Dr. Balvant Roy Kanugo and his wife Vijayagauri. He was not interested to hold any Government job. So when Sir Basil Scott, the Chief Justice of the Bombay High Court requested him to join either as a Judge or a Professor, Vallabhbhai turned him down and preferred to pursue independent legal practice which had enough opportunities for both name and fame. Hence, unlike Vithalbhai, who had then switched over to a public life by entering into the Bombay Legislative Council, he immediately settled down in a known place like Ahmedabad, with less competition and better scope for early success. True to his expectation, very soon he established himself as one of the best criminal lawyers of Ahmedabad basically for his personal skill, extra degree of a barrister and old contacts. He never felt the necessity of using his association with Godfrey Davis, one of his Middle Temple friends, posted as the Assistant Commissioner in Ahmedabad. His earnings of the period managed to cover the expenditure of Vithalbhai in Bombay, his own family in Ahmedabad and that of the family in the native place of Karamsad. Death of father Jhaverbhai in 1914 and sister who shouldered responsibility of his two children after passing away of his wife and the involvement of Vithalbhai in politics made him more committed towards the family. All these developments might have influenced him not to marry again.[35]

Vallabhbhai's high profile as a lawyer and his keen interest in the game of Bridge made him a regular member of the Gujarat Club. There, he met with active public workers like Govind Rao Patil, Shivabhai Patel, Chimanlal Thakore, Maganbhai Chaturbhai Patel etc. Given his success as a lawyer, all of them except Chimanlal Thakore encouraged him to become part of public life.[36] The environment of the Gujarat Club and the success of Vithalbhai motivated him to think of diverting his attention towards public activities. But he was little influenced by Gandhi in this regard when he first met him in the Club in the mid 1916. Gandhi had then just returned from South Africa and was looking for opportunities to repeat his successful Natal experiment of challenging the political authority in India. Vallabhbhai was also little affected by the Political Conference which was organised by the Gujarat Sabha in October 1916 to bridge the gap within the Congress, the most prominent political organisation of the period. He was disillusioned over the bifurcation of the organisation into the 'Moderate', and 'Extremist' groups who advocated different strategies to resist the British authority[37]. But the success of Gandhi in Champaran in April 1917, changed his perception towards him and defined further his slowly changing outlook towards public activity and made him confident to defy the British political set-up in an organised way.

At this juncture, due to the colonisation of India by the British authority, all public bodies were in a state of doldrums. The Municipality of Ahmedabad was no exception. Though, the civic bodies were created in India in 1884 to reflect the spirit of devolution of power, they had become defunct due to lack of fund, public apathy, nepotism and high-handedness of the Government. The decline of the Ahmedabad Municipality was reflected in the frequent succession of its Presidents, suspension of the body from 1910-1915 and appointment of a Government officer to supervise its functioning. The situation deteriorated further as the local administrative set-up hardly had any scope for reforms. "Until the election of Vallabhbhai Patel in 1917, Municipal politics had no relation to wider national or provincial issues. The Municipality was not popular with the rate-payers. They thought it a nuisance which harassed them for petty interactions of Municipal by-laws and taxed them for unwanted innovations like modern drainage and water supply."[38] Vallabhbhai, encouraged by his success in professional career, motivated by friends and endowed with the Vaishnovite conservative approach of a Patidar, decided to enter into the Municipality at an advanced age of 42 to wrest the substance of civic authority. Success of Gandhi might have acted as a catalyst for him. He fought the election in January 1917 from the Dariapur constituency and won by a narrow margin of just one vote. But the election was declared invalid. Subsequently, in May 1917 he was declared elected unopposed.

The whole span of Vallabhbhai's municipal career (1917-28) can be divided into two parts on the basis of the activities taken up during the period. In the first phase (1917-22), he concentrated on challenging the authority by protesting against the high-handedness of the officers. While in the second one (1924-28), he carried out several developmental projects and supervised the relief operations for the flood affected people. In this context, Pathak and Sheth comment: "If the first phase shaped the formative period in the Municipality to remove the cobwebs in the administration and improve the civic amenities, the last could be characterised as Vallabhbhai's commitment to 'Municipal Socialism', as reflected through a series of social welfare measures for the poor and backward communities in the cities and the low-paid employees in the Municipality"[39]. In the first phase, he followed the politics of 'confrontation' to drive out the arrogant officers like Shillidy, Master, Pratt etc. Any dereliction of duty or high-handedness by any officer was resisted. Even Indian officers like Wadia were challenged for the gross negligence of duty. Moreover, he boycotted the Government grant for education. His success at carrying out various town planning measures in the second phase made the civic body more people-oriented. The very presence of the Imperial set-up encouraged him to move beyond the civic body and reconcile the strategies of cooperation and confrontation. He successfully shifted the scale of politics to enhance its scope. The Memorandum of the Government of Bombay admitted: "It is gratifying to note that good progress has been made during the year in the task of providing for the chief needs of the town. On the whole, the record of the Municipal administration shows a steady progress in almost every branch and Government concur with the Collector and Commissioner, that the Municipality is pursuing a sound and progressive policy."[40] Thus, with the skillful use of many local factors Vallabhbhai set a new standard. He belonged to the group of leaders "who innovate ways requiring skills and resources not widely available, yet they set the styles and impose performance standards which once demonstrated can be initiated by others."[41]

In the Municipality, the strategy of confrontation enabled Vallabhbhai to come closer to Gandhi. Though, initially he was sceptical about Gandhi, later on he was touched by the latter's innovations made to convert the Gujarat Sabha, a semi-political elite organisation, into a mass based one. The transformation of the Gujarat Sabha into an extended branch of the Congress Party at the all-India level in 1920, reiterated the Champaran success of Gandhi. Thus, in the given situation, Gandhian politics with an emphasis upon non-violence, spirituality, discipline, moral strength etc. became the best method for Vallabhbhai to challenge the British authority, the process which he had already initiated independently in the Ahmedabad Municipality. So, he became mentally ready to quit the roaring legal practice and to become a full-time public worker. He admitted: "No doubt, my practice is flourishing today. I am also doing something big in the Municipality. . . . But, my practice may or may not be there tomorrow. My money will be blown tomorrow, those who inherit my money will blow it. Let me leave them a better legacy than money."[42] The decision became one of the most significant in the life of Vallabhbhai as it crystallised his future course of action and gave a new dimension to his leadership. At this crucial hour, besides Gandhi, he came in contact with other

Congress leaders like Bal Gangadhar Tilak, Aurobindo, etc. whose conviction of superiority of the 'inner domain' and the Indian culture made him more firm against the British exploitation[43].

In between 1918-28, Vallabhbhai was involved in various grass root mobilisations to express his resentment against the colonial power. This phase of his life characterised two contradictory tendencies like extending support to the Government through the Municipality and boycotting it through Gandhian agitations. Though, he launched his struggles within the broad framework of the Gandhian ideology, he got ample scope to bring innovations in it due to his access into the rural areas and busy engagements of Gandhi outside Gujarat. During the period, the Gujarat Province was affected by acute problems like recurrent epidemics, frequent tax hikes by an insensitive authority, population explosion and unplanned industrialisation. All these conditions made it receptive for changes. Vallabhbhai raised voice against the British exploitative policies, meant for harassing people and entrenching the regime on the foreign soil. He demanded tax relaxation for the peasants of Kheda (1918), lifting of imposition of punitive tax in Borsad (1923) and the restrictions on hoisting of the National Flag in Nagpur (1923), and the revision of the arbitrary taxation policy in Bordoli (1927). Vallabhbhai deliberately chose the local issues on which he had complete grip. Except in Kheda, in all other cases he mobilised people independent of Gandhi. Initially, he organised people with the help of semi-political bodies like the Gujarat Sabha but later on he sought the help of the Gujarat provincial Congress Committee, to set right the injustices perpetuated by the authority. His mobilisation created political consciousness at the grass root level. Of all the struggles, Bordoli happened to be the most crucial one as its decisive impact was felt at the all-India level. Though organised on a local issue, its success resulting out of Vallabhbhai's army like organisation of the local unit and involvement of the people beyond the province especially through the branches of the Congress Party, created tremendous political awareness. It catapulted him from a mere provincial to a national leader who henceforth started being recognised as the 'Sardar' of India.

Besides the mobilisations at the local level, Vallabhbhai simultaneously became part of the all-India freedom struggle pursued under the leadership of Gandhi. Irrespective of their differences, the struggle by both to fight out British injustices required the same level of organisation and to some extent the same techniques. Hence, they became complimentary to each other. Vallabhbhai's participation in the Non-Cooperation Movement (1920), launched as a protest against the Rowlatt Act and the Jalianwala Bagh Massacre helped extend it to the grass root level in the form of boycott of grant for education by the civic body of Ahmedabad and strengthened the struggle. The movement had a long term effect. The curbing of the speech (Rowlatt Act) and violation of right to life (Jalianwala Bagh Massacre) motivated Vallabhbhai to use the public body against the British authority. Vallabhbhai started associating himself with Gandhi from 1917. He helped him in abolishing forced labour in some part of Gujarat province, providing justice to the peasants of Kheda and in making Recruitment drive for the Ist World War. He came forward to collect money for the Tilak Swaraj Fund to carry out the Non-Cooperation Movement. When he had mustered enough strength and support especially after the Bordoli, he supported Gandhi during the Civil Disobedience Movement (1930) to demand more constitutional opportunities. He became one of the prominent members of the party who stood behind Gandhi in initiating the Quit India Movement (1942) to save the country from the likely Japanese aggression. His experience of mobilising the local people helped him a lot in all these measures.

Vallabhbhai also proved to be a great help to Gandhi in reorganising the Congress. He felt the necessity of organising the party not only for the agitation but also for the coming electoral politics. He began the process in 1921 as the President of the Gujarat Provincial Congress Committee. He proved his mettle in

1921 as the Chairman of the Reception Committee of the 36th Session of the Congress and in 1931 as the President of the 46th Session of the Party. In fact, due to the success in Bordoli, his name was first proposed as the President for the Lahore Congress in 1929. However, tussle within the party compelled him to give way to Jawaharlal Nehru. Subsequently, he managed to hold the post of the party President from 1930-34, when the party was banned by the authority and elections could not be held. Vallabhbhai assumed office in an adverse atmosphere. It was marked by developments like the shifting of power equation in England from the Labour Government to an apparently anti-Indian Conservative Party dominated political set-up, replacement of Lord Wellingdon by Lord Irwin, a critic of India as the new Governor General, repression of the Civil Disobedience Movement and hanging of freedom fighters like Bhagat Singh and his associates. But his tenure was marked by an attempt to bridge the gap between the old and young leadership and spread the message of communal harmony. It also approved the resolution on the Fundamental Rights.

The changed situation of the mid-thirties coincided with the opening of new constitutional opportunities. It changed the perception towards power politics. Vallabhbhai's grasped the changing realities quickly. He supported Gandhi's decision in 1934 on his withdrawal from active power politics. He came forward to organise the party for the coming elections and the possibility of acceptance of office. Such a bold decision confirmed the view that he was not a 'blind follower' of Gandhi.[44]

Following the decision on the Council-entry programme, Vallabhbhai became the Chairman of the All-India Congress Parliamentary Board. It was formed to supervise the forthcoming elections for the Central Legislative and Provincial Assemblies. In his new capacity, he played a decisive role in monitoring every stage of the election. Under his supervision the party secured a convincing majority in six out of the eleven Provinces and formed Government in eight Provinces. With regard to the responsibilities of Council-entry and office management, he was challenged both from within and outside the Party. As a result, he became ruthless and imposed disciplinary measures. Again, as the Chairman of the Parliamentary Board, he supervised the functioning of the Congress ministries. As the whole agenda of office acceptance was supposed to carry forward the freedom struggle, he urged all the Congress Ministers to resign from office in 1939, when the British authority imposed upon India the decision of participation in the Second World War.

The ongoing War had its impact upon the Indian political scenario. During such a fluid situation, the Indian leadership was divided into three groups. The first one, inspired by M.N. Roy the Communist leader, advocated for unconditional support of India to England, the second under the leadership of Rajagopalachari a veteran Congress leader, demanded conditional cooperation with the British authority and the third led by Gandhi stood for the unconditional moral support to England. In such a situation, Vallabhbhai had become flexible enough to change his stand frequently as per the need of the hour. He deviated from the Gandhian path the in the mid-thirties and stuck to the second group of leadership. Like many other leaders of the Congress, he wanted to check the rise of the undemocratic forces of the Axis Power. He intended to do so by encashing the dilemma of England which was then attacked both in Europe and Asia. He tried to extract the maximum possible constitutional incentives from the authority. But, the cold response of the authority expressed through the 'August Offer' in 1940, compelled Vallabhbhai to return to the Gandhian fold and to extend support to him to launch the Quit India Movement. In the meantime, the gradual emergence of the Muslim League as a political party with a strong base, especially after the resignation of the Congress ministries, made him more aggressive and suspicious of the intention of the British authority.

The end of the Second World War had a far reaching repercussion upon the international situation in general and India in particular. The British authority had started declining due to the war burden and for the political consciousness generated in India as a result of the INA (Indian National Army) trial and the Naval Mutiny. If in the mid-thirties, interest in politics was generated by the emerging constitutional opportunities, in the mid-forties it was for the compulsions of the withdrawal of the British power. The arrival of the Cabinet Mission Plan in 1946 generated huge political interests. Vallabhbhai clearly realised the limitations of the British authority. He argued: "You have not understood the state of the British mind today that is in 1946 and 1942. In 1942, the British under the Tories led by Sir Winston Churchill were fighting to maintain their empire and therefore, the British game then was to play the role of an apparently disinterested broker between the Hindus and Muslims, all the time keeping the main springs of power in their own group. But, the position is now that the Tories have been ousted from power and there is a Labour Government in England[45]. Vallabhbhai, much against the wishes of Gandhi, convinced the Congress to accept the Cabinet Mission Plan, which though envisaged the balkanisation of India, yet had some positive attributes like the immediate transfer of power to an Interim Government and formation of the Constituent Assembly. His persuasive ability enabled him to take popular leader like Nehru into his fold.

Vallabhbhai's strategy helped the Congress to form the Interim Government. In the new political set-up, he became the Minister of Home and Information and Broadcasting. His responsibility was onerous as he had to tackle the communal violence unleashed by the Muslim League which failed to realise the goal of Pakistan. Subsequently, he became the Minister of States and initiated the process of integration of the Princely States. As the Chairman of the Congress Parliamentary Committee, he supervised the electoral strategy of the Congress, and monitored the election for the Central and Provincial Legislative Assemblies in 1946. Vallabhbhai, with a deep foresight could visualise the consequences of the victory of the Muslim League in a contiguous zone in the election to the Provincial Assemblies and the tacit support given to the League by the British authority to make it part of the Interim Government. His apprehension came true, when the League did not cooperate both as part of the Government and the Constituent Assembly. Then, the majority of the Congress leaders including Vallabhbhai had no option but to accept the June 3rd Partition Plan, articulated by Lord Mountbatten, the last Governor General with the help of V.P. Menon, the Reform Commissioner.

After independence, Vallabhbhai continued to assume the responsibilities of the Department of Home, States, and Information and Broadcasting. He also became the Deputy Prime Minister in the new Cabinet led by Jawaharlal Nehru. In addition to his ministerial responsibility, he played an active role in the framing of the Constitution, especially as the Chairman of the Committees for Fundamental Rights, Minorities and Provincial Constitution. He was known to have incorporated provisions like the right to Private Property, Privy Purse for the princes and constitutional guarantees for the Civil Service. As one of the members of the Partition Council, he helped in the allocation of the liabilities and dividends between India and Pakistan. He played the most crucial role in the integration of the states. Due to his long association with the Princes he managed to convince them by invoking their patriotic sentiments and harping upon their limitations like economic backwardness and need for democratisation. In fact, except Junagarh, Kashmir and Hyderabad where he had to apply force, in all other cases his negotiating skill could integrate the whole of India in the quickest possible time.

Vallabhbhai's health was affected both prior to and after independence because of the physical and mental strain. He had the first major heart attack in 1948 immediately after the death of Gandhi. Two years, later he had another massive attack and finally he succumbed to it on 15 December 1950.

2.3 Sources of Influence

Vallabhbhai's personality was shaped by many persons. It was also defined by several developments which took place in his life both in the pre-adulthood and adulthood phases.

2.3.1 The Family

Vallabhbhai was deeply influenced by his parents Jhaverbhai and Ladba. He inherited the strong physique of his father.[46] His medium height, bold skull, penetrating eyes and serene look were almost like his father. It used to have a decisive impact on the people coming in contact with him. Vallabhbhai was born and brought up in a conservative and religious atmosphere. The influence of the Swami Narayana cult, which Jhaverbhai accepted with utmost dedication, had immense impact upon the family members. The cult preached the spirit of *Vairagya* not in terms of renunciation of activities but by cultivation of a spirit of detachment, to be accrued in course of fulfilling one's duty. It was quite akin to the secular values of the Protestant ethics, giving birth to capitalism in the West.[47] The impact of religion made Jhaverbhai quite conservative and stoic and it was thoroughly inherited by Vallabhbhai. He wrote in one of his letters to Maniben, his daughter: "There is no point in continuously remembering the past and being miserable. The essence of the past is that remaining life should be considered as new life and correct the mistakes. That is the right duty. So, think that whenever you awake, it is morning time and have faith in God and restructure the remaining life... serve the people without any expectation and try to be as much pure as possible by mind and deed"[48]. It revealed his emphasis on the present and concern for duty which echoed the sense of humanism preached by the Vaishnava sect. This faith in the Almighty made him a tolerant man subsequently.[49] Devotion to religion constantly reminded him of his duties in every field of life. It was further revealed when as a student he defied his teachers in protest against dereliction of duty, as a lawyer fought the case of his clients even leaving Jhaverba, his wife on the death bed and as the Sanitary

Committee Chairman of the Ahmedabad civic body he moved around the plague affected city. In subsequent period, he confided: "I accept without reservation that I served the Ahmedabad Municipality to the best of my capacity. I had unalloyed happiness in the task which I performed then. After all, to all of us to serve our city must give unmitigated pleasure and mental satisfaction, which we can not get in another sphere."[50] In fact, such a duty-oriented attitude might have been further refined by the communitarian approach of his parents.[51] In this backdrop, his faith in religion appeared to be quite secular. He used to observe some rituals in his younger days in Karamsad. But he abandoned those once his pragmatic *Patidar* mind was exposed to Western education. Like his parents, he had a deep faith in an invisible power which enabled him to internalise qualities like determination, infinite ability to bear physical pain, fearlessness, and an instinct to serve others. All these qualities in him were refined with age and exposure to diverse challenges. Vallabhbhai was also influenced by his father's ability to give patient hearing to others and make quick decisions. Like his father's obsession for Chess, he was quite inclined towards Bridge.[52] It sharpened his *Patidar* calculative mind, known for taking risk and making way through skillful negotiations. It came in good stead when he pursued dialogue with the authority during the freedom struggle. He was also deeply inspired by the communitarian approach of his mother and dedicated his whole life for the country.

Vallabhbhai learnt mutual understanding and sense of obedience in his typical *Patidar* joint family system.[53] It was clearly evident as he accepted the decision of his marriage while he was still a student, allowed elder brother Vithalbhai to move to England ahead of him even at his own expense and bowed before his father's wish to take up the case of Yangpurushdas, the village priest to pursue it in the court of law. His respect for the eldest brother was revealed from one of his correspondences while in London. He wrote: ". . . .You have written about the mortgage of sister's ornaments; that does not behove you. You are elder and so you must have done whatever you must have thought proper. . . . You have written that you are in debt. But I understand that your debt is my debt. So you write to me the name of creditors, I will relieve you as quickly as possible from the debt, so that you have a sigh of relief"[54]. The sense of obedience rooted in the family hierarchy enabled him to work under Gandhi and Nehru in subsequent periods.[55] No doubt, it was the same joint set-up which deterred him from mixing freely with his wife or children. It became a major obstruction in marrying off his daughter, which was the basic responsibility of a *Patidar* father.[56] Once, he confided: "I am somewhat at fault. But, my works keep me out of the house till late at night. . . She (Maniben) is unable to talk frankly with me and feels uncomfortable if I try to talk frankly with her. But it is not her fault. It is a tradition in the family. Until I was thirty, I did not utter a word if elders were around."[57] But his inherent sense of duty consciousness hardly kept him aloof from his children and it was reflected in the correspondences he made with them from the Jail.[58] As John Campbell narrates: "Nearly all the Indian leaders are surrounded by women members in the family who have an extremely powerful influence on their careers… Not all of them would be content so quietly in the background as Maniben, but it is doubtful whether the influence of any of them in their respective household exceeds her with her father."[59] The same feeling might have been experienced by Vallabhbhai in relation to his wife Jhaverba. His decision not to marry again even though he had become a widower in the early thirties was sufficient to prove it.[60] The lack of any display of emotion in this regard might be due to the family set-up and his reserved temperament. He himself once confessed, "Other people can find relief in tears. But, I can not weep and that reduces my brain into pulp."[61] Besides the sense of responsibility, the middleclass backdrop of the family made Vallabhbhai acquire simplicity which helped him accept the challenge of quitting his roaring legal practice to join Gandhi. If he had learnt the habit of obedience and quality of sharing in the family, it also taught him to assert before others. The independent mindset of his father and the sense of negligence he felt as the middle child in the family made him so.[62] He argued: "As a child, it always pays one to be either the eldest or youngest. As the eldest, a child is the centre of paternal hopes; as the youngest, he is the object of paternal affection. Having been born between these two extremes, I naturally had the usual independence, initiative and resources of a middling."[63]

2.3.2 The Community

Vallabhbhai was deeply influenced by his *Patidar* community. The Patidars have grown homogenous over the years.Their migration to a new area, settlement in the compact Charotar region, dependence on agriculture for self-sustenance, acceptance of hypergamous marriage between the higher and the lower Patidars unified them further to influence hy and large each and every member of the community. All these factors had an indelible impact upon the patidars and motivated them to behave in a similar manner. Characterised by "Bluntness in speech, unconcerned about dress and appearance, a sense of equality within the fold that turned the villages into a collectivity of *Patidar* brothers and a sense of superiority towards the non-Patidars, a self-image of tough and independent man,"[64] the community appeared to be simple but firm enough to maintain its identity. It could tide over the challenges experienced during its migration from the Punjab to Gujarat and introduction of the British policy of the individual land ownership system. Thus, fights against adversities developed its sense of independence which was further shaped by the rustic agrarian set-up. As Vallabhbhai argued, the open space in the village provided him with opportunities to explore himself. He admitted: "It was in this atmosphere of equal give and take that I grew up with all the zest in life that only a village child can have and all that sturdiness and determination which grow out of a healthy atmosphere of daredevilry and juvenile buoyancy and impish pranks, mirth and laughter."[65] The relatively lower status in the social hierarchy influenced the community to become pragmatic. In the mid-nineteenth century, it deliberately picked up various taboos like vegetarianism, dowry practices, child marriage, etc. to maintain its exclusivity and arrest the declining status of the community. Though all these made the community conservative, yet in the long run it proved its determination to withstand the new British agrarian practices and to become more independent by going beyond the mere 'middle peasantry' status.[66] Thus, it was quite natural to find the community endowed with a utilitarian approach. Vallabhbhai's choice of legal profession for quick success, a trip to London for better position, joining with Gandhi and again differing from him in the mid-thirties for a larger objective, reflected this *Patidar* trait in him. Such an outlook motivated him to be patient during the Freedom Struggle while negotiating with the mighty British Empire. The conservative traits adopted by the *Patidar* community as a matter of expediency also encouraged him to resist a number of rituals relating to his father's death[67]. In this context, the impact of the reform movement like the Arya Samaj Movement upon the community could hardly be ignored.[68] Again, the inherent political consciousness of the community was quite well known. It was acquired over a period of time due to its association with various administrative set-ups, contact with outside world and exposure to the Swadeshi Movement in the early part of the twentieth century for which even Gandhi too reposed confidence in it.[69] The independent bent of mind of Vallabhbhai could hardly have remained immune from it. In fact, his very birth in such a community at a crucial time marked by the consolidation of the British authority following the shifting of political power from the East India Company to the Parliament and the birth of the Indian National Congress might have acted as catalysts to motivate him. The period witnessed rapid socio-economic modernisation of Gujarat as the British started leaning upon the province to overcome the 'cotton famine' which it had been facing since the American War of Independence. The changes in the surrounding might have influenced the adventurous *Patidar* Vallabhbhai to grab the opportunities.

All these traits had started developing in Vallabhbhai since his childhood. In fact, he himself at a later date credited this phase of his life for shaping his personality to a large extent. He confessed: "Child is the father of a man. I do not know how much I owe to these blissful days. I know this much however, that my constitution today is what I built up as a child and the many qualities or defects of characters which I might exhibit today can probably be traced to the characteristics which I displayed, when I was a child. This does not however mean that I kept my development in a straight line . . . I had my share of these incidents and experiences, but in the main I am what I was or tried to be seventy years ago."[70]

2.3.3 Educational Institutions

The school environment too influenced the life of Vallabhbhai. His sense of independence emboldened him to challenge the teachers for not doing their duties and during the process he picked up leadership qualities and team spirit. He admitted: "As far as I remember, I yielded to none in the captaincy of mischief or of sly attempts to hoodwink one's elders. As far as I can recall, however, it was almost always in a good cause. . . . I had no patience with an indifferent teacher and never spared a lazy one."[71] His keen interest in sports enhanced his team spirit. His independent thinking was further refined because of the thrust of some teachers to read without assistance. His inclination for English education as a way to enhance one's status created a positive attitude in him towards the Western liberal values. He acknowledged the contributions of the British system of education in creating a highly motivated and self-confident class of people capable of ruling over a foreign land. It strengthened his commitment to the notion of merit being given due prominence in the society.[72] The study of Bar-at-law in the Middle Temple of England further strengthened his view.[73]

His exposure to the British jurisprudence refined his *Vaishnovite* conservative mindset further, which might have come in good stead in the mid-thirties when the Congress decided to switch over to electoral politics in order to realise freedom. During the period of his toiling in England, he was not only influenced by the Western liberal values of discipline and nationalism but also became aware of the colonial attitude of the authority, known for following different standards towards the individuals both in England and India.[74] He was shocked to see the British pursuing policies like the Rowlatt Act to snatch the freedom of the Indians.

2.3.4 Semi-political and Political Associations

Vallabhbhai in his adulthood, got the opportunity to acquaint himself with many semi-political and political associations due to his success in the legal profession. It provided him with the opportunities not only to learn legal intricacies but also to fight against the authorities with due use of newly acquired advantages. All these helped him gain more self-confidence.

Vallabhbhai's legal career took a new turn after his return from England. The elevation from a simple public pleader to a sophisticated Barrister legitimised his status in the society. It helped him to raise voice against any form of exploitation. His transformation from a private individual to a public person was possible basically due to the influence of the Gujarat Club of which he became a regular member. Its members made him realise that it was the responsibility of the leaders to instil confidence in the public. It motivated him to enter into the Ahmedabad Municipality and to challenge the arrogant British officers. His involvement in an apolitical organisation like the Sanitary Association encouraged him to take such a decision. During the period, his ability to utilise social discipline, public spirit and the influence of Jainism and Vaishnavism[75] not only nurtured the growth of the civic political culture of Gujarat but also redefined his leadership.[76] He was further motivated by other semi-political bodies like the Gujarat Sabha and the Bombay Political Conference. All of them helped him to shift his focus from the local problems to the national cause.

Vallabhbhai was deeply influenced by the prominent leaders of the Congress. Influences of great leaders like Bal Gangadhar Tilak, Dayananda Saraswati, Aurobindo and Lajpat Rai, broadened his political horizon and made him acquaint with the search for India's identity and need for freedom. If he was indebted to Dayananda Saraswati and Lajpat Rai for their attempt to revive the past glory of India,[77] he remembered Aurobindo and Tilak for giving shape to Indian nationalism.[78] Over and above, the impact of Gandhi the most promising leader of the Congress in the late twenties, appeared to be most decisive for Vallabhbhai as it gave a new direction to his life in his adulthood. The three decades of their interactions appeared to be quite complex one which was strengthened significantly due to the physical proximity of both the leaders and for their mutual dependence.

Vallabhbhai's association with Gandhi began in Ahmedabad. It was a coincidence that both Gandhi and Vallabhbhai belonged to the same place. Both of them decided to opt for the place as their area of operations on different grounds. For a person like Vallabhbhai who was little comfortable in an unknown world, it was quite natural on his part to lean upon and nurture Ahmedabad his own native place.[79] But Gandhi found the place to be a confluence of both tradition and modernity and to have a fertile soil for both unrest and mobilisation.[80] Kenneth Gillon observing the potential of the emerging industrial city of the period wrote: "Before the Ist World War, Ahmedabad was an unknown parochial place, lightly ruled by the British. But, soon after, it was to become in fact, if not now, a financial and political base for the Indian National Congress and a leader and a prototype of new India."[81] Commenting upon the city of Ahmedabad, Mavalankar, one of the close associates of the two leaders observed: "while Ahmedabad can not be permitted the exclusive claim of having given Gandhiji to India and the world, it can legitimately claim so as regards the Sardar."[82]

Vallabhbhai was influenced by the message of non-violence of Gandhi. He was moved by it due to the ineffectiveness of other existing methods adopted against the British authority and the magnetic impact of the leader upon the mass. Prior to the rise of Gandhi, there were virtually two recognised methods of making political protests, such as the gradualist constitutionalism with an inadequate following and terrorism with an unacceptable base. In this context, the Gandhian innovations of making synthesis of the courage of renunciation and right action became the best available method to remove any sense of inferiority and infuse determination as needed for any non-violent struggle. In the given traditional society which was characterised by mechanical solidarity and communal bond, Gandhi's method of protest by means of non-violence, spirituality, discipline etc. not only generated awareness among the people but also created confidence in the authority to be negotiated with. The Champaran success proved his unique ability to blend religious purification with political resistance. In the initial part of his public career, Vallabhbhai's conservative and pragmatic mindset was obviously attracted towards method to gain legitimacy in the shortest possible time. He argued: "Long before I met Gandhiji, I was interested in politics. But no school of politics at that time attracted me. There were many arm-chair politicians of course and there were also the anarchists, very often in Bengal and Maharastra. Then came Gandhi on the scene and in him I see a leader worth following."[83] He extended cooperation to Gandhi and worked very closely with him during the freedom struggle. In fact he was quite aggrieved when at a later date some people pointed out his incapability as the Home Minister of India and held him responsible for the assassination of Gandhi."[84] His sincerity towards the leader was revealed from his own acknowledgement: "With one voice, the world acclaimed him as the greatest and purest of his times . . . . When we look back on our lives, we are reminded of what we were and what he made of us, what a revolution he brought in our lives, not in individuals, but in tens of millions . . . . What he preached, he practised. Smaller men like us could only try to follow in his footsteps as best as he could."[85]

Despite the dedication and dependence it would be too sweeping to brand Vallabhbhai as 'a blind follower of Gandhi'[86] or to consider him to have been just picked up by the great leader.[87] He came in contact with Gandhi in his 1940's, when he had already started asserting himself at the grass roots level independently. Moreover, there was little doubt that Gandhi was dependent on Vallabhbhai in all the grass roots movements for the latter's command over the rural hierarchies. Vallabhbhai's innovations like use of caste and flexible approach towards Khadi and non-violence contributed immensely to the success of the Gandhian *Satyagraha* in Gujarat. His ability to play the role of a linkman in between the national leadership and the local *Patidar* leaders, and to reconcile the impracticalities of the Gandhian philosophy with the realities of peasant politics, made him indispensable[88]. It was revealed from Gandhi's view given at the time of the Kheda struggle. ". . . .If it were not for his (Vallabhbhai's) assistance, I must admit that this campaign would not have been carried through so successfully."[89] With his distinct ability to contribute, Vallabhbhai dared to differ from Gandhi's injunction and self-experiment which involved notions of spiritual purification, cosmic withdrawal and redemption.[90] He criticised Gandhi's style of making continuous experiments. Once commenting upon the latter's effort to spin cloth with his left hand, he said: "I can not see any advantage in this. Why can not you stick to that to which you are accustomed? You can not acquire a new skill after certain age."[91] His views reflected the *Patidar* mindset which was more practical and was inclined towards mundane affairs. Vallabhbhai realised the ideological burden of Gandhi in the age of power politics and took a neutral stand in the Bombay session of the Congress to pave the way for the latter's retirement.[92] With his tremendous sense of self-confidence, he argued: "Many call me a blind devotee of Gandhiji. I wish that in fact I had the strength to become his devotee, but, that alas is not the case. I claim to have the average intelligence and understanding. I have seen something of the world, so it is not likely that I would follow this half-naked person like a man without understanding.... I keep Gandhiji away from my work. We are not likely to develop a capacity for initiative and independent action, if we always look to him for guidance."[93] The difference in approach between the leaders became more apparent as the British withdrawal came nearer leaving behind a deep-rooted communal animosity. Gandhi reacted sharply against Vallabhbhai's hard stand on the Muslim League and keenness to negotiate with the authority. But justifying his stand Vallabhbhai said: "I do not want to take different path... but if I had not done what I did, the Congress would have been held to blame afterwards"[94]. Regarding their different approaches to power politics, Pyreylal observes: "The final phase of negotiations with the Cabinet Mission marked the beginning of that cleavage between Gandhiji and some of his closest colleagues, which in the final phase of the transfer of power left them facing different ways."[95] Anyhow, despite the difference in perception, both Gandhi and Vallabhbhai, over a period of time learned to realise and accommodate each other's limitations and to share their responsibilities as a thinker and a doer respectively. Thus, they provided a collective leadership before the country.

Besides Gandhi, Vallabhbhai was also inspired by many other contemporary political leaders. In the mid-thirties, his style of functioning was shaped by the radical approach of the Socialist faction and hawkish attitude of the Muslim League. True to his *Patidar* mindset, he became more calculative in response to the strategy of Subash Chandra Bose, the leader of the Socialist group in the Congress which was advocating a different path for the socio-economic change and liberation of the country. L.N. Sarin observes: "Whereas patriotism was concerned, neither Bose nor Patel were lukewarm and wavering. Their methods however differed. Bose believed that Gandhi's leadership, if necessary, was not indispensable. To Patel, it was the brain and the soul of the struggle of the Congress."[96] Vallabhbhai successfully weaned away Nehru, a prominent votary of the Socialist thinking into his fold by incorporating a set of socio-economic principles in the Karachi Congress Resolution on Fundamental Rights.[97] Again his ability to negotiate with the authority cornered the League to a large extent. He was also greatly helped by C. Rajagopalachari and K.M. Munshi, the stalwarts in the Congress in course of making constitutional dialogues with the British authority and framing the Constitution so as to ensure the goal of independence[98]. He was assisted by them in ensuring Commonwealth status for the country, guaranteeing Privy Purse for the native Princes incorporating the Right to Private Property in the Constitution and carrying out military operation in Hyderabad.

Thus, over a period of time, Vallabhbhai appeared to have become more and more matured by making due synthesis of diverse roles such as that of a simple Gujarati, ambitious Patidar, the hair-splitting moffussil lawyer, a Municipal Councillor, an effective provincial leader, the nationalist, the uncompromising anti-League and above all that of a power politician. Hence, he could take up larger responsibilities in the liberation of the country and its consolidation subsequently. It has been rightly observed: "Without Patel, Gandhiji's idea would have had less practical influence and Nehru's idealism less scope. Patel was not only the organiser of the fight for freedom, but also the architect of the new state, when the struggle was over. The same man is seldom successful as rebel and statesman; Sardar Patel is an exception."[99]

2.4 The Emerging Pattern

All these influences upon Vallabhbhai and the socialisation experiences gained by him during the process seem to have conditioned his mindset, perception and personality. The ideas and belief system of his parents and traits of his *Patidar* community have probably contributed towards the formation of an individualistic and conservative mindset in him. At the same time his exposure to the Western culture and involvement in the socio-political process of India seem to have developed in him liberal democratic and humane ideas. Accordingly, a fine synthesis of conservatism, liberalism and humanism seem to characterise his personality.

Notes and References

1. Fred, I. Greenstein, "The Benevolent Leader: Childen's Images of Political Socialisation", *American Political Science Review*, 54, 1960, pp. 934-47.
2. Jan Breman, *Of Peasants Migrants and Paupers Rural Labour Circulation and Capital Production in West India* (New Delhi: 1985, pp. 83-4).
3. B. Krishna, *Sardar Vallabhbhai Patel: India's Iron Man* (New Delhi: Indus, 1995, p. 6).
4. David F. Pocock, *Kanbi and Patidar: A Study of the Patidar Community of Gujarat* (London: Oxford, 1972, p. 80).
5. Charotar, a tract of sandy but fertile land in Central Gujarat, is bordered on its east and south by the river Mahi, on its north by the river Shedhi and on its west by the black earth of the Bhal tract.
6. Swami Narayan Cult, a popular Vaishnovite movement was launched in Gujarat in the mid-nineteenth century. It provided opportunity for upward mobilisation to the pragmatic Leva Patidars which was then challenged by the new British agrarian practice of individual land ownership system. The 1931 census recognised their elevated status and replaced the caste name 'Kanbi', the original name of the broad migrated group with 'Patidar'. For details refer David F. Pocock, *Kanbis and Patidars, op. cit.*, p. 64.
7. D.V. Tharmankar, *Sardar Patel* (London: George Allen and Unwin Ltd., 1970, p. 23).
8. Chhagam group of villages includes six prominent settlements such as Karamsad, Nadiad, Vaso, Sojitra, Dhamaja and Bhadran which represent the dominance of the Patidars.
9. David Hardiman, *Peasant Nationalists of Gujarat: Kheda District, 1917-34* (London: Oxford, 1981, p. 44).
10. D.V. Thamankar, *Sardar Patel, op. cit.*, p. 27.
11. Narahari, D. Parikh, *Sardar Vallabhbhai Patel*, Vol. I (Ahmedabad: Navajivan, 1953, p. 6).
12. Vallabhbhai Patel, "When I was a Child" in G.M. Nandurkar (ed.), Commemorative Volume (Ahmedabad: 1974, p. 168).
13. David F. Pocock, *Kanbi and Patidar, op. cit.*, p. 90.
14. G.M. Nandurkar (ed.), *Sardar Shri na Patro*, Vol. 3. (Ahmedabad: 1976.)

15. Vallabhbhai to Narshibhai, 15 January 1904, *Ibid.*
16. D.V. Thamankar, *Sardar Patel, op. cit.*, p. 29.
17. Narahari D. Parikh, *Sardar Vallabhbhai Patel*, Vol. I, *op. cit.*, p. 9.
18. Rajmohan Gandhi, *Patel: A Life* (Ahmedabad: Navajivan, 1991, p. 12).
19. Narahari D. Parikh, *Sardar Vallabhbhai Patel*, Vol. I, *op. cit.*, p. 9.
20. D.V. Thamankar, *Sardar Patel, op. cit.*, p. 33.
21. Vallabhbhai Patel, "When I was a Child" in G.M. Nandurkar (ed.), Commemorative Volume, *op. cit.*, p. 168.
22. G.M. Nandurkar (ed.), *Birth Centenary* Volume I (Ahmedabad: 1974, p. 206).
23. Alice W. Clark, *Marriage Investment, Credit, Networking and the Demography of Central Gujarat: 1825-1905* (Chicago: 1982).
24. Rajmohan Gandhi, *Patel: A Life, op. cit.*, p. 9.
25. Narahari D. Parikh, *Sardar Vallabhbhai Patel*, Vol. I, *op. cit.*, p. 11.
26. G.I. Patel, Vithalbhai Patel, *Life and Times* (Bombay: 1950, p. 19).
27. Narahari D. Parikh, *Sardar Vallabhbhai Patel*, Vol. I, *op. cit.*, p. 14.
28. G.M. Nandurkar (ed.), *Sardar Shri na Patro*, Vol. 3 (Ahmedabad: 1977).
29. K.L. Panjabi, *The Indomitable Sardar* (Bombay: Bharatiya Vidya Bhavan, 1962, p. 13).
30. Narahari D. Parikh, *Sardar Vallabhbhai Patel*, Vol. I, *op. cit.*, p. 13.
31. Raojibhai Patel, *Hind Ke Sardar* (Ahmedabad: Navajivan, 1972, p. 30).
32. Narahari D. Parikh, *Sardar Vallabhbhai Patel*, Vol. I, *op. cit.*, p. 20.
33. Indulal Yagnik, *Atmakatha*, Vol. 2 (Ahmedabad: 1955).
34. G.V. Mavalankar, "Sardar Vallabhbhai Patel", in P.D. Saggi, (ed.), *A. Nation's Homage: Life and Works of Sardar Vallabhbhai Patel* (Bombay: Overseas Publishing House, p. 9).
35. G.M. Nandurkar (ed.), *Sardar Shrina Patro*, Vol. V. (Ahmedabad: 1978).
36. Narahari D. Parikh, *Sardar Vallabhbhai Patel.* Vol. I, *op. cit.*, p. 27.
37. The Policy adopted by the Congress to counter the Bengal partition

decision, divided the organisation. While the Moderate group under the leadership of Surendranath Benarjee and Dada Bhai Naoroji demanded constitutional reform, the Extremist group led by Tilak insisted on pursuing radical alternatives like non-cooperation to resist the British authority.

38. Kenneth Gillon, *Ahmedabad: A Study in Indian Urban History* (California Press: 1968, p. 130).
39. Devavrat Pathak and Pravin Sheth, *Sardar Vallabhbhai Patel: From Civic to National Leadership* (Ahmedabad: Navajivan, p. 33).
40. The Memorandum Submitted by the Government of Bombay to the Indian Statutory Commission, *The Times of India*, 27 November 1926.
41. Dwain Marwick, "Political Decision Makers in Contrasting Milius" in Marwick, *Political Decision-Makers: Recruitment and Performance* (Free Press of Glencoe: 1961, p. 27).
42. Raojibhai Patel, *Hind Ke Sardar, op. cit.*, p. 39.
43. P.N. Chopra,(ed.), *The Collected Works of Sardar Vallabhbhai Patel,* Vol.I. (New Delhi: Konark Pvt. Ltd., 1990, p. 40).
44. Narahari D. Parikh, *Sardar Vallabhbhai Patel,* Vol. 2. (Ahmedabad: Navajivan, 1956, p. 175).
45. R.K. Murthi, *The Man and His Contemporaries* (New Delhi: Sterling Publishers, 1976, p. 144).
46. P.U. Patel, *Sardar Patel: India's Man of Destiny* (Bombay: 1964, p. 134).
47. Devabrat Pathak and Pravin Sheth, *Sardar Vallabhbhai Patel: From Civic to National Leadership, op. cit.*, p. 371.
48. G.M. Nandurkar (ed.), *Sardar Shri na Patro*, Vol. III. (Ahmedabad: 1976).
49. P.U. Patel, *Sardar Patel: India's Man of Destiny, op. cit.*, p. 136.
50. Devavrat Pathak and Pravin Sheth, *Sardar Vallabhbhai Patel: From Civic to National Leadership, op. cit.*, p. 379.
51. G.M. Nandurkar (ed.), *Sardar's Letters Mostly Unknown*, Post-Centenary Volume II. (Ahmedabad: 1981).
52. Narahari D. Parikh, *Sardar Vallabhbhai Patel,* Vol. I, *op. cit.*, p. 25.

53. Vallabhbhai to Dayabhai, 4 July 1924, *Patel Papers.* Navajivan, Ahmedabad.
54. G.M. Nandurkar (ed.), *Sardar Shri na Patro*, Vol. III. (Ahmeabad: 1976).
55. Howard Spodek, "Sardar Vallabhbhai Patel At 100", in Verinder Grover, (ed.), *Political Thinkers of Modern India*, Vol. 18 (New Delhi: Deep and Deep Publication, 1992, p. 357).
56. David, F. Pocock, *Kanbi and Patidar, op. cit.*, p. 101.
57. Raojibhai Patel, *Hind Ke Sardar, op. cit.*, pp. 26-8.
58. G.M. Nandurkar (ed.), *Sardar Shri na Patro*, Vol. V. (Ahmedabad: 1978).
59. Johnson Alan Campbell, "The Gentle Hindu", in P.D. Saggi (ed.), *A Nation's Homage: Life and Works of Sardar Vallabhbhai Patel, op. cit.*, p. 48.
60. G.M. Nandurkar (ed.), *Sardar Shri na Patro*, Vol. III. (Ahmedabad: 1976).
61. Pyarelal, "The Incomparable Sardar" in G.M. Nandurkar(ed), The Commorative Volume, *op cit*, p.147
62. Narahari D. Parikh, *Sardar Vallabhbhai Patel*, Vol. I, *op. cit.*, p. 7.
63. Vallabhbhai Patel, "When I was a Child", in G.M. Nandurkar (ed.), Commemorative Volume, *op. cit.*, p. 167.
64. David Hardiman, *Peasant Nationalists of Gujarat: Kheda District, op. cit.*, p. 43.
65. Vallabhbhai Patel, "When I was a Child", in G.M. Nandurkar (ed.) Commemorative Volume, *op. cit.*, p. 168.
66. Middle Peasantry status refers to the economic independence of the peasants. For details refer Eric R. Wolf, "On Peasant Rebellion in Teodor Shanin (ed.), *Peasants and Peasant Societies: Select Readings.* (London: 1971); Hamja Alvi, "Peasants and Revolution" in A.R. Desai (ed.) *Peasant Struggle in India.* (Bombay: 1979). David Hardiman's 'caste-cum-class factor' as the basis of peasant independence advocates a contrary view. For details see David Hardiman, "The Roots of Rural Agitation in India, 1914-47: A Rejoinder to Charlesworth", *The Journal of Peasant Studies*, Vol. 8, 1980-1.
67. Devavrat Pathak and Pravin Sheth, *Sardar Vallabhbhai Patel: From*

Civic to National Leadership, op. cit., p. 352.

68. David Hardiman, *Peasant Nationalists of Gujarat, op. cit.*, p. 64.
69. Ambelal Gopalbhai Desai, *Dakshina Gujaratana Anavil Brahmanas* (Surat: 1969, p. 90).
70. Vallabhbhai Patel, "When I was a Child", in G.M. Nandurkar (ed.), Commemorative Volume, *op. cit.*, p. 168.
71. *Ibid.*
72. Narahari D. Parik, *Sardar Vallabhbhai Patel*, Vol. I, *op. cit.*, p. 11.
73. V.B. Kulkarni, *The Indian Triumvirate: A Political Biography of Gandhi-Patel-Nehru* (Bombay: Bharatiya Vidya Bhavan, 1963, p. 263). Michael Lyon, Sardar Patel and Indian Independence (New Delhi: Konark Pvt. Ltd., 1996, p. 18).
74. K.L. Panjabi, *The Indomitable Sardar, op. cit.*, p. 17.
75. Ali Ashraf, Politics of Development and Decay: A Study of Politics and City Government in Ahmedabad and Kanpur (Kanpur: 1975).
76. Devavrat Pathak and Pravin Sheth, *Sardar Vallabhbhai Patel: From Civic to National Leadership, op. cit.*, p. 371.
77. *The Hindustan Times*, 20 November 1950.
78. P.N. Chopra,(ed.), *The Collected Works of Sardar Vallabhbhai Patel*, Vol. I, 1990, *op. cit.*, p. 40.
79. Rani Dhavan Shankardass, *Vallabhbhai Patel: Power and Organisation in Indian Politics* (New Delhi: Orient Longman, 1988, p. 18).
80. Erik Erikson, *Gandhi's Truth* (London: Faber and Faber, 1970, pp. 261-2).
81. Kenneth Gillon, *Ahmedabad: A Study in Indian Urban History, Op. cit*, p. 131.
82. G.V. Mavalankar, "Sardar Vallabhbhai Patel" in P.D. Saggi, (ed.), *A Nation's Homage: Life and Works of Sardar Vallabhbhai Patel, op. cit.*, p. 8.
83. *The Illustrated Weekly of India*, 8 October 1939.
84. Maulana Abul Kalam Azad, *India Wins Freedom* (New Delhi: Orient Longman, 1959, p. 244).
85. R.K. Murthi, *The Man and His Contemporaries, op. cit.*, p. 131.
86. Narahari D. Parikh, *Sardar Vallabhbhai Patel*, Vol. 2, *op. cit.*, p. 175.

87. Maulana Abul Kalam Azad, *India Wins Freedom, op. cit.*, pp. 216-25.
88. David Hardiman, *The Peasant Nationalists of Gujarat: Kheda District, op. cit.*, p. 128.
89. Narahari D. Parikh, *Sardar Vallabhbhai Patel,* Vol. I, *op. cit.*, p. 92.
90. Michael H. Lyon, *Sardar Patel and Indian Independence, op. cit.*, p. 40.
91. K.L. Panjabi, *The Indomitable Sardar, op. cit.*, p. 96.
92. In the mid-thirties, crushing of the Civil Disobedience Movement, dissension within the Congress regarding the forthcoming strategy, growing popularisation of the Congress Socialists, introduction of the constitutional opportunities and uprisings of Prajamandal groups in the Princely States questioned the viability of the agitational strategy of Gandhi. For details refer Bombay Chronicle 29 September 1934. D.V. Tahamankar, *Sardar Patel, op. cit.*, p. 140. Rani Dhavan Shankardass, *Vallabhbhai Patel: Power and Organisation in Indian Politics, op. cit.*, p. 123.
93. Narahari D. Parikh, *Sardar Vallabhbhai Patel,* Vol. I, *op. cit.* pp. 392-393.
94. R.K. Murthi, *The Man and His Contemporaries, op. cit.*, p. 124.
95. *Ibid.*, p. 123.
96. L.N. Sarin, *Sardar Patel* (New Delhi: S. Chand & Co. 1972, p. 62).
97. B. Krishna, *Sardar Vallabhbhai Patel: India's Iron Man, op. cit.*, p. 181.
98. Rajmohan Gandhi, *Patel: A Life, op. cit.*, p. 504. K.L. Panjabi, *The Indomitable Sardar, op. cit.*, p. 189.
99. *The Manchester Guardian*, 16 December 1950.

3

Pattern of Political Values

Values are emotional preferences conditioned by one's life experiences. These preferences relate to societal objects and are formed by the individual during his life as a consequence of his experiences and observation of societal phenomena and also of his interactions with fellow members of the society. Values then characterise the individual's mindset and constitute an integral part of his personality and get manifested in his behaviour, activities and roles. When values are related to political objects, these may be termed as political values. These are also formed by the individual through his political socialisation, as a reflection of his observation and experiences of political phenomena. As political values tend to condition an individual's political behaviour and roles it seems imperative to undertake an inquiry and analysis of these to comprehend the political thought of leaders like Vallabhbhai Patel. In this context, his perception and notion of political values like rights, liberty, equality and justice have been analysed.

3.1 Rights and Liberty

Rights and Liberty are two essentially related concepts. Rights ensure the conducive atmosphere required for the growth of the human personality and pave the way for the enjoyment of liberty or freedom with due regulation. Given the enterprising outlook and independent approach of the *Patidar* community, it was quite natural on the part of Vallabhbhai to reflect upon and articulate his views on these concepts. He became obsessive about one's privileges because of his insecure mindset developed due to the alleged self-perceived sense of negligence as the 'middle child' in the family, and exposure to the Western education loaded with liberal values. A glance over the life sketch of Vallabhbhai reveals his concern for rights like the right against exploitation, freedom of speech and expression, right to life, right to property, right to religion and for some specific political rights. In order to assess the pattern of political values of Vallabhbhai, his view points on all these have been analysed.

3.1.1 Right against Exploitation

Vallabhbhai, a true *Patidar*, was never accustomed to servility. He raised voice against every form of exploitation throughout his life. As his life sketch reveals, even prior to his involvement in the freedom struggle he used to resist the teachers in schools and judges in the Court for making undue encroachment upon the rights of individuals. His effort to protect the individual from exploitation can be discerned in his fights against the high-handedness of the authority, the exploitative revenue policies and maladministration in the Princely States.

On the High-handedness of the Authority

In an age, when the British legal system was couched with restrictions against the Indians, Vallabhbhai's struggle to set it right became an epitome of self-pride. In the initial stage of his legal career, he was highly indignant over the arrogant judicial authority for the whimsical shifting of the court of the Resident Magistrate from Borsad to Anand, restricting the Indian clients from having a face to face contact with the judges in the court room and debarring the lawyers from legal practice for participating in the anti-Rowlatt Act agitation (1919). Vallabhbhai invariably appeared as the defence lawyer. His dedication could be assessed from the fact that he gave priority to attending the court trials than to his wife even when she was in her death bed. His presence as a defence counsel not only inspired confidence in his clients but also kept the judge and prosecution straight in the narrow path of justice. Mavalankar, one of his associates aptly observed: "Patel would never allow a judge to overstep even in the least, the limits of courtesy nor would he allow or tolerate any unfairness, injustice or improper leaning on the part of the court in favour of the police or the prosecution .... He would spare neither the judge nor the prosecutor nor the police and called a spade a spade . . . . He thus safeguarded the self-respect of the bar and the public."[1] His robust commonsense, courage, foresight, unruffled temperament and the ability to understand human psychology often held him in good stead and helped him in his crusade for justice.

The self-confidence acquired by Vallabhbhai as a successful criminal lawyer emboldened him to set right the crippled civic body. He was very much keen to ensure the provision of basic amenities to the tax-payers. The state of affairs of the Ahmedabad civic body was deplorable. An Administrative Report observed: "there was little organisation, duties were carelessly defined and procedure was negligible . . . . the efficiency of the Municipal staff is at a low ebb. Complaints on the part of the public against the delays and corruption by Municipal servants have been rife . . . . It can not be denied that they were founded on a substratum of truth."[2] The decline was attributed to its structural loopholes like the domination of the nominated members, groupism amidst the elected ones and low public morale. All these resulted in the high-handedness of the British officials demanding very often forced labour from the people. Personnels like Shillidy, Master, Pratt etc. were arrogant enough to give priority to the private than the public interests. Vallabhbhai's strong concern towards such issues encouraged him to enter in to Municipal politics. Subsequently, he manoeuvred to oust Shillidy, the Municipal Commissioner from the office for giving tenders, fixing salaries and misusing public property by keeping the elected civic body in dark. He was also critical of Pratt, the Commissioner of the Northern Division for instigating the people to burn the houses of the elected members for any inconveniences.[3] He reacted against Pratt's vindictive policies such as the withdrawal of efficient officers like P.K. Desai, the Secretary of the School Committee, and P.N. Gore, the Engineer for Water Works who were on deputation to the Municipality, manipulation to prevent appointment of the Indian officers, and seising of public money worth Rs. 72,000 from the exchequer of the civic body. Such measures were adopted to make the elected body a defunct one and also to harass the public for supporting the Non-Cooperation Movement. Vallabhbhai criticised the officers for demanding extra perks, installing statue of Queen Victoria in the city, keeping an unregulated and huge inspection staff, sparing the influential people from the tax net and supplying water to the posh Cantonment locality at the cost of the ordinary tax-payers. Such a reaction particularly directed against the high-handedness of the authority was in tune with his *Patidar* business ethics. He was convinced: "If it is a personal account, one need not be miserable about it, but if in the trust, there is any irregularity, it is regrettable."[4] In this context his repeated warning to son Dayabhai to handle public money carefully, appeared to be quite natural.[5] Subsequently, he not only refrained himself from but also advised Rajagopalachari, the Governor General of independent India against using public money for personal security.[6] Again, on assuming the charge of the Ministry of Information and Broadcasting, he was quite emphatic against the use of the All India Radio for private causes like raising subscription for the Jai Prakash Narain and Gandhi Memorial Funds.[7] Morarji Desai, one of his close associates, substantiated it further by revealing Vallabhbhai's hesitation to make telephone calls to the Provincial Congress Chiefs from the party fund.[8] Besides the regulation of the public purse, his keenness to restrict the authority was felt from the way he criticised the existing special privileges for the outgoing British administration and advised M.O. Mathai, the Railway Minister of the first Cabinet to get rid of them.[9] His sincerity in resisting official high-handedness was reflected in his insistence on devolution of power to the civic body. He urged for financial autonomy and division of authority between the officials and elected representatives at the local level.[10] At the time of independence, he advocated for proper codification of the authority of Bureaucracy and due regulation of the privileges of the legislature to protect people from official excesses.[11]

On the Exploitative British Revenue Policies

Vallabhbhai was highly critical of the exploitative revenue policies of the British. The alien power did not hesitate to hike and extract agricultural taxes from the farmers arbitrarily, especially when the country was reeling under the adverse impact of the First World War. It was also least bothered about the frequent epidemics and unpredictable monsoon affecting the agricultural output. It preferred to ignore both the British convention of 'no taxation without representation' and the prevailing Indian practice of contractual obligation between the ruler and the ruled on the protection of people's interests in lieu of payment of taxes. Such policies had affected the peasants of all strata directly or indirectly. Leaders like Vallabhbhai contributed to peasant mobilisation against the authority. Highlighting the exploitative British revenue policies, he argued: "The question today is not a few lakhs of rupees, but it is a question of self-respect. It is one of the fundamental principles of government, no taxation without representation. They should do nothing without having heard your views in the matter. You have to resist the arbitrary system of fixing the revenue according to Government's own whim and fancies."[12] He criticised the authority in Kheda (1918) for ignoring the natural calamities and the claim of compensation. He raised voice against the authority in Bordoli (1927) for overlooking the peasants' demand for tax restructuring. The issue of Bordoli had a greater repercussion as it involved arbitrary hike in tax collection made on the basis of different yardsticks like the gross value product and rental value as suggested by Jayakar, the Settlement officer and Anderson, the Settlement Commissioner. In both the cases Vallabhbhai was critical of the authority's policy of forcible confiscation of land and cattle of the defaulters[13]. Besides the land tax, he was also against the punitive measures like the riot tax imposed by the authority as a deterrent measure to recover the loss of property during any riot. He had to bear the brunt of such exploitation during the anti Rowlatt Act agitation (1919) and the Quit India Movement (1942). He reacted against another punitive measure like the levy of tax in Borsad (1923) imposed to counter the threat of the dacoits. In all these cases, he was basically dependent upon the socio-economic groups like the upper caste *Patidars*. At the same time he mobilised people through the Congress Party. During the Bordoli struggle he linked the provincial unit of the party with the all-India level and got a decisive victory against the British authority.

On the Maladministration in the Princely States

Vallabhbhai was equally critical of the exploitation perpetuated in the autocratic Princely States. He reacted against the indifference of the ruler of Baroda towards his own people at the time of the Gujarat Flood.[14] He criticised the Princes for exploiting the people though he failed to address the problem directly till the late-thirties. But then he was in favour of the people of these States to have their own responsible governments.[15] He was convinced that in most of the cases the dictatorial set-ups were flourishing under the British influence. He believed: "The responsibility for these happenings is therefore not only of the Thakore Saheb (local ruler), but in the ultimate analysis rests with the Parliament of Britain which while claiming to peak in the name of democracy permits the grossest form of medieval autocracy to flourish in India and place the life and liberty of people at the mercy of the little despots."[16] Most likely this conviction made him realise that victory in the freedom struggle would put an end to the exploitation in states. Even, in course of pursuing the struggle for independence, he formed Civil Liberty Union in states like Rajkot and applied pressure tactics upon the Limbdi ruler to create political awareness against the autocratic regimes.

3.1.2 Freedom of Speech and Expression

Vallabhbhai was an ardent advocate of freedom of speech and expression. It was clearly reflected in his outburst against the Jalianawalbagh massacre (1919) carried out by the British government to silence the people protesting against the draconian Rowlatt Act. The policy intended to restrict all freedoms and the right to appeal against the judgement of a Jury. Vallabhbhai decried: "We were given the Rowlatt Act which deprived us of freedom of action. When the people protested against such a tyrannical piece of legislation, the Government decided upon a policy of suppressing all resistance by force . . . .and the government officers exceeded all processes to exonerate those officers from the legal consequences of their actions."[17] While raising voice on the freedom of speech and expression he expressed his deep concern over the British policy of education, restrictions on political prisoners and unwanted regulation of the press.

On the Policy of Education

Vallabhbhai believed that the individual must get required education to develop his proper articulation. He believed: "If a medical practitioner is evil, health of a limited number of persons shall be impaired; if a merchant is evil, he will go bankrupt and will damage a few persons; if an advocate is evil, he will spoil a few suits; but if a teacher is evil, he would spoil many lives."[18] He argued that the prosperity of a country was dependent neither on the abundance of its revenue nor on the beauty of its public buildings but consisted of the number of its cultivated citizens. With this mindset, Vallabhbhai could easily foresee the colonial design of influencing the system of education and thereby penetrating into the young impressionable minds to entrench itself more firmly. He admitted: "I had been taught to think that the people of our country were of poor character and unworthy of and that it was only the foreigner ruling over us, who was good and had the ability to improve our condition. We could only be slaves. This was the sort of poison which was being instilled in our mind"[19]. The exposure to the Western way of life in England opened his eyes regarding British dualism. Hence, on his return, he made the Ahmedabad Civic body the medium to set the system of education right. He supported the

Non-Cooperation Movement of Gandhi in 1920 to motivate the members of the Municipality to refuse the Government grant for education. No doubt, it was a symbol of non-cooperation, but in reality it succeeded in reforming the system of education. He was influenced by the Sikh League which was demanding religious and educational freedom in 1919 to protect its identity. Throughout the agitation, he involved the people to develop a national ethos oriented system of education by insisting upon the refusal of the Government grant for education, prevention of routine inspection of the authority and formulation of the school curricula independently. He was also apprehensive of the administration's retaliatory measures like indiscreet retrenchment and withdrawal of grants from the sectors other than Education. So he created pension fund, organised privately managed schools, motivated people for new taxes and raised donations with the help of local leaders like Darbar Gopaldas, Gokuldas Talatis, etc. He supported organisations like the Gujarat Vidyapitha and the Kelavani Mandal to indianise the system of education. Hence, despite the suspension of the civic body by the Government, Vallabhbhai succeeded in withstanding the pressure of the authority and reforming the education system which created political awareness among the masses in the long run. His unique ability of synchronising the operations at the local and national level helped him get the desired result to a large extent.

On Prison Reforms

Vallabhbhai's concern towards the condition of the inmates in jails reflected his longing for the freedom of speech, expression and movement. During the Civil Disobedience Movement (1930), he reacted against the British policy of putting him behind bar with no valid reasons. While attacking the Government he said: "As for the conviction, I am quite sure that it was wrong. The magistrate was too tense to understand the law. He did not know under which section he was to convict me. He took about an hour and half to write a judgement of eight lines"[20]. He criticised the British Government for the imprisonment of Swami

Narayana Nanda, a member of the Andhra Provincial Congress Committee in 1931 and Khan Abdul Ghaffar Khan, a Congress worker from the North West Frontier Province in 1934. He also did not fail to criticise the Princely State of Kashmir for preventing Nehru to enter the state in 1946.

Time and again, Vallabhbhai reacted against the inhuman conditions prevailing in the jails, namely Yervada, Surat, Mathura etc. He expressed deep anguish over the death of Jatin Das, a prominent freedom fighter inside a jail in 1930. He criticised the categorisation of the political prisoners into A, B and C categories and imposition of restriction on their reading and writing books. He argued: ". . . .Whether legal and authorised, these can only be described as inhuman and barbarous. If it is legal and authorised, it condemns the whole administration as unfit and makes the condemnation all the worse"[21]. He protested against the ongoing practice of censoring of letters of the jail inmates.[22] He was extremly hurt over the censorship of his letter written on the eve of the death of his elder brother Vithalbhai. It was a question of self-respect for him. He opined: "The short statement was quite colourless and was in no way intentional or was likely to sense as propaganda. As however, government have thought fit to suspect mischief even in such harmless and innocent statement and as the mutilated statement makes it vague and meaningless, I have decided though not without regret not to publish any statement at all."[23] He not only raised voice for his daughter Maniben, who was compelled to put out her bangles in jail[24], but also for the I.N.A (Indian National Army) detenues, imprisoned in course of discharging their duties.[25] He impressed upon the Congress party to raise fund for such prisoners and tried to reform the judicial system through legislations. After independence, he took initiatives to abolish the provisions of mixed jury and separate High Court for the Europeans and insisted upon proper use of the habeas corpus. He was in favour of providing legal aid for the under trial prisoners and criticised handcuffing of the women prisoners.[26] He advised the Provincial governments to set-up administrative tribunals to scrutinise the actions of the executive to detain people.[27]

On the Press

Vallabhbhai's consistent cordial relationship with the press substantiated his genuine concern for freedom of speech and expression. He was highly critical of the British policy which intended to control it. He believed: ". . . . the press has at last been confiscated and is now in the possession of the government. The action of the government is intended to suppress truth of which it is terribly afraid, but no ordinance can confiscate truth."[28] He tried time and again to bring out the regular editions of the 'Satyagraha Akhbar' in 1919, 'Young India' in 1930, 'The Harijan' in 1948 and the 'Indian Opinion' in 1949. He tried to ensure the freedom of press when the Congress assumed power in various provinces in the late thirties. He warned against its violation in the Princely States of Kathiawar, Limbdi and Rajkot. Later on, as the Minister of Information and Broadcasting he gave a clear enunciation of the Language Policy of the All India Radio, reorganised the Public Division and initiated steps for the creation of a Research and Reference Division under the Ministry of Information and Broadcasting to make the official agencies relating to Press more effective in dissemination of news and information.

3.1.3 Right to Life

Vallabhbhai always appeared to be consistent on the value of the Right to Life. Though, the utilitarian mindset of his *Patidar* community and the middle class family existence most likely brought some moderation in his fine taste, it was still reflected in his way of life. Observing his life style in Borsad, Narahari Parikh, a close friend of Vallabhbhai said: "The furniture was neither modern nor fashionable, but for Borsad it was good and was well arranged. The floor was covered with a mat. There were a few chairs around the office table and along one wall were a soft mattresses and bolsters for those who preferred to sit on the floor in the Indian fashion".[29] Vallabhbhai used to love good food, though he had not much inclination for its variety and refinement. J.B. Kripalani, one of his co-workers observed "he (Vallabhbhai) had often to content with plain diet, but, I have an idea that he was always partial to good food"[30]. Until he came in contact with Gandhi, his fascination for good clothes was quite known to all. Even a few opined that his switching over to khadi in subsequent period was part of a new alignment strategy[31]. Given this background, K.M. Munshi was quite right to comment: "Vallabhbhai is in a sense an ascetic. His life is as simple as a peasant; his wants are always under complete control. But, he knows life in all respects and appreciates its variety and richness."[32] His longing for the Right to Life can be assessed from his hatred towards fasting, keenness to tackle food crisis, weakness for good health, obsession for self-defence and anxiety for the people affected by various calamities.

On Fasting

Vallabhbhai's least faith in fasting reiterated his conviction in the value of life. Hence, it was quite natural on his part to have resisted Gandhi, as the latter used it not simply as a technique, but as a means of purification. Once reacting to Gandhi's decision on fasting he said: "why should I fast? If I fast people will let me die. They are your friends and they exert themselves to end your fast. Not for me."[33] Vallabhbhai never glorified sacrifice as a matter of virtue. He got rid of all these practices as the symbols of rituals soon after leaving his native place Karamsad.[34] However, he was of the opinion that fasting could be resorted to sparingly to maintain good health. He advised Abdul Bari, the Bihar Congress legislator: "I am not an expert in fasting and I do not understand its philosophy. But, I think a few days fast will improve your mental condition and physical balance and it would do a lot of good."[35] Thus, he advocated for a sparing use of fasting. His attitude towards fasting seemed to be purely symbolic.

On Food Crisis

Vallabhbhai expressed deep concern over food shortage faced by the country every now and then. He extended every possible help to the British authority as he was convinced that food should be kept above party politics.[36] He reiterated the same view when the Government of India met with such a situation again after independence. It was further aggravated by population explosion, destruction of the cottage industry leading to excessive pressure on land, artificial shortage of food due to hoarding and the economic imbalances that developed after the Second World War. He argued: "the first duty of the government is to make people happy by giving them plenty of food and clothing."[37] His eagerness to ensure adequate food for people was reflected in his much articulated remedial measures such as raising productivity with due harnessing of the irrigational facilities, making fruit cultivation as an alternative, establishing cooperatives like Anand for dairy development and crop innovation, developing a centralised public distribution system and abolishing unwanted regulation on essential food items.[38] He was instrumental in motivating and convincing Nehru and Le Henderson, the US Ambassador to agree upon a mutual understanding by which the Government of India could procure a loan to finance the import of two million tons of wheat from the United States and reduce the gravity of the impending food crisis.[39] In fact, he was in favour of the involvement of both governmental and non-governmental organisations in tackling the food crisis.

On Health

Vallabhbhai had great obsession for good health. He argued: "Health should be given top priority, everything else comes next."[40] His attitude in this regard was clearly reflected in his letters to daughter Maniben. Once he wrote to her: "I knew from Mahadevbhai's letter that, though you travelled in Class III, your journey was not difficult. It was not necessary to take such a risk. One has to incur necessary expenses for maintaining health. If you try to economise then ultimately it proves to be expensive."[41] "On another occasion he discouraged her from spinning as it might affect her eyes."[42] For him, health was a holistic concept which must include the weight and vitality of the body. 'To ensure it, he gave importance to cleanliness. His belief in 'cleanliness to be next only to Godliness'[43] was basically inherited from his parents[44] and was strengthened subsequently during his involvement in the municipal politics in Ahmedabad. He criticised the British authority for turning a blind eye to the poor health condition of the people resulting out of unplanned industrialisation, population explosion and recurrent epidemics like plague. He also found the public to be responsible to some extent. They neglected the basic rules of health and cleanliness[45]. When Ahmedabad was gripped by plague, he tried his best as the Chairman of the Sanitary Committee to provide relief to the people even at the cost of putting his own life at risk. He argued: "I have undertaken the job as the Chairman of the Sanitary Committee . . . how can I leave the conservancy staff to risk plague and seek safety for myself?"[46] His sincerity to create a better atmosphere was reflected in the plan of actions he implemented as the Chairman of the civic body. He pursued schemes like the City Wall Improvement Plan, Kalupur Relief Road Project and the Ellis Bridge Scheme to make the city free from congestion. His success in this regard was attributed to his ability to take into account the financial constraint, cultural dimension and utility aspect of the plans. Again, his decision to impose Betterment Tax upon the rich people, retrench the corrupt officials and restrict the high-handedness of the authority helped him create a better atmosphere for a sound town planning mechanism. Besides cleanliness, he harped upon a balanced growth of various streams of medicines like allopathy, homeopathy and naturopathy to provide people with suitable alternatives.[47] He was very much progressive as he wanted to use science and technology to improve the standard of living of people. He was also keen on the growth of infrastructures especially in rural areas even with the help of private donations.[48]

On Self-defence

Vallabhbhai was very much concerned about the right to life of the people. So he supported the Recruitment drive in 1918 to provide the people with an opportunity to learn the operation of arms necessary for self-defence. He believed that it was an obligation on the part of the authority to protect the life of the people.[49] He exposed the British Government in 1923 for having nexus with the dacoits of Borsad and demanding punitive tax from the people on the pretext of giving them protection. Further, his hesitation to use the Gandhian techniques of boycott and picketing indiscreetly proved his concern for the right to life. He argued: "We can not stop anybody's essential service like drinking water, health services . . . . If we do, we cease to be human beings."[50] With a firm conviction that "self-defence is the elementary duty and one should do it violently or non-violently or in both ways in times of insecurity", Vallabhbhai criticised the hanging of prominent freedom fighters like Bhagat Singh and his associates in 1931, though he had lot of ideological differences with them.[51] He argued: "The boast of the English law was that upon evidence, untested by cross examination, no one could be convicted. Yet a man has been hanged and killed upon the evidence that came long after the event and without any cross examination, a man may be made to sacrifice to suffer for perversity or obstinacy but surely not hanged."[52]

On the Distressed People

Vallabhbhai was highly concerned about the people who were affected by the natural and man made calamities. He gave priority to the rehabilitation of such people and held that it was one of the moral obligations of the government.[53] Hence, he did not hesitate to criticise the native ruler of Baroda for his slackness in giving succor to the flood victims in 1927. He warned: ". . . . if the state fails in its duty, then it will be a black spot on the native state and people will be crippled. This is not a political matter, it is humanitarian and matter of piety. If the state fails in rendering adequate help, then people shall have to think about the next step."[54] He initiated measures to reorganise the provincial Congress unit in Gujarat to ensures smooth supply of seed for next cropping, to generate employment and to provide food and clothing at a cheaper rate. In fact, his efforts were also appreciated by the British authority.[55] Vallabhbhai showed the same concern when Bihar came under the spell of earthquake in 1934. While reminding the authority of its responsibility, he handled the problem not as a political issue but as one of compassion and for human life and humanism.[56] Even after assuming power, he appeared to be quite consistent in his approach as he showed the same concern towards the drought-stricken people in Saurastra and the earthquake affected people of Assam. Vallabhbhai was also very much eager to protect people from the havoc of communal violence which seized the country at the time of independence. To tide over the man-made crisis, he urged the Sikhs to provide 'safe passage' to the Muslims, formed Emergency Committee to control the riot, constituted the Punjab Relief Fund to mobilise resources and initiated the construction of the Gandhidham and Sind Resettlement Corporation to rehabilitate the affected people. Thus, if during the British administration he reminded the British authority of its obligation to protect the right to life, subsequently after its withdrawal, he motivated both the Government of India and voluntary organisations to take up the same responsibility.

3.1.4 Right to Property

Vallabhbhai was a consistent supporter of the individual's Right to Property. The deep-rooted conviction of the *Patidar* community that the security of life depends upon the possession of private property might have influenced him to become a strong votary of it. He interpreted property as the creation of God which could be enhanced by the use of one's intelligence and labour.[57] His longing for private property could be assessed from his aversion towards the policies of confiscation of personal belongings, hasty land reform, arbitrary nationalisation and the initiative to introduce measures such as 'Privy Purse'.

On Confiscation

Vallabhbhai was quite firm throughout his life against the appropriation of private property by the authority. Here, by property he referred to both movable and immovable belongings like cow, house, land, etc.

Vallabhbhai's concern for the cow was in tune with his agrarian backdrop. He reacted sharply against the British authority's decision to torture cows in order to pressurise the farmers against participating in the Kheda agitation (1918). Narrating a Patidar's concern for his cow he wrote: "*Patidars* consider the cow as members of their families. The wives of farmers wake up from deep slumber, in the night twice or thrice to feed their animals."[58] After independence, he supported the formation of the cooperative societies to look after the cows. He extended help for the establishment of a cooperative society at Anand, in Gujarat. During the inauguration of the Cooperative Society he made his intention quite clear and said: "In India, cow is worshipped, but their condition is pitiable . . . . when we are on death bed, we buy cow and donate it. Then, the person who received the donation sells the cow in the slaughter house and from the money he buys four more cows to sell again... It is said that one cannot afford to keep cows. We want to show by our experiment that one can afford keeping a cow."[59] Because of this attitude of people he found the Bill on Cow Protection to be inadequate. He appealed to the Hindus to show genuine concern for the cows by getting rid of the money making attitude first.

Given his obsession for private property, Vallabhbhai argued that the Government had no right to compel the Municipal employees to invest their Provident Fund in the Government securities.[60] As a true *Patidar*, who displays his passion fully in house building, he understood the significance of a house for the owner.[61] He dissuaded the Government of India from converting the house of Manilal where Gandhi had spent sometime, into a memorial. He argued: "Acquisition of private properties in such an arbitrary manner teaches a lesson that no one should keep a great man in his or her house as a guest. In a house, so many things happen, in which the owner is emotionally attached and from which it is difficult to dissociate. I do not think it is justified to acquire private property in the name of nation.[62]

Besides all the movable assets, Vallabhbhai was keen to protect the land of the peasant folk. His concern was partly motivated by the huge contribution of the farmers towards the society. He believed: "The peasant does not belong to the third or the last estate, but to the first estate . . . . Character always depends on whether a man works for his own bread or others work for his bread and the peasant is the least dependent among all mankind. I resent the description of the peasant as a poor, wretched creature."[63] Endowed with such an attitude, Vallabhbhai became more vocal on the issue of protection and restoration of lands of the peasants affected during the *Satyagrahas* or peaceful agitation. He was convinced: "if we do not support them . . . . we could justly be charged of failing in our duty."[64] He managed to restore the confiscated lands of many peasants by organising the villagers against the Japti operation, exerting pressure of caste to prevent the selling of the confiscated land and negotiating with the authority for the earliest restoration. In fact, he expressed his displeasure with the Congressmen who were engaged in the relief operation for the earthquake affected people in Bihar. He appealed to them to give equal attention to the plight of the peasants of Ras in Gujarat whose lands were confiscated by the British authority during the Civil Disobedience Movement.[65] His concern was further reflected when he expressed reservation over the Gandhi-Irwin Pact (1931) for sidelining the land restoration issue. He also motivated the Provincial Congress Ministries to promulgate the Forfeited Land Restoration Act (1938) and criticised the Parsees for buying the confiscated land. It was alleged that he went to the extent of sidelining K.F. Nariman, the President of the Bombay Congress unit for being in touch with Mr Garda, who dared to buy lands from the authority during the Civil Disobedience Movement.[66]

On Land Reforms

Vallabhbhai expressed reservation over any hasty land reform initiatives. He was highly critical of the Kishan Sabhas for demanding radical land reforms from the Provincial Congress Ministries in the late thirties. He even supported the government to resist the excessive demands of peasants who expected too much from the Congress Ministries."[67] He initiated the move in the Haripura Congress (1938) for the rejection of the proposed affiliation of such Kishan Sabhas with the Congress. Vallabhbhai's apprehension on bringing social justice at the cost of individual freedom was substantiated by the failure of the U.P. Jagirdari Act. He was all along aware of the reality that the *Zamindars, Jagirdars, Talukdars*, money lenders etc. were not merely the intermediaries but were inalienable parts of the agrarian system. Hence, as the Chairman of the Congress Parliamentary Sub-committee, he tried to balance the demands of both the landlords and tenants.He used the good office of the Nawab Sir Ahmed Said of Chhatari for bringing about a compromise. He emphasised on giving compensation for any loss of private property acquired for public purposes as otherwise it would be mere looting and cause resistance.[68] He believed: "You can not build the prosperity of the tenants on the misery of landlords."[69] Keeping with the logic, as the Home Member, he tried to arrange interim relief for the Kashmiri landlords for the outright abolition of the *Zamindari* right and advised the Government of India not to make any distinction between the *Zamindari* and other property at the time of land reform. He fought hard in the Constituent Assembly to have the the right to property as one of the fundamental rights in the Constitution of India.[70] In this context, his aversion towards indiscreet distribution of land and emphasis upon creation of private property appeared to be quite natural. He argued: "I myself want to distribute land equitably all over India, but you must realise how much land is available and how many people there are amongst whom it is to be distributed. The question is not taking away the riches from the rich and distributing them amongst the poor, it is that of raising the capacity of the poor to earn. If you take over the small amount, which a few rich peasants have and distribute among the poor, you will not make any appreciable difference to the poverty of the masses. At the same time, you will have killed the goose that lays the golden eggs."[71] Asoka Mehta, a prominent Socialist leader who once criticised Vallabhbhai for his soft corner for the upper section, subsequently admitted that the latter was realistic and offered solutions as per the compulsions faced by the country.[72]

On Privy Purse

Vallabhbhai was concerned about the fate of the Princes who were no doubt finally given back their status of paramountcy through the Cabinet Mission Plan, but were compelled at the time of independence to be part of either of the dominions[73]. Vallabhbhai argued: "It is easy to sacrifice by going to jail, but it is difficult to sacrifice one's own hearth and home. We can therefore, realise how much sacrifice entailed in the ruler in giving up their power and authority."[74] He wanted to compensate the Princes for the loss of their territories which symbolised their identity. He praised them for joining with the Indian State and in the process saving it from balkanisation. In order to compensate them adequately he not only secured some privileged postings for them, but also ensured their maintenance through a compensation scheme called the 'Privy Purse'. To guarantee its effectiveness, he even incorporated it in the Constitution of India.

On Nationalisation

Vallabhbhai was highly critical of the policy of indiscreet nationalisation of industries[75]. It was rooted in his soft corner for profit motive. He believed: "Profit motive is a great stimulant to exertion and rules human conduct in whatever walk of life it may be whether it is the capitalist, the middle class, the labourer or the agriculturists, with whom we may have to deal."[76] Hence, at the personal level he hardly ever dissuaded son Dayabhai from pursuing his private business interest[77]. At the same time, in the public sphere he fought for the interest of the traders by striving to ensure secrecy of their property account from the British authority, retrieving their lost property during *Satyagrahas*, urging the Provincial Congress Ministries to remain non-committal towards the Excess Profit Tax Bill and criticising Liaquat Ali, the Finance Minister of the Interim Government for restricting the scope for the growth of the Indian industries in the very first budget.[78] He continued to maintain his concern for profit motive even after independence. It was clearly reflected in his support for the Industrial Policy Resolution of 1948 envisaging the growth of Private Sector, channelisation of the unrevealed income of the industrialists by keeping their names anonymous, introduction of various saving measures like the Saving Certificate Scheme, the policy of decontrol in certain areas and backing for limited nationalisation.[79] He argued: "I shall be the first to ask for the end of capitalism, if I were convinced that, that way lay the interest of the country. . . . Nationalisation is worthwhile only if we can manage to run the industries."[80] Vallabhbhai had great reservation over the Socialists' vision of large scale nationalisation with a planned economy. Even Socialist leaders like Jaya Prakash Narain and Asoka Mehta who had suggested the Government to follow their plan immediately after independence, subsequently realised the impracticalities of their views especially during the transition period.[81]

3.1.5 Right to Religion

Unlike all other rights, Vallabhbhai's sincerity towards Right to Religion appeared to be dubious to some people. It was his Hindu conviction dominated *Patidar* way of life, limited exposure to the outside world, little knowledge about other religions and hard attitude adopted towards the Muslims since the 1940's that compelled a few to dub him a pro-Hindu leader. Ironically it was the very Hindu way of life based upon a synthesis between hierarchy and egalitarianism, and principle and practice that taught Vallabhbhai to be realistic and accommodative.[82] In fact, he found religion as a means for infusing sincerity, tenacity, discipline and organising public sentiment for a greater cause. His commitment to the right to religion was reflected in his suggestion of reforming the Hindu faith, supportive outlook towards the Muslims and concern for the other minorities.

On Reform of the Hindu Religion

As the life sketch suggests, Vallabhbhai's pragmatic *Patidar* community was deeply influenced by the popular Vaishnava sect. It picked up some orthodox religious practices only for its survival. Hence, Vallabhbhai could abandon many family rituals once he got a chance to move out of the village. It was evident when he reacted against many such rituals which were to be followed after his father's death. This apparently secular attitude was pointed out by K.M. Munshi from the way Vallabhbhai used to read the holy book the Gita. He observed: "Sardar is fond of Gita, but in his own way. He does not worry about the philosophical aspect; he concerns himself only with its inspirations."[83]

With this secular mindset, Vallabhbhai was determined to remove the existing superstitions in his own faith. He said: "The Hindu religion is at present divided and it now exists only in outward shows, such as applying religious or sectarian marks on the forehead, glimpses of deities and in undertaking religious tours of sacred places of pilgrimage. It consists in practising control of the senses, abstaining from sensual pleasures and in realisation of the supreme being such as God."[84] He criticised the ongoing Hindu practices like performing *Shraddhas* after death, taking bath in the Ganges, making the habitable areas congested by erecting wooden structures for animals in the name of religion and worshipping of the cows. He reacted against the *Sadhus* for exploiting the innocence of the people. He advised his father not to advocate the cause of Yangpurush Das, the village priest entangled in a property dispute, as he believed: "those who intrigue and quarrel and rush to the court of law themselves were unlikely to look after us in this world and still in the next."[85] He criticised the Hindu community for allowing the display of perversion on the temple in the name of religion. While pointing out such things in the Puri temple he said: "The presence of such figures in any place or public resort and particularly their exhibition in temple is most revolting and humiliating to the aesthetic sense of every pure-minded person."[86] Vallabhbhai's secular outlook was reflected in his zeal to renovate the existing dilapidated shrines. He was not in favour of building new ones as it would drain away the resources which could be used for the education of the children.[87] His support for the renovation of the Somnath temple in Gujarat had a larger goal of reviving the cultural heritage of the country and bringing proximity among the Princes of the newly formed Saurastra Union[88]. But he did not want it to be built out of funds from the Government exchequer. Rather a Public Trust was created for the purpose under the supervision of Jam Saheb, the ruler of Nawanagar. Further, Vallabhbhai insisted upon the codification of the Hindu law to prevent exploitation of people. He believed that faith in the predictions of astrologers was a sign of weakness. He ignored the opinion regarding the date of independence for India and accepted the one mentioned in the Indian Independence Act. He also criticised C.P.N. Singh, the Ambassador to Nepal for being guided by such persons.[89] He appealed to the Hindu Mahasabha, a prominent Hindu organisation not to spread any misgivings regarding the religion. He urged them: "If you think you are the only custodian of Hinduism, you are mistaken. Hinduism preaches a broader outlook of life. There is much more tolerance in Hinduism than is usually supposed."[90]

On Sympathy for the Muslims

Vallabhbhai not only thought of reforming the Hindu religion but also expressed concern for the protection of the Islamic faith. He realised the contribution of the Muslim community during the Khilafat agitation and the Recruitment drive. He also admitted the important role played by Maulana Mohammed Ali in bridging the gap between the 'no-changer' and 'pro-changer' factions of the Congress.[91] His concern for the community was reflected in the early 1930's during the Karachi Presidential address (1931), where he appealed: "As a Hindu I adopt my predecessor's formula and present the minorities with a Swadeshi fountain pen and paper and let them write on their demands. And I shall endorse them . . . . what we want is a heart unity not a patch of paper unity that will break under the slightest strain. The unity can only come when the majority takes courage in both hands and is prepared to change place with the minority."[92] In subsequent periods, he transformed his vision into action by making alliance with the Nationalist Muslims and protecting the interest of the community particularly in provinces run by the Congress. He requested his colleague Shankar Rao to investigate a complaint levelled against the Hindus for converting a burial ground into a school. His sincerity was also acknowledged by the British authority, who refused to accept the report of the Pirpur Committee, constituted by the Muslim League to verify the communal leanings of the Congress.[93]

Vallabhbhai continued to show the same concern, even after independence. He tried to maintain a balance between the Hindus and the Muslims. If at the time of the integration of the country he was critical of the Muslim rulers of Bhopal, Junagarh and Hyderabad for their soft corner towards the Muslim League, he also criticised the ambitious Hindu ruler of Travancore. While disapproving the celebration by some Muslims over the escape of Laik Ali, the last Prime Minister of Nizam of Hyderabad to Pakistan, he also expressed reservation over the rejoicing by certain Hindu communal bodies on the assassination of Gandhi. During this period, as the Information and Broadcasting Minister he addressed the nation over radio as"Gandhiji has been killed by a Hindu." Had the word Hindu not been used a lot of Muslims would have been killed in the aftermath. He expressed concern for the security of Hindus in East Bengal and was equally worried about the Muslims in the Hindu dominated areas of India. Further, he warned the Muslims against 'riding two horses' and showing disloyalty.[94] At the same time, he appealed to the Hindus to be compassionate towards the minority community to make the freedom worthwhile[95]. Vallabhbhai's aversion towards the idea of making India a Hindu state, demonstrates the genuineness of his stand. He argued: "Ours is a secular state. We can not fashion our policies or shape our conduct in the way Pakistan does it. We must see that our secular ideas are actually realised in practice."[96] In pursuance of the policy, he reacted against the unorganised exodus of population on both the sides, segregation of one community from the other and deployment of exclusively Muslim personnel for the protection of the members of the same community during rehabilitation.[97] He criticised the policy of communal representation and reservation for the minorities. But, he clarified his stand and said: "Everyone thinks that I am anti-Muslim, but, that is not the case at all. I am quite ready to guarantee the safety and well-being of the Muslims all over India."[98] He ensured the safe passage for the Muslims for their migration to Pakistan. He also arranged for the renovation of the mosques and protection of the Dargah of Nizamuddin in Delhi during the communal riot, supported the Nehru-Liaquat Pact (1950) for the safety of the minorities in India and Pakisthan and guaranteed the right of the Muslims to propagate their religion and preserve their script and culture. His defence for the Urdu language was another evidence of his sympathy for the community. He argued: "If we have to make All India Radio effective as an instrument of publicity and promotion of ideas of a secular state and culture amongst a large majority of Muslims and refugees, we must, for the time being, assign a portion of our All India Radio programme from Delhi to Urdu."[99] He wanted an amicable solution of the Ayodhya dispute which involved the interest of both the Hindu and Muslim over the disputed site of Babri Masjid.[100] Vallabhbhai's confidence in the ability of the Muslims was reflected in his support for their absorption into the mainstream. He supported the appointment of Basir Ahmed as the Chief Justice of the Madras High Court, Josh Mallhabadi as the Editor of the Ajkal, Khurshid Ahmed Khan as the Chief Commissioner of Delhi and Gulam Ahmed as the Deputy Director of the Intelligence Bureau. Observing his concerns, even Gandhi commented: "I know the Sardar. His method and manner of approach to the Hindu-Muslim question is different from mine and Pandit Nehru, but it is a travesty of truth to describe him as anti-Muslim."[101]

Concern for Other Minorities

Vallabhbhai was also quite vigilant over the safety of other minorities. Reflecting his concern for the Sikhs, he said: "It is true to our own folly that there have been distinctions between Sikhs and other communities. We all are one. This is a land of variety of religions, dress and even of hair styles. We have to evolve unity to run through this variety."[102] He was aware of the contribution of the community made during the freedom struggle and was sympathetic towards it for the division of the Punjab at the time of independence. As the Home Minister, he constituted a judicial inquiry committee to probe into the death of a Sikh police sub-inspector killed by a frenzied mob. He advised the foreign embassies to retrieve the lost image of the Sikhs tarnished by the British propaganda, holding them responsible for the violence against the Muslims at the time of transfer of power. He also negotiated with the Government of Pakistan to get back the copies of the Guru Granth Saheb from the West Punjab. He suggested reservation for the neglected Scheduled Caste population among the Sikhs. He also fought hard for the representation and reservation of the Anglo-Indian community. His appeal to protect the Ajanta and Ellora caves proves his concern for the minorities like the Buddhist and the Jains. He was equally concerned about the Parsees. Ironically, Vallabhbhai as the Chairman of the Congress Parliamentary Board had taken disciplinary measures against K.F. Nariman, the President of the Bombay Congress unit.[103] Azad used the incident to say that Vallabhbhai was against the Parsees. But an inquiry conducted by an Independent Tribunal constituted by the Congress Party under the supervision of D.N. Bhadurji, a prominent Parsee, rejected all charges against him and held Nariman responsible for anti-party activities. Interestingly, Vallabhbhai agreed to Nariman leading the Bombay

Municipal Corporation after independence. Moreover, he advised Nehru to accommodate C.H. Bhabha as the representative of the Parsee community in the first Cabinet of the country. All these measures amply confirm his concern for the minorities.

3.1.6 Political Rights

Vallabhbhai was equally conscious of the need to provide political rights to the people to enable them to participate in the political process. So he gave emphasis on participation in election, holding of public office and resistance to the political authority.

On Election

Vallabhbhai had tremendous faith in democratic election as it allowed the individual to become part of the political process and also gave scope for gradual and peaceful transformation of the society. It was perfectly in tune with the conservative *Patidar* spirit. From the beginning he showed inclination for peaceful change and participated in the civic election of Ahmedabad in order to reform the body. He was highly critical of the British policy of limiting franchise with the help of communal representation, property qualification and segregation of women. His resistance to the 1918 Council election and participation in the Gandhian agitation reflected his lack of faith in the existing limited opportunities. Expressing his resentment over the system of communal representation or compartmentalisation of both seats and electorates he said: "Let those who talk of communal representation and seats in the council, come with me to rural India, where there was no communal problem to solve. The only problem that faced part of India was the problem of hunger and bread."[104] He reacted against the British policy of Communal Award as it would not only strengthen the system of separate electorate but also divide the Hindu votes by recognising the 'untouchables' as a separate category. He also criticised the denial of the right to franchise in various Princely States such as Kathiawar, Bhavnagar, Mysore, Rajkot etc. He argued: "It is a known maxim that a right once granted to the people should never be withdrawn save for extraordinary reasons capable of being justified before the public . . . . I therefore, earnestly appeal to the state to cancel nominations which are to take the place of election."[105] During the elections of 1936 and 1946, he reacted against the British policies of restricting women franchise and neglecting deliberately the task of updating the electoral lists.

Besides pointing out the loopholes in the existing system, Vallabhbhai harped upon the remedial measures like the organisation of the Congress Party and due encouragement to other political parties with different lines of thinking. Though he avoided nexus with the Hindu Mahasabha for its least winning prospect yet he made alliance with the Nationalist Muslims to ensure smooth victory[106]. Vallabhbhai's faith in the electoral process was also revealed from his attitude towards other political parties. Despite his ideological differences with the Socialists particularly on the issue of Council-entry, he incorporated their views in 1931 in the Karachi Resolution, suggested their names as the Congress candidates for the election of 1937 and made some of them such as Yusuf Meherally, the Mayor of Bombay and Asoka Mehta, the Chief of the Congress Volunteer Corp. After assuming charge of the Home Ministry, he appealed to the Socialist factions of the Congress to suggest measures for specific programmes which they expected the Government to follow.[107] A true democrat, Vallabhbhai expressed his desire to bring change in new post-independence political scenario only through election. He emphatically said: ". . . . the only way to change the Government is through the ballot box not by revolution. Bomb attacks do not symbolise revolution. All these are cults of lunatics and the work of mad men."[108] He was eager to introduce the universal adult franchise to overcome the prevailing limitations in the electoral system, and to enable the highest and the lowest to have a share in the Government.[109]

On Holding of Public Office

With this attitude it was quite natural on the part of Vallabhbhai to have inclination for public office to be able to influence decision making. He never hesitated to accept public office at the grasroot level even while participating in the Non-Cooperation Movement of Gandhi. During his first term in civic politics, he remained as the Chairman of the Sanitary Committee and in the second term he became the President of the Municipality. He found both the roles quite constructive which provided him opportunities to be in touch with the public. In the thirties, largely due to the opening of constitutional opportunities he realised further the significance of the public office in the fight against the British authority. He did not reveal his agenda in detail in the Lucknow Session of the Congress (1936) which approved the Council-entry programme as it would have invited resistance from the Socialist faction of the Congress. Strategically, he selected candidates for the Provincial legislatures in such a way that he would be able to approve the office-acceptance plan smoothly.[110] He allowed Nehru to become the Party President in 1936 to alienate him from the Socialist influence and resisted the candidature of Subash Bose in 1939 who was opposing the office-acceptance plan. In the 1937 Provincial election, Vallabhbhai because of his organisational ability enabled the Congress to secure majority of votes in five provinces and to become the single largest Party in three other States. With this success, approval of office-acceptance which had been kept pending since 1936 by the party became a mere formality.[111] Then the Congress demanded an assurance of non-interference from the British authorities before assuming office. Some alleged that Vallabhbhai's strategy to link office-acceptance with the non-interference assurance from the Governors of the States was an eye-wash, as the Party assumed office in eight States without it.[112] He encouraged the Party to form coalition where it was not in majority. His rejection to accept the office of the Bombay Premier was to provide the party his service as an organiser to help it run the ministries smoothly.[113] His desire to stick to office was revealed in 1939 when the Congress ministries were forced to resign due to the imposition of the war decision. Vallabhbhai as the Chairman of the Parliamentary sub-committee, instructed the Speakers to adjourn the houses sine die to prevent the opponents from getting the opportunity to assume office.[114] Finally, during the negotiation with the British power for the formation of the Constituent Assembly, he insisted on accepting the 16 May plan of the Cabinet Mission (1946) to enable the Congress to accept the long term measure and form the Interim Government by isolating the Muslim League, another contender for power. On assuming office after independence, he became more conscious of the responsibility attached with the office and desisted Nehru from giving frequent threat of resignation.[115]

On Resistance

In the early part of his political career, Vallabhbhai, a supporter of the agitational strategy of Gandhi, vehemently resisted the political authority. He convinced the civic body of Ahmedabad to refuse Government grant on education during the Non-Cooperation Movement. He reacted against the British power in 1923 for putting restrictions on the hoisting of the Indian Flag and launched the Nagpur Satyagraha. Time and again, he encouraged the students community to resist the authority at various levels. He fought for the students in Gujarat who were debarred from appearing in the examination for their participation in the protest against the Simon Commission (1928) demanding the involvement of the Indians in the reform process.[116] While he challenged the authority by breaking the Salt Law during the Civil Disobedience Movement, he also encouraged the use of violence against the administration during the Quit India Movement.[117] He appealed to the Congress to oppose the controversial measures of the 1935 Act and involvement of India in the Second World War.

3.1.7 Rights and Liberty: Correlationship

Vallabhbhai's concern for the rights of the individual made him realise the need for their regulation. As a professional criminal lawyer, he observed the fallible human nature from a close range. He said: "It is true that man has the divinity in him. But does not the Gita also say that a man harbours his worst enemy within himself? If there is God in every man, there is also devil in him"[118]. He wanted regulation of human behaviour through a representative political set-up. His intention was to maximise freedom in the true sense. True to his pragmatic *Patidar* nature, he could foresee the link between the demand for rights and enjoyment of liberty needed for peaceful co-existence. Accordingly, in the mid-thirties when elected Governments were formed by the Congress in various provinces, he dropped the earlier idea of seeking absolute rights from the British authority and thought of putting due restrictions on them. He then opined: "Civil liberty must have the full scope in Congress regime. Please note the adjective civil before liberty. The moment you drop the word civil liberty then it means licence. No responsible Government can allow licence or unlimited liberty to the people. If the criminal liberty of a few persons should be restrained for the exercise of the civil liberty of lakhs of law-abiding citizens, and if the Congress Ministers fail to impose restrictions on these few, then they will be failing in duties"[119]. Hence, Vallabhbhai, who was demanding enjoyment of absolute individual rights from the Imperial authority, subsequently changed his stand on the eve of independence. He realised that the duly elected Government needed to be empowered to enable it to tide over the various problems like communal tension, refugee influx, and uneven economic growth etc. Thus, fallible human nature, compulsions of power politics, the freedom struggle and nation-building activities made him realise the necessity of making liberty compatible with a legitimate authority. All these motivated him to implement regulatory mechanisms and incorporate preventive measures in the Constitution accordingly.

Regulation of Right against Exploitation

Vallabhbhai's fight to protect the right against exploitation underwent changes in course of assumption of political power by the Congress. During the freedom struggle, the demand for unity within the Congress compelled him to express reservation over temple-entry by the untouchables. Aware that the Congress Nationalists were then determined to oppose the Temple Entry Bill and thereby expose factionalism within the party, he advised the Party to go slow on the issue[120]. His earlier stand to protect the individual from undue encroachment of the authority changed as he favoured granting of constitutional privileges to the Civil Servants after independence to enable them to take up the responsibilities of Nation-building activities. Further, he favoured reservation for certain disadvantaged section[121]. Vallabhbhai's eagerness to protect the peasants from exploitation was constrained by the compulsion of power politics. He realised it when he became the Chairman of the Congress Parliamentary Board. The long term goal of removal of the British regime led him to seek political rapprochement. In the process, he did not hesitate at times to sideline the issue of retrieval of confiscated land of the peasants. He advised the peasants: "True sacrifice is where what is done for the good of others and in such sacrifice there can be no balancing of gains and losses nor can there be any expectations of reward"[122]. He suggested the peasants of Mansa not to take any radical steps like the no-tax campaign against the ruler as it could affect the law and order situation not only in the state but also in the nearby provinces. Rather he advised them to seek justice through arbitration[123]. His attempt to bring in the Tenancy Act proved his desire to provide justice to the aggrieved peasants through amicable settlement. Further his fight against the maladministration in the Princely States was hindered as he was aware of the fact that many of the Princes were victims of British exploitative policies. He also knew that many of them had contributed financially to the Freedom Struggle. Hence, he requested the people in these states to bear with them. Justifying his friendship with some of them, he said: "If patriotism consists in becoming enemies of and unfriendly towards the states then I must confess I am not a patriot. I do not think it unpatriotic to have friendly relations with officers of the states. On the contrary, it often has been helpful for us in our struggle"[124]. The

Haripura Resolution of the Congress (1938) reflected the limitations of the Party which harped upon the need for a gradual change to be made on the basis of an amicable settlement between the people and ruler. Vallabhbhai, a staunch opponent of abrupt change, echoed the same approach and reiterated: "The people of India and the states know their duty to their Rajas. If the Rajas forget or disregard their sacred duty to their subjects, it is the fundamental duty of the subjects to bring them by constitutional means back to the right path"[125].

Regulation of Freedom of Speech and Expression

Vallabhbhai's concern for Freedom of Speech and Expression was affected by the need to infuse a sense of nationalism during freedom struggle and maintain discipline after independence. In the pre-independence period he was critical of the British education policy and encouraged the growth of private bodies which would contribute to the development of a policy on National Education aiming at the balanced mental and physical growth of the students. But after independence, he not only advocated for a Government supervised education system but also discouraged the students from going abroad for higher studies.[126] While urging students to concentrate exclusively in studies he reminded them: "It is not for you to involve yourself in controversies. Studies must claim your prior attention. It behoves the students to make most of their time and opportunities, so that they may equip themselves for the responsibilities they have to shoulder in their future career."[127] Besides education, his cautious approach was reflected in his views regarding the political prisoners. Vallabhbhai, who favoured the release of political prisoners in the mid-thirties felt the necessity of keeping such prisoners in jails after independence for the maintenance of law and order. Justifying maintenance of public decency, he even criticised the prisoners raising revolutionary slogans in the jails[128]. He was in favour of imposition of a code of conduct for them. He moved the Preventive Detention Bill while he was the Home Minister to keep people in jail without trial in order to restore peace. All along Vallabhbhai considered the Press to be the eyes of the Government and urged for its regulation. He was always critical of the misreporting of facts and premature publications. On the issue of the early publication of the Nehru-Jinnah talk he opined: "Premature publication may temporarily give some advantage to newspapers of news agencies publishing or circulating such news, but in the end besides causing harm to the national cause, it is bound to react on them"[129]. He also reacted against the Bombay Chronicle for its misrepresentation of facts especially on the issue of the future leadership of the country[130]. Hence, if prior to independence he was critical of the papers like Kaiser-I-Hind, Mumbai Samachar etc. during the partition years he did not hesitate to take action against The Dawn, Anjam, National Call, Janata, Janasakti etc. He reacted strongly against of some of the newspapers for their divided allegiance, attempt to leak information and use of scurrilous writings. He was opposed to the spreading of rumors by them and considered it to be worse than plague.[131] So he pressed for their regulations. He told: "I was dreaming of an atmosphere in which the press would carry on without any irksome and irritating restrictions . . . . I want you to think of some agreed measures of restraint and discretion in publishing news and offering comments . . . . but if there is no agreement, Government will unwillingly be driven to the necessity of taking action, however, unpalatable it might be to the press, public and Government alike.[132] As the Minister of Information and Broadcasting, he invoked the Press to use moral pressure for self-discipline, supported the use of the Official Secrets Act by the Bombay Government, brought a Press Ordinance and piloted a Press Bill for the purpose. In the same vein, he also supported the Government's right to withhold information in the public interest.[133]

Regulation of Right to Life

Vallabhbhai's earlier support for the Right to Life was affected by the grim law and order situation which threatened the very existence of the newly created Nation–State. As a responsible member of the political set-up, he could hardly afford to support the absolute right of self-defence of the individual. In fact, he had started developing such an attitude since the mid-thirties, when the Congress assumed the responsibility of maintaining law and order in many provinces. Then, he had not hesitated to instruct the Bombay Government to withdraw the licence of holding gun and revolver, allowed for self-defence.[134] He supported the Bombay Government to initiate the Industrial Dispute Bill and to use force to control the labour strikes[135]. Supporting the curbing of the 1938 industrial strike in Bombay he argued: " . . . . Until the Government is able to generate the atmosphere of non-violence, it has no alternative but to use minimal force including firing for the protection of the life and property of those who are innocent."[136] He believed that it was the duty of the Government to protect the life of the people. Subsequently, he rejected the suggestion of Gokul Narang, a Hindu Mahasabha leader, who was in favour of raising civil guard for the protection of the life and liberty of the Hindus.[137] He strongly objected to the creation of any private army by the organisation like the R.S.S. (Rastriya Swayamsevak Sangha) independent of the government.[138] At the time of independence, he criticised the unleashing of violence by the people of certain ideological convictions, insisting upon the inevitability of social change. Realising the need for Government's control over them, he said: "When we think of civil liberties of an extremely small number of people, let the House think of the liberties of millions of people, threatened by the activities of individuals whose civil liberties we have been forced to curtail. I am using the word civil liberties in connection with these people with some reluctance because for them liberty is synonymous with licence and there is hardly any difference between civil and criminal."[139] Thus, in the context of maintenance law and order he supported police firing. It was resorted to control the student unrest, refugee influx and to manage the public distribution system effectively at the time of the food crisis.[140] He brought the Preventive Detention Bill to overcome the loopholes of the existing Public

Safety Act. He also advised the Government of India to go for an army operation in Hyderabad to protect its people from the Razakars who were spreading communal violence with the help of the Nizam. In this backdrop, Vallabhbhai did not hesitate to support the use of capital punishment as a deterrent measure and criticised the section of people claiming clemency for Nathuram Godse, the assassin of Gandhi. He argued: "The moment the Congress took to the art of Government, it had to give up that creed of non-violence in all essentials. It would be a mere hypocrisy to put that creed into practice, when it has to deal with the worst crime that any individual could have committed"[141]. Thus, he preferred to support the curtailment of right to life through a legitimate authority only.

Regulation of Right to Property

Vallabhbhai's longing to protect the private property of an individual was equally curtailed by the challenges of the uneven economic development, assumption of office by the Congress and the complications developing out of the partition of the country. In the thirties when the Congress assumed office in many provinces, the priority of the Party shifted from the retrieval of the confiscated land to the other larger issues as assured in the Party election manifesto. Though, he advocated in favour of guarded land reform, he was quite categorical on the regulation of private property. His effort to spread education, establish cooperatives, land revenue leagues and rural banks for the farmers were part of the strategies to enable the state to regulate the concentration of private property.[142] In this context, he preferred imposition of the Betterment and Terminal Taxes as the President of the Ahmedabad Municipality and supported the levying of the Property Tax in the Provinces as the Chairman of the Congress Parliamentary Board.[143] Such measures not only helped in the redistribution of resources but also enabled the Government to overcome resource deficit caused by the burden of development projects and prohibition programmes. Vallabhbhai was also critical of the amassing of resources by the industrialists. He believed it to be a 'national crime.'[144] He argued: "I have no prejudice against such persons, though I am opposed to hoarding of money... It is our duty to see that those who have amassed wealth shall have to use it for the benefit of the society . . . . There was a question of balancing the budget and find out ways and means of getting money to fill the gap between income and expenditure. There was no difference of opinion about taxing the wealthy people. There was no question of poor being asked to pay. Money can be taken only from the rich people that also by direct tax."[145] Hence, as part of the political setup, he encouraged the imposition of Income Tax in proportion to one's income.[146] He emphasised upon the streamlining of the Income Tax Department for proper tax collection. He criticised the industrialists like Seth Ramakrishna Dalmia for giving donation to the Gandhi Memorial Fund to get tax exemption. He appeared quite harsh when he said: "I am not aware of any donor who misled himself to such an extent as you seem to have done. Nor do I see any possible connection between contributions to such a sacred object and escape from punishment or consequences of evasion of income tax. After all, the contributions were from business firms and not individuals and I do not think any of the industrialists would sink as low as you to try to profit for their own selfish ends from the contributions made out of shareholder's money."[147] With this backdrop, the allegation made against Vallabhbhai that as the Deputy Prime Minister he pressurised Sanmukham Chetty, the then Finance Minister to show special favour to a few industrialists appeared to be quite baseless.[148] In fact, V. Shankar, his private secretary revealed that both Nehru and Patel had to change their mind regarding protecting Chetty after going through the files.[149] In fact, Chetty who had to tender his resignation on the episode, too admitted it to be an unintentional mistake on his part.[150] Vallabhbhai, despite his initial support for the policy of decontrol, reposed faith in the elected Government to regulate at least the supply of essential commodities to retrieve the public distribution system of the country from the clutches of the black marketers. He also supported the policy of guarded nationalisation which was in pursuance of his policy of protectionism, declared much prior to the independence.[151] He wanted nationalisation of the key industries to balance the profit motive with the deficit of essential commodities.

Regulation of Right to Religion

Vallabhbhai's support for the Right to Religion was hindered by the political developments taking place in the country since the mid 40's. The rise of the Muslim League in connivance with the authority became a major obstruction for the communal harmony. The resurgence of the Muslims in India had its genesis in the thirties in the rise of Pan-Islamism and the Mopala Massacre. But, it grew substantially with the open support of the authority. The decline of the Imperial power during the Second World War was further encashed by the Muslim League. In the Shimla Conference (1945), the Muslim League was recognised by the British as the spokesperson of the Muslim Community. The purpose was to create a rift between the Hindus and Muslims to foil the process of transfer of power. In subsequent periods, the Cabinet Mission Plan (1946) with provisions like weak centre and 'group clause' strengthened the League further. The invitation to the League to become part of the Interim Government ignoring its involvement in communal violence reflected the inclination of the authority towards it. Vallabhbhai was greatly disturbed by the ongoing political developments. He reacted against communal violence unleashed by the League in the sensitive areas, changing allegiance of the Arhar Party candidates from the Congress to the League, decisive victory of the League in the election of 1946, migration of prominent Muslim leaders like Choudhary Khaliquazzaman, Syed Mamud and Jos Mallihabadi into Pakistan and by the growth of the Hindu communal bodies. The first casualty of all these changes was the partition of the country the next was the assassination of Gandhi. Vallabhbhai's earlier critical approach towards the Hindu religion and sympathies for the Muslims and other minorities was adversely affected by the prevailing state of affairs. He was concerned about conversion among the Hindus, encouraged by the Missionaries. But he exerted moral pressures upon the protagonists of Hindu religion to set their own house in order.[152] He initiated the process of incorporation of legal provisions against conversion in the Constitution of India. As the Minister for Mome Affairs he imposed ban on Hindu organisations like the Rastriya Swyamsevak Sangh in 1948, for indulging in some objectionable activities. S. Gopal has observed: "Patel is usually depicted as a supporter of Hindu chauvinism, but actually his major concern was national unity."[153] Vallabhbhai's sympathy for the Muslims was hampered by the activities of organisations like the Muslim National Guard and Khaksars. Hence, he strongly recommended their banning.[154] To ensure communal harmony he stuck to his earlier decision on the denial of the facility of religious education for the Muslims in schools,[155] and insisted upon the regulation of the use of loudspeakers in the mosques.[156] As the Home Minister, he brought legislative measures to control the Dargah of Khawaja Saheb to prevent anti-social activities. He recommended the exchange of people beyond the Punjab and Bengal[157] at the time of partition and supported measures like the Property Evacuee Bill and Permit System to rehabilitate the refugees[158]. In the Constituent Assembly, he found no justification of making reservation for the Muslims in terms of both jobs and representation because of their migration from many parts of the country. He restrained Nehru from introducing communal representation in the legislative body of Hyderabad.[159] He influenced the Government in 1950 to delete the provisions incorporated in relation to the reservations for the Muslims in the Nehru-Liaquat Pact.[160] He also reacted sharply against Syed Ali Zaheer, India's Ambassador to the International Labour Organisation, for his alleged objectionable role which helped the Ambassador of Iran to become the Chairman of the Organisation.[161] In case of other minorities too Vallabhbhai took a balanced approach. As the Chairman of the Ahmedabad civic body he ignored the parochial sentiment of the Jain community and took measures against the stray animals.[162] Again as the Home Minister of the country, he detained Tara Singh for instigating the Sikh community. He admitted: "Nothing has pained me more than my having to detain Master Tara Singh . . . . He wanted to destroy what we wish to construct. That way I saw the death of India."[163] He criticised the indiscreet use of reservation policy and denied its benefits to the Sikh community as a whole. He did not favour its extension to the converted Indian Christians.[164]

Regulation of Political Rights

The prospect of independence and subsequent responsibilities had tremendous impact upon Vallabhbhai's concern for political rights. It made him skeptical about political parties and organisations who were looking for quick solutions. Initially he was critical of the Kishan Sabhas, labour associations, Gandhi Seva Sangha, etc. for obstructing the Provincial Congress Governments. He criticised them for not realising the constraints imposed by the Imperial authority. He argued: "It was an abuse of freedom on the part of those who never wished the Government well, who never participated in the country's freedom struggle, who all along placed impediments in the way of Government, have been joined in the positive criticisms by others, who were once upon a time friends".[165] In fact, he believed that the growth of such parties on the ground of ideological differences should take place after independence.[166] He criticised the Muslim League for its narrow religious base and admonished the Communists for spreading the cult of violence.[167] He failed to appreciate the heterogeneous stands of the Socialists. He argued: "Firstly, the Socialists were not agreed upon even regarding the definition of Socialism; there are 85 different types of Socialists. Secondly, they were wasting time speculating about the social and political organisations in the future independent Government of India.... Thirdly, some Socialists merely talk with such persons I shall never be able to get on."[168] He did not spare the Congress Party either. He put all his efforts during the freedom struggle to sideline the Socialist faction within the Congress and instill discipline within the Party. After independence, the ongoing political upheavals deterred him to encourage the mushroom growth of political parties. He assured: "In all humility, I would point out that the opposition would be worthwhile when the country settled down."[169] He appealed to the political parties against making frequent changes and said: "If you change the ministry, thinking that you would be better than others, you have to make sure that you are not falling from the frying pan into fire."[170] In the fluid situation in which universal adult franchise was yet to be effective in the absence of an updated electoral list, he found it was difficult to conduct election in the provinces like West Bengal. He also justified central interference in Hyderabad and Madhya Bharat as a temporary measure.[171] Vallabhbhai was highly protective of the national symbols. In pursuance of his earlier stand on admonishing the Muslims for not paying respect to the national song 'Vande Mataram',[172] he considered the defiant attitude of the Rastriya Sayamsevak Sangh towards the National Flag, a matter of resistance.[173] He advised the Princely state of Mysore to show restraint and pay allegiance both to the Flags of Mysore and the Nation.[174] He wanted imposition of restrictions on the hoisting of the National Flag in order to maintain its sanctity. He argued: "I can neither understand nor appreciate the attempts that are being made in various places to hoist the National Flag on buildings against the wishes of the proprietors. To hoist the Flag on building of the Bar Association has no meaning. In fact, I regard it as an unseemly demonstration of our intolerance"[175]. Vallabhbhai believed strike in any form was a resistance to the authority. He even criticised the Indian Naval Ratings (1946) for providing opportunities to some vested interests to weaken the process of transfer of power. He was instrumental in introducing measures like the Bombay Trade Dispute Bill (1938), the Prevention of Strikes in Essential Services (1949) and the Preventive Detention Bill (1950) to regulate strikes. He was highly critical of the strikes especially by teachers, police, labour, railway and postal employees which affected general administration, refugee rehabilitation, public distribution system, industrial scenario etc. Though critical of fasting he found it to be an effective technique of resistance to the political authority. However, he wanted it to be used sparingly.Urging caution over its use, he said: "I have always maintained that fasts can not be the instrument of action except by a man who is fully conversant with its whole philosophy and can be dependent upon to make use of those fasts for rightful purposes"[176]. He criticised fastings resorted to by persons like as Abid Ali on labour problems, Bansali on Hyderabad issue, Karpatrji over his inability to get into the Constituent Assembly and Sibbanlal for pressurising the Government.[177] Further, he considered sending of Jathas from the Punjab to New Delhi by the Sikh leader Tara Singh to highlight the demand of the community a sign of resistance.[178] His firmness revealed his intention to ensure political stability in the fluid condition which seized the country after independence.

3.2 Equality and Justice

Equality and justice as human values and principles of socio-political organisations are complimentary to each other. Equality stands for individual dignity in inter-personal relationships despite differences in socio-economic conditions whereas justice refers to fairness in the distribution and sharing of societal resources required to correct the inegalitarian order. As the patterns of distribution of societal resources are contained in the public policies made and implemented by the Government, establishment of justice seems to depend mostly upon the will and activities of the Government. Therefore, equality and justice are inseparably associated with each other in the context of establishment of a just and welfare society. As such, individuals, leaders, statesmen and policy makers engaged in nation building activities think of and undertake measures for updating the value of equality and justice for ending exploitation and creation of a just political society. Hence, an inquiry has been undertaken to assess the ideas of a prominent statesman like Vallabhbhai on the values of equality and justice especially in respect of the societal issues like gender equality, caste relationship and dignity of labour.

3.2.1 On Gender Equality

Vallabhbhai observed an imbalanced gender equation in the contemporary society. The *Patidar* community in which he was born into accorded a low status of women. It further aggravated with the decline of the *Patidar* community in the mid-nineteenth century following the replacement of collective land ownership system by individual land holding system. If compelled them to pick up many social taboos like vegetarianism, dowry system, male supremacy etc. to maintain their exclusive and superior status in the society. Women were "not only believed to be physically subject to pollution but also to be morally more subject to temptation"[179]. The prevailing practices like child marriage, dowry system, purdah culture, restrictions on widows etc. confirmed their lower status.

Among the *Patidars*, early marriage was dictated by the time honoured customs. The attraction of dowry strengthened it further. Both Vithalbhai and Vallabhbhai got married at very early ages. In the long run such practices affected the mortality of women. It could hardly be a coincidence that in the family, wives of all the five Patel brothers including their only sister Dahiba met with early death. Kashibhai, the youngest of all the brothers commented: "We are a brood of widowers"[180]. For Vallabhbhai, it was sharply in contrast to the British way of life where a woman used to remain unmarried until she was in her mid-twenties to become self sufficient first. He considered the system of child marriage to be a sin and emphatically said: "If I were in power, I would have a law passed to provide that those who marry off their daughters when they are twelve or thirteen should be shut or hung. If a girl of fourteen or fifteen becomes a mother and a large number of such daughters became widows, what else do you expect except a famine"?[181] Vallabhbhai reacted against the abduction and selling of girl child, pursued for managing livelihood in some Princely States like Kathiawar.

Commenting on the slight of such girls, he said: "when I see the conditions of the image of the wolves with a ferocious look to attack the poor flock of sheep and pounce them, my heart bleeds."[182] He reacted against the alleged misbehaviour shown to the girl inmates in the name of celibacy in the institutions like the Arya Kanya Vidyalaya.[183] He did not hesitate to highlight the rape of a *Harijan* girl in the state of the Central Province, which was then run by the Congress Party and termed it "a heinous crime."[184]

The status of the *Patidar* women was affected by the dowry practice, followed meticulously as part of the hypergamous marriages. These ceremonies were performed between the superior and inferior *Patidar* villages. If the attraction of wealth, given as dowry was the consideration for the former, the prospect of upward mobility by tying knot with the higher category was the objective of the latter. Thus, marrying off the daughter which happens to be an obsession of a *Patidar* father, had an 'investment' potential. Though 'gols' were formed by the lesser *Patidar* villages to prevent such marriages, yet the interested persons from both the sides managed to overcome such regulations by paying a substantial punitive sum. Vallabhbhai himself had such a marriage when his father Jhaverbhai decided to have an alliance with Desaibhai Punjabbhai of Gana which was outside the Chhagam village. Obviously, his father preferred dowry to status and his wife's father was keen to secure an alliance with a superior village.[185] He was conscious of the emotional strain on a girl's father which might have been responsible for the prevalence of the female infanticide practice in the contemporary society.[186] Hence, he was highly critical of the lavish expenditure incurred in the *Patidar* marriages, compelling the girl's side to be trapped by the moneylenders.[187]

Vallabhbhai was also against the purdah practice. He believed that such system of segregating women from the rest of the society was a symbol of distrust which would distort the growth of their personality. He asked the protagonists of such system:

"Are you not ashamed that you keep your women behind *purdah*? Who are these ladies? Your mothers, sisters and wives? Do you really believe that only by keeping them behind *purdah* you can look after their chastity? ... You distrust their capacities of protecting themselves and their honour and you have turned them into stricken animals afraid of their own shadows. You are born of those very creatures whom you, love to keep cribbed, cabined and confined.[188]

Vallabhbhai was extremely concerned about the fate of the widows. During his period, the *Patidar* community had become harsher towards them in order to protect its superior status in the society.[189] Traditionally she had to shave her head and wear black or dark purple clothes. The society considered her inauspicious for being responsible for the early death of her husband. She was supposed to end the rest of her life as expeditiously as possible by doing fastings and other rituals. Vallabhbhai was deeply moved to comment: "Those who have gone through such a horrible state of things will not ask to send them to human world again. The society will be getting her shaven and keep her in dark corner for twelve months. There are hundreds and thousands who believe that a sight of a widow is an evil omen. So, she has to live always in a state of fear. If her husband has left some property then other relatives will come forward to claim and make her life miserable."[190]

3.2.2 On Caste Relationship

Vallabhbhai was aware of the uneven caste relationship existing in the contemporary society. During his time, the age-old rural agrarian society was sharply divided into the '*Ujaliparajas*' (the fair skinned people) comprising of the Anavil Brahmins, Patidars, *Vanias*, etc. and the '*Kaliparajas*' (the dark skinned people) consisting of the *Kolis*, *Dubalas*, *Dhondias*, *Dheds*, *Bhangis* etc. The '*Ujaliparajas*', had some degree of homogeneity due to its control over land. It had not only become affluent over a period of time, but also had moved upward by following several ritual practices in order to command respect, from the society. On the other hand, the *'Kaliparajas'*, being an impoverished and unorganised section, was virtually dependent upon the former. The one-sided dependence, rooted in the mutual reinforcement of economic power with status, was partly responsible for the imbalanced caste relationship. It was so deep rooted that the Kaliparaja Inquiry Committee, constituted by the Congress in 1927 found that even Gandhi's 'constructive programme' could hardly have any impact upon it.[191] Vallabhbhai expressed deep concern over the prevailing evil social practices like untouchability, conversion, bonded labour, etc. resulting out of the exploitative social relationship.

Vallabhbhai reacted against the practice of untouchability. He found that it had socially segregated a section of the society and meted out inhuman treatment to them in the name of religion. In the traditional society of Gujarat the prominent untouchable communities were the Dheds and Bhangis. The Dheds were mostly the weavers who switched over to agriculture due to the introduction of mill clothes by the British and the Bhangis were the outdoor servants or the conventional scavengers. Vallabhbhai found it was a travesty of religion perpetuated to exploit a section of the society who was believed to be poor and ignorant. He argued: "In India many superstitions exist in the name of religion. We give food to the scavengers, but we throw food articles to them from a distance. When we give them water it is poured in their hands from above. Thus a person who considers others as untouchables, despises them with an eye of contempt."[192] He was highly critical of the British policy like the MacDonald Award (1932) introduced to legitimise the practice of untouchability by dividing the electorates in to caste Hindus and the untouchables. He also pointed out the prevalence of such practice in the Princely States like Mysore. He observed: "It is regrettable that many devasthanams (Hindu temples) in the state were closed to the so-called depressed classes. Do not these *Harijans* bear the brunt of the work in every village in the state? . . . . It is definitely not possible to make progress with the village uplift work unless that effort is at the same time accompanied by the *Harijan* uplift work."[193]

Vallabhbhai was also worried about the conversion of the low caste people of the Hindu community into other religions. The practice was followed with a hope of making an upward mobility. He pointed at the role of the Christian Missionaries who were taking advantage of the loopholes in the Hindu religion and the dismissive attitude of the upper section of the society. He criticised the Missionaries for wooing people by giving them services. He condemned the caste Hindus for perpetuating caste violence upon the low caste people in places like Kavitha village in Gujarat.[194] He warned: "Hindus wake up! You are in the wrong. These untouchables embrace Islam or Christianity when they are maltreated by you and then when they become Christian you kowtow to them."[195]

Besides conversion, Vallabhbhai was deeply moved by the fate of the *Halis* or the bonded labours. It affected mostly the *Kolis, Dublas, Dhondias, Chodhras,* etc. who were landless and were dependent upon the upper castes for their survival. In the absence of effective cooperative societies and lack of awareness, the low caste people used to mortgage themselves before the land holders to get financial assistance. The upper castes legitimised the practice to make up the deficit of labour force. The purdah system prevented women of the upper strata to come to the field. Vallabhbhai criticised the practice as it affected the dignity of human being. He said: "It is believed that your owner is somebody else. There is no other malady in this world which is greater than that. As the cattle has its owner similarly today one man has become the owner of another man. The only owner of man is God and God alone who has given you birth in this world and created you . . . . Man becomes the owner of animals but when one man becomes the owner of another man, then the situation becomes most dangerous."[196] Vallabhbhai condemned the '*Vedh*' practice in Kheda district, which was as exploitative as the *Hali* system. It used to encourage the Government servants posted in rural areas to extract free service from the people of the backward communities. He expressed deep concern for the tribals affected by economic indebtedness, alcoholism and the system of bonded labour. He said: "From their faces I can discern that nobody is as miserable as they are. I desire to remove that misery and we fear for that we must seek for self- rule and achievement."[197]

3.2.3 On Dignity of Labour

Vallabhbhai realised the significant contribution that the workers made to the state. It made him conscious of their plight and think of measures to ensure their well-being. He believed: "Indeed labour is a real chariot to lead us towards Swaraj: the real independence, for it is they who work for the well-being of the Nation and earn their livelihood by the sweat of their brow."[198]

Vallabhbhai got a chance to involve himself in the problem of the labour force at the time of the Ahmedabad Mill strike, launched in 1918 by Gandhi, seeking justice for the mill workers. Subsequently, he became more acquainted with their problems in course of managing the Municipality of Ahmedabad. He found them denied of the basic human existence because of the unregulated industrialisation policy followed by the British. The resulting unplanned expansion of the city, acute congestion, shortage of water, recurrent epidemics, etc., had led to the creation of an unhealthy atmosphere, especially for the downtrodden working in the mill areas. He also highlighted the problems of the jobless people migrating to industrialised areas from the rural belt of the Princely States especially during the slack season.[199] Vallabhbhai came across a new dimension of the labour problem with the assumption of power by the Congress in the Provinces. He was perturbed over the frequent strikes especially in the sensitive areas allegedly initiated by a section of leaders with a purpose to bring radial change in the society. In fact, rapid migration to the urban areas, residential clustering based on the districts of origin and the internal hierarchical structures of the mills, created conducive atmosphere for these leaders to have easy access into the mill areas. The alienation of the Congress because of its engagement in the freedom struggle and management of the provincial offices provided them with further space. When the country became independent, Vallabhbhai found the same trend continuing which put the labour force at 'cross road'. He believed "Labour has fallen on evil days. Its organisers know only one thing and believe in one method only; to prop up their leadership by strike. They do not seem to realise that if we killed industries, labour itself would cease to exist."[200]

3.2.4 Equality and Justice: Correlationship

Vallabhbhai responded variously to all these social inequalities, if not created but left untouched by the British authority. The deep sense of humanism of the *Vaishnava* cult diverted his attention towards such issues in the society. He was encouraged by the changing outlook of the pragmatic *Patidar* community which had then come under the influence of the social reform movement like the Arya Samaj. The exposure to the Western egalitarian values and the Gandhian 'constructive programme' motivated him further. So, he argued: "if one still believes in the saying that a drum, an ignorant person, a person belonging to a low caste and above all women—all those describe physical chastisement, then we are bound to be slaves."[201]

Measures against Gender Bias

Vallabhbhai wanted to correct the gender bias in order to shape the posterity of the nation. He urged the people to emulate the British way of life and to imbibe the habit of giving respect to women. He said: "None of the Englishman leaves his wife alone in his country. When he goes for his work, riding a horse, his wife accompanies him riding another horse. Where there is such love and thrust on the wife, there will be different behaviour with her . . . . Only then can be born and brought up proper children.[202] With such concern for equality, he could hardly appreciate dowry practice and the custom of child marriage. He deviated from such practices at the time of the marriage of his own son and encouraged the latter not to attend such marriages as a matter of protest.[203] He urged the youth of the country to build up their character to ward off the temptation of dowry and to set examples needed for nation-building.[204] Vallabhbhai had great faith in the potential of women which was hampered by the prevailing *purdah* practice. He argued that because of their faith in religion, they had tremendous internal strength which could have been utilised for constructive purposes. He appealed to them to march ahead with man and become part of the freedom struggle. He urged them: "Do not let anybody stay at home. Let not any young man be he your brother, husband or son stay at home. Do not be afraid. Divorce those who are afraid. Do not marry them who are afraid of firing, being beaten or going to jail."[205] Vallabhbhai also believed that besides purdah, the way of living of women too obstructed the overall development of their personality. Hence, he suggested them: "Sisters, I do not like the signs of slavery on your hand and feet. Your heavy brass ornaments accumulate a lot of dirt, produce all sorts of skin diseases and interfere in your free movements."[206] He also wanted to improve the fate of the widows. As he was least confident of the involvement of a step mother in bringing up children, he did not prescribe second marriage as a solution.[207] Rather he believed that they would get comfort in the service of the nation. He argued: "She will be able to heal her pain quickly, and bear it bravely and cheerfully if she gets the requisite training for service – social, political or otherwise. Selfless service has its own way of giving peace of mind and happiness, which is equal, if not superior to any other happiness in the world."[208] Vallabhbhai encouraged institutions like Jyotisangha and Kasturba Trust to impart education and training to women so as to make them self-sufficient. He observed: "The woman is not aware of her right. The society fears if she is educated, she would have knowledge of her rights and will shake off the problem. But that fear is uncalled for. What is good for men is equally good for women also. The result of education is always sublime."[209] He was practical enough to suggest empowerment of women to upgrade their status in the society. In fact, he enabled the first woman member to be in the General Board of the Ahmedabad Municipality. At the time of the 1936 provincial election, he cited the example of England and pleaded for equal right of enfranchisement to ensure the status of womanhood[210] and also appealed to increase their representation in the legislative assembly.[211] He urged the Government of India after independence to create job opportunities for women if not in all fields but especially in the field of health and administration.[212]

Measures against Caste Exploitation

Vallabhbhai had deep hatred for the use of the word 'backward' against certain communities as it used to affect their self respect.[213] Hence, it was natural on his part to believe: "India's independence would be incomplete until every *Harijan* can claim and obtain complete equality with the most highly placed persons in the country."[214] Vallabhbhai had launched his drive against untouchability even during the freedom struggle. He convened the Kathiawar Political Conference and the Raniparaj Conference in 1922 and 1935 to highlight the problems of the untouchables. In an attempt to change the outlook of the people, he exposed the British policy of popularising alcoholism and machine produced clothes which contributed to further backwardness of such people. He promoted measures like prohibition and use of *Khadi* to provide them economic independence and boost their self-confidence. Besides the *Patidars*, he involved the backward communities like the *Bariyas* and *Patanavadiyas* during the Borsad agitation. His effort was recognised by Gandhi as a measure of social change which was more valuable and difficult than simply fighting against the Government.[215] He also encouraged the backward communities to use violence in their fight against the local landlords to ensure their position in the society. He suggested: "The first thing for the Raniparajas to do is to get rid of the fear of landlords, which has become ingrained in them. When they are infused with courage and feel strong, there will come the time to teach them the virtue of non-violence. But, till then they must be taught to meet the force with force."[216] Vallabhbhai thought of providing education to the backward communities to remove the stigma levelled upon them. When the Congress assumed offices in the provinces, he supported the opening of the Lokshalas or the special adult education schools for these people.[217] He supported the *Harijan* Sevak Sangha not only by raising donations for it every now and then, but also by recommending its suggestions to the Government to release money necessary for the education of the *Harijan* students. His sincerity in this regard became evident as he went to the extent of giving instructions for the closure of the schools for not admitting the *Harijan* candidates.[218] He thought of securing their position by empowering them. In the Ahmedabad Municipality itself he supported the candidature of a Harijan[219]. Moreover, he made special efforts as the Chairman of the Congress Parliamentary Board to ensure the victory of the *Harijan* candidates in the elections of 1937 and 1947.[220] Vallabhbhai supported the move to include such people in the administration. Though he was not keen on the appointment of a commission to safeguard the interests of these people, yet he was instrumental in laying down the provisions in the Constitution of India to reserve jobs for the backward communities.[221] He said: "I will be highly pleased if the Harijans are given quota in the administration… The state can not abandon its responsibility towards them.[222] He even instructed the Home Ministry that the educationally qualified Scheduled Caste employees, fit for permanent retention in the service should be retained in preference to the members from other communities."[223] Vallabhbhai tried to change the mindset of the society towards the role played by the people of such communities. While addressing the Bhangi community in the All Gujarat Conference of Sweepers Association, he said: "Though the profession of sweeper is treated as low and unclean, it is undoubtedly a noble work of service to the society. Is not cleanliness next to godliness? Hence, those who are engaged in the profession must *ipso facto* be nearer to the God."[224] He emphasised upon the need to incorporate provisions like Article 17 as a Fundamental Right in the Constitution of India to make the practice of untouchability a cognizable offence. He instructed the state governments to cancel the licence of vehicles and hotels who were denying entry to the untouchables.[225] Vallabhbhai urged the advocates of the Hindu community to reform their religion to enable the backward communities to enter into the temples. He believed that in the long run, it would check the process of religious conversion.[226] He emphasised upon removing the practice of bonded labour to improve the fate of the exploited section. He took initiative in 1938 to convene a joint conference of the Halis and their owners to regulate the life styles of the former. He was actively involved in the working of the Mirakhadi Bhil Ashram in Ahmedabad to improve the condition of the tribals.[227]

Measures against Plight of Labour

Vallabhbhai was an ardent supporter of dignity of labour. So he felt the necessity of organising the labour force. He was proud enough to admit: "I can claim longer association with organised labour than probably many labour leaders of today. I served my apprenticeship under the great leader of men and great friend of labour, Mahatma Gandhi."[228] In the early part of his public career, he became the President of the Municipal Employee's Union, B.D. and C.I. Railway Employee's Union and the Postman's Union. He supported the Railway Union in its demand for recognition from the Government so that it would be able to put its grievances directly before the authority.[229] He helped the union of the postmen to fight against the pressure of forced labour.[230] He not only protected the Employees of the Ahmedabad Municipality from the whimsical retrenchment of the authority for participating in the Non-Cooperation Movement but also created pension fund for the purpose. He acceded to their demands of investing personal savings at their own discretion.[231] With such concern, it was quite natural on his part to have argued in favour of introducing uniform for the employees of certain sections to enhance their organisational ability and ensure their dignity. He argued: ". . . . I am sure it is a disgrace to us all if telegraph peons or for that matter other peons go about in such filthy conditions . . . . I see no difficulty in the issue of uniforms. If there are any difficulties, they must be overcome, in the fair name of the country."[232]

Vallabhbhai was more concerned about the exploitation of the workers in the mills and industries. He attributed it to their lack of organisation. While working in the Ahmedabad Municipality, he showed great concern for the workers. He tried to ensure a better life for them by extending the facilities of hospitals and dispensaries, constructing public latrines and supplying potable drinking water. During his tenure as the Chairman of the Ahmedabad civic body, out of the total 92 proposals, he implemented 24 measures relating to the upliftment of the workers.[233] He took initiative to impose proportional taxation to generate revenue at the local level to meet such expenditure. He also supported the Gandhian technique of arbitration to ensure justice for the workers of the Ahmedabad Mill. He became actively involved in the formation of the Ahmedabad Labour Association or the Majdoor Mahajan. While arguing for the existence of such Unions needed for the upliftment of the workers, he said: "Majdoor Mahajan puts up labourer's schools, night schools as well as hospitals. I am bitterly opposed if someone speaks about breaking such a labour association and declares that if someone executes a bigger work than this, I am prepared to serve him."[234] Subsequently, to improve the status of workers he recommended the formation of a committee, endorsed the plea of Gandhi for a reasonable wage for the unorganised *Khadi* spinners, extended support to the Village Industries Association and encouraged the role of the Gandhi Seva Sangha. Vallabhbhai participated in the All India Trade Union Congress formed in 1920 by the Congress Party itself. But very soon he became disillusioned with its ventures. He argued that the preoccupation of the Congress with the political struggle gave an opportunity to certain sections of the political leadership to exploit the situation to their advantage and place before the labour the vision of unrealisable utopia.[235] He believed: "We saw the danger, however, that this trade union movement was developing on foreign lines. The difference was that while we were particular about the means we employed, for them the end justified the means. Their tactics were to bring about confusion and compel the police to open fire."[236] He was convinced that the Hindustan Mazdoor Sangh formed in 1935 largely under his initiative should be groomed further to counter such tendency. In fact, he was instrumental in bringing measures like the Bombay Trade Dispute Bill (1938) and Prevention of Strikes in Essential Services (1949) to diffuse strike and prevent the workers from falling into the trap of the political leaders. He argued: "I have been accused of being a friend of rajas, capitalists and the *Zamindars*. But, I claim to be a friend of Labour and the poor. Since I followed Gandhiji, I resolved not to own property and I have none. But, like Gandhiji I want to make capitalists understand where their duty lies."[237] He tried to assure the labour through adoption of measures like arbitration and balanced industrialisation. At the same time, he also made the capitalists aware of the Government's intention of running the administration for the benefit of all.[238] After liberation, he played a key role in monitoring the industrial truce between the workers and industrialists to diffuse tension and enhance production. He initiated the move in 1948 to replace the All India Trade Union Congress (AITUC) with the Indian National Trade Union Congress (INTUC) to prevent the organisation from being exploited for a party cause. He claimed: "The INTUC will save the labour from interested and self-seeking leadership of the past and will save the labour and the country from injurious uncertainties and hesitations of the present. It will safeguard both for the country and the labour, industrial peace and prosperity of the future, without which we can never hope to attain the place which our motherland is entitled to having with due regard to its potentialities and resources."[239]

3.3 The Emerging Pattern

Thus, Vallabhbhai endowed with a deep sense of self-respect and an independent mindset of a *Patidar*, was found to be obsessed with the protection of rights of individuals, an essential condition necessary for the growth of one's personality. His sincerity in this regard further increased because of his exposure to the liberal value-loaded British system of jurisprudence. He raised his voice on several issues which were sufficient to prove his liberal inclination. Emphasising the Right against Exploitation, he criticised the high-handedness of the authority, exploitative revenue policies of the Government and maladministration in the Princely States. He also demanded reforms in the education policy, improvement of living conditions in the prisons and regulation of the Press in order to ensure Freedom of Speech and Expression. Again, his keenness to protect the life of a person was reflected in his criticism of fasting as a technique to pressurise the authority or adopted as a measure of penance. He came forward for the individual's right for self-defence and expressed seriousness to improve the public health scenario of the country. His *Patidar* conviction revealed his desire to safeguard the private property of an individual. He not only criticised the arbitrary policies of confiscation of both movable and immovable properties, but also insisted upon guarded regulations on land reform, nationalisation of key industries and annexation of the Princely States. His effort to reform the Hindu religion and protect the people of other faiths reflected his longing for the Right to Religion. His democratic inclination was supported by his urge for political rights like participation in the electoral process, holding of public offices and resisting the authority wherever required. But Vallabhbhai, true to the pragmatic spirit of his community, realised that rights could hardly be enjoyed in abundance. So he supported empowering the legitimate authority to regulate rights. He was even more convinced in this regard with the withdrawal of the British power from India which left behind the problems of communal tension, refugee influx, national disintegration and uneven economic development. So, he encouraged the duly elected authority to bring reasonable restrictions through various legislative measures to ensure freedom for all even at the cost of restricting rights of certain segments.

Besides having liberal inclinations Vallabhbhai also expressed concern over social inequalities manifested in gender bias, caste segregation and exploitation of the workers. He emphasised upon the involvement of both the Government and the non-Government sectors to ensure social justice. He was instrumental in the incorporation of provisions like reservation in the Constitution of India for the upliftment of the Scheduled Caste and Scheduled Tribes. But the compulsions of the freedom struggle and that of the nation-building activities affected his efforts. He was confident that a stable legitimate authority could ensure the political values. Like a conservative and pragmatic Patidar, he preferred to wait and slowdown the drive for social change. So during the freedom struggle he was hesitant of demanding changes in the social hierarchy. Then he insisted that the Congress should remain non-committal in the provincial legislature on the issue of temple entry by the low-caste people. Even after independence, he supported a guarded reservation policy to ensure the merit of the individual. He even postponed the formation of the Commission for the Scheduled Caste and Scheduled Tribe in view of the impending challenges of national unity.

Thus, the pattern of political values of Vallabhbhai is found to be characterised by a blending of liberalism and welfarism. He was not only a liberal-democrat but also a prudent and pragmatic welfarist. A stern advocate of individual rights and liberty, a sympathetic welfarist, and a fiery champion of state-authority, he could not sacrifice one ideal for the other. He realised the importance of individual rights and liberty as necessary attributes for development of human personality and acknowledged the importance of state authority as an essential condition for the maintenance of law and order, social justice, and political stability in a newly created Nation–State. He therefore synthesised the needs for individual rights, social justice, and State-Authority for the development of the individual as well as for the stability, unity, integrity and development of the state. Hence, the pattern of Vallabhbhai's political values may be said to represent a fine blending of liberalism, democracy, conservatism, welfarism and nationalism.

Notes and References

1. N.D. Parikh, *Sardar Vallabhbhai Patel,* Vol. I (Ahmedabad: Navajivan, 1953, p. 23).
2. Administrative Report 1916-17 quoted in A.R. Tiwari, *Making of the Leader: Sardar Vallabhbhai Patel* (Ahmedabad: Sardar Patel University, 1967, p. 6).
3. Devavrat Pathak and Pravin Sheth, *Sardar Vallabhbhai Patel From Civic to National Leadership* (Ahmedabad: Navajivan, 1980, p. 32).
4. P.N. Chopra,(ed.), *The Collected works of Sardar Vallabhbhai Patel,* Vol. IV (New Delhi: Konark Pvt. Ltd., 1994, p. 29).
5. P.N. Chopra (ed.), *Ibid.*, Vol. IX, 1997, p. 77.
6. P.N. Chopra (ed.), *The Collected Works of Sardar Vallabhbhai Patel,* Vol. X, 1997, *op. cit.,* p. 174.
7. P.N. Chopra (ed.), *Ibid.*, Vol. XIII, 1998, p. 238.
8. Rani Dhavan Shankardass, *Vallabhbhai Patel: Power Organisation in Indian Politics* (New Delhi: Orient Longman, 1988, p. 303).
9. G.M. Nandurkar (ed.), *Sardar's Letters Mostly Unknown,* Post Centenary Series, Vol. I (Ahmedabad: 1980, p. 49).
10. *Hindustan Times,* 2 March, 1950.
11. P.N. Chopra (ed.), *The Collected Works of Sardar Vallabhbhai Patel,* Vol. XIV, 1999, *op. cit.,* p. 208.
12. *Young India,* 16 February, 1929.
13. N.D. Parikh, *Sardar Vallabhbhai Patel,* Vol. I, *op. cit.*, pp. 87-8.
14. *Bombay Chronicle,* 9 September, 1927.
15. *Ibid.*, 8 September 1938.
16. Vallabhbhai Patel, "Lawless Limbdi', File 47/1, Patel Papers, Navajivan, Ahmedabad.
17. N.D. Parikh, *Sardar Vallabhbhai Patel,* Vol. I, *op. cit.*, pp. 123-4.
18. *Gujarat Samachar,* 6 January, 1935.
19. N.D. Parikh, *Sardar Vallabhbhai Patel,* Vol. I, *op. cit.*, p. 11.
20. *Young India,* 12 March, 1930.
21. P.N. Chopra (ed.), *The Collected Works of Sardar Vallbhbhai Patel,* Vol. X, 1997, *op. cit.*, p. 81.

22. P.N. Chopra (ed.), *Ibid.*, Vol. III, 1993, p. 39.
23. Home Department (Special) MSA, 4 November, 1933.
24. P.N. Chopra (ed.), *The Collected Works of Sardar Vallabhbhai Patel*, Vol. III, *op. cit.*, p. 122.
25. P.N. Chopra (ed.), *Ibid.*, Vol. X, p. 222.
26. P.N. Chopra (ed.), *Ibid.*, p. 20.
27. *The Hindustan Times*, 18 March, 1949.
28. *Ibid.*, 10 July 1930.
29. N.D. Parikh, *Sardar Vallabhbhai Patel*, Vol. I, *op. cit.*, p. 18.
30. P.N. Chopra (ed.), *The Collected Works of Sardar Vallabhbhai Patel*, Vol. I, *op. cit.*, 1990, p. xvii.
31. Indulal Yagnik, *Atmakatha*, Vol. 2 (Ahmedabad: 1955).
32. K.M. Munshi, "A Day with Sardar" in Verinder Grover, (ed.), *Political Thinkers of Modern India*, Vol. 18 (New Delhi: Deep & Deep, 1992, p. 480).
33. K.L. Panjabi, *The Indomitable Sardar* (Bombay: Bharatiya Vidya Bhavan, 1969, p. 94).
34. N.D. Parikh, *Sardar Vallabhbhai Patel*, Vol. I, *op. cit.*, p. 4.
35. P.N. Chopra, *The Sardar of India* (New Delhi: Allied Publishers Ltd., 1995, p. 296).
36. Abdul Majid Khan, *Leader by Merit* (Lahore: 1945, p. 285).
37. *The Hindustan Times*, 26 February, 1949.
38. P.N. Chopra (ed.), *The Collected Works of Sardar Vallabhbhai Patel*, Vol. XV, 1999, *op. cit.*, p. 248, P.N. Chopra (ed.), *Ibid.*, Vol. XII, 1998, p. 54, 15, 124.
39. V. Shankar, *My Reminiscience of Sardar Patel*, Vol. 2 (New Delhi: MacMillan, 1975, p. 122).
40. P.N. Chopra (ed.), *Ibid.*, Vol. XIV, 1999, p. 335.
41. P.N. Chopra (ed.), *Ibid.*, Vol. I, p. 335.
42. G.M. Nandurkar (ed.), *Sardarshri Na Patro*, Vol. III (Ahmedabad: 1975).
43. *The Hindustan Times*, 22 January, 1950.
44. N.D. Parikh, *Sardar Vallabhbhai Patel*, Vol. I, *op. cit.*, p. 7.

45. *Ibid.*, p. 278.
46. G.M. Nandurkar (ed.), *Sardar's Letters Mostly Unknown*, Centenary Vol. I, (Ahmedabad: 1974, p. 135).
47. G.M. Nandurkar (ed.), *Sardarshri Na Patro*, Vol. III (Ahmedabad: 1976).
48. *The Hindustan Times*, 23 May, 1950.
49. *Navajivan*, 9 December, 1923.
50. Prajabandhu, 20 May, 1928.
51. *Bombay Chronicle*, 16 March, 1931.
52. *Ibid.*, 25March, 1931.
53. G.M. Nandurkar (ed.), *SardarPatel: In Tune with the Millions*. (Ahmedabad: Navajivan, 1975, p. 132).
54. *Navajivan*, 11 September, 1927.
55. N.D. Parikh, *Sardar Vallabhbhai Patel*, Vol. I, *op. cit.*, p. 301.
56. P.N. Chopra (ed.), *The Collected Works of Sardar Vallabhbhai Patel*, Vol. IV, *op. cit.*, p. 108.
57. *Gujarat Samachar*, 11 January 1935.
58. P.N. Chopra (ed.), *The Collected Works of Sardar Vallabhbhai Patel*, Vol. I, *op. cit.*, p. 15.
59. P.N. Chopra (ed.), *Ibid.*, Vol. XII, 1998, p. 126.
60. *Bombay Chronicle*, 25 March, 1931.
61. David Pocock, *Kanbis and Patidars* (London: Oxford, 1972, p. 76).
62. G.M. Nandurkar (ed.), *Sardarshri Na Patro*, Vol. II (Ahmedabad: Navajivan).
63. *Prajabandhu*, 20 December, 1929.
64. *Vallabhbhai Patel's Appeals to the People of Gujarat*, 27 July, 1934, AICC Papers, NMML, New Delhi.
65. G.M. Nandurkar (ed.), *Sardarshri ke Patro*, Vol. 2 (Ahmedabad: 1981, p. 119).
66. *Bombay Chronicle*, 7 June 1930.
67. *Vallabhbhai Patel to Rajendra Prasad*, 4 December, 1937, Prasad Papers, File II of 1937, National Archives of India, New Delhi.

68. P.N. Chopra (ed.), *The Collected Works of Sardar Vallabhbhai Patel*, Vol. XIII, 1996, *op. cit.*, p. 202. *Times of India*, 15 May 1950.
69. *The Hindustan Times*, 28 November, 1950.
70. *Vallabhbhai Patel to Jawaharlal Nehru on 16 August 1949*, Patel Papers: Navajivan, Ahmedabad.
71. *The Hindustan Times*, 7 October, 1950.
72. Asoka Mehta, *Oral History Transcript*, 4 December, 1980, NMML, New Delhi.
73. The Subsequent Mountbatten Plan had left them with no options but to be part of either India or Pakistan.
74. *The Hindustan Times*, 31 March, 1949.
75. *Bombay Chronicle*, 11 September, 1937.
76. *The Hindustan Times*, 13 November, 1949.
77. P.N. Chopra (ed.), *The Collected Works of Sardar Vallabhbhai Patel*, Vol. XV, 1999, *op. cit.*, p. 201.
78. *Prajabandhu*, 15 September 1918, P.N. Chopra (ed.), *The Collected Works of Sardar Vallabhbhai Patel*, Vol. VIII, 1996, *op. cit.*, p. 221. N.V. Gadgil, *Government from Inside* (Meerut: Meenakshi, 1965, p. 31)
79. K.H. Kabbur, "Swadeshi Movement" in P.D. Saggi, (ed.), *Life and Works of Sardar Vallabhbhai Patel* (Bombay: 1951, p. 55. *The Hindustan Times*, 13 November 1949. *Ibid.*, 3 January, 1948).
80. P.N. Chopra (ed.), *The Collected Works of Sardar Vallabhbhai Patel*, Vol. XIII, 1998, *op. cit.*, p. 297.
81. Jayaprakash Narayan, in G.M. Nandurkar (ed.), Commemorative Volume (Ahmedabad: 1974, p. 216).
82. Michael H. Lyon, *Sardar Patel and Indian Independence* (New Delhi: Konark Pvt. Ltd., p. 59).
83. K.M. Munshi, "A Day with Sardar" in Verinder Grover, (ed.), *Political Thinkers of Modern India*, Vol. 18, *op. cit.*, p. 479.
84. *Gujarat Samachar*, 24 October, 1935.
85. N.D. Parikh, *Sardar Vallabhbhai Patel*, Vol. I, *op. cit.*, p. 4..
86. Vallabhbhai Patel's to Gopabandhu Choudhury, 14 November, 1931, AICC Papers, New Delhi.

87. *Gujarat Samachar*, 10 March, 1935 *Ibid.*, 3 January, 1935.
88. N.V. Gadgil, Government from Inside, *op. cit.*, p. 185.
89. P.N. Chopra (ed.), *The Collected Works of Sardar Vallabhbhai Patel*, Vol. XII, 1998, *op. cit.*, p. 151. P.N. Chopra (ed.), *Ibid.*, Vol. XV, 199, p. 206.
90. Susana Heredia, *A Patriot For Me* (Bombay: Orient Longman, 1972, p. 195).
91. In the twenties, in response to the Montegu Chelmsford Reform, the Congress was divided internally into the 'no changer' and 'pro-changer' groups. While the former under the guidance of Gandhi preferred to stick to the agitational path, the latter under the leadership of Motilal Nehru and C.R. Das wanted to enter into the Council to challenge the British authority.
92. S.R. Bakshi, *Sardar Patel: His Political Ideology* (New Delhi: Anmol, 1990, p. 79).
93. Rajmohan Gandhi, *Patel: A Life* (Ahmedabad: Navajivan, 1991, p. 289).
94. V. Shankar, *My Reminiscence of Sardar Patel*, Vol. I, *op. cit.*, p. 145.
95. P.N. Chopra, *The Sardar of India, op. cit.*, p. 150.
96. Bipan Chandra, *Essays in Indian Nationalism* (New Delhi: Har Anand Pvt. Ltd., 1999, p. 202.)
97. P.N. Chopra, *The Sardar of India, op. cit.*, p. 168.
98. Rajmohan Gandhi, *Patel: A Life, op. cit.*, p. 435.
99. V. Shankar (ed.), *Sardar Patel: Select Correspondence (1945-50)*, Vol. I (Ahmedabad: Navajivan, 1978, p. 408).
100. The Hindu organisation have laid a claim to the Babri Masjid as being the original birth place or Lord Rama. Hindu-Muslim conflict over the Ramajanm Bhumi-Babri Masjid issue flored up in early 1948 when an idol of Lord Rama was found in the precincts of the Masjid. It led the Hindus to claim that the site was originally a temple which was destroyed by Babar and converted into a Mosque. For details, refer to Rafiq Zakaria, *Sardar Patel and Indian Muslims* (Bombay: Bharatiya Vidya Bhavan, 1996, p. 87).
101. P.N. Chopra, *The Sardar of India, op. cit.*, p. 263.
102. *Ibid.*, p. 150.

103. Adul Kalam Azad, India Wins Freedom (Calcutta: Orient Longman, 1959, p. 17).
104. *Bombay Chronicle*, 25 February, 1931.
105. *Ibid.*, 19 November, 1941.
106. Vallabhbhai Patel to Rajendra Prasad, on 8 October, 1945, Rajendra Prasad Press, National Archives of India, New Delhi. *Bombay Chronicle*, 20 November, 1936,
107. P.N. Chopra, *The Sardar of India, op. cit.*, pp. 219-20.
108. *The Hindustan Times*, 16 January, 1950.
109. *Ibid.*
110. Rajula Jain, *Vallabhbhai Patel and the Indian National Congress* (New Delhi: Gyan Sagar Publications, 1997, p. 25).
111. *Bombay Chronicle*, 3 March, 1937.
112. *Sardar Patel's Circular*, 5 May, 1937, AICC, E-I(4), 1936-37, NMML, New Delhi.
113. P.N. Chopra (ed.), *The Collected Works of Sardar Vallabhbhai Patel*, Vol. V, 1994, *op. cit.*, p. 43.
114. Rajula Jain, *Vallabhbhai Patel and the Indian National Congress, op. cit.*, p. 205.
115. P.N. Chopra (ed.), *The Collected Works of Sardar Vallabhbhai Patel*, Vol. XII, *op. cit.*, p. 4.
116. Home Department (Special), F. 321/165, 3 February 1929.
117. P.N. Chopra (ed.), *The Collected Works of Sardar Vallabhbhai Patel*, Vol. X, 1997, *op. cit.*, p. 157.
118. K.L. Panjabi, *The Indomitable Sardar, op. cit.*, p. 248.
119. *Bombay Chronicle*, 31December, 1937.
120. Vallabhbhai tried to convince Gandhi that the Bill on temple entry would be passed with least effort and time only after independence. True to his apprehension the Bill was withdrawn after 18 months. For details see Raj Mohan Gandhi, *Patel : A Life, op. cit.*, p. 230.
121. *The Hindustan Times*, 2 March, 1950.
122. *The Times of India*, 17 January, 1935.
123. *Bombay Chronicle*, 25 April, 1938.
124. *Ibid.*, 10 May, 1938.

125. *The Times of India*, 29 November, 1938.
126. *Gujarat Samachar*, 5 November, 1976.
127. *The Hindustan Times*, 2 March, 1950.
128. P.N. Chopra (ed.), *The Collected Works of Sardar Vallabhbhai Patel*, Vol. XII, 1997, *op. cit.*, p. 232. *The Hindustan Times*, 18 January, 1948.
129. *Bombay Chronicle*, 13 June, 1938.
130. P.N. Chopra (ed.), *The Collected Works of Sardar Vallabhbhai Patel*, Vol.XII, *op. cit.*, p. 136.
131. *Bombay Chronicle*, 4 June, 1938. *The Hindustan Times*, 13 February, 1939, *Ibid.*, 19 May, 1950.
132. *Bombay Chronicle*, 13 November, 1946.
133. *The Hindustan Times*, 1 April, 1950.
134. *Vallabhbhai Patel's to Kanubhai*, 24 February, 1939, AICC Papers, NMML, New Delhi.
135. *The Times of India*, 11 November, 1938.
136. *Ibid.*, 8 November, 1938.
137. Durgadas, *Select Correspondence*, Vol. I (Ahmedabad: Navajivan, 1971, p. 283).
138. *The Hindustan Times*, 20 December, 1948.
139. *Ibid.*, 20 February, 1950.
140. *The Hindustan Times*, 15 January 1950 *Ibid.*, 22 March, 1950 *Ibid.*, 10 October, 1950.
141. G.M. Nandurkar (ed.), Sardar Patel's Centenary Volumes (II) (Ahmedabad: 1975, p. 136).
142. *Harijan Bandhu*, 1 May, 1938. Home Department (Special), F.355/1929. *The Hindustan Times*, 13 November, 1949.
143. Devavrat Pathak and Pravin Sheth, Sardar Vallabhbhai Patel: From Civic to National Leadership, op. cit., p. 342. *Hindustan Times*, 22 July 1939.
144. *The Hindustan Times*, 15 Novembe, 1949.
145. Narahari Parikh and Uttam Chand and Dwarikadas Shah, *Sardar Patel Ke Bhashon* (Ahmedabad: Navajivan, 1950).
146. *The Hindustan Times*, 13 November, 1949.

147. P.N. Chopra (ed.), *The Collected Works of Sardar Vallabhbhai Patel*, Vol. V, *op. cit.*, pp. 132-3.
148. M.O. Mathai, *Reminiscence of Nehru Age* (New Delhi: Vikash Publishing House Pvt. Ltd., 1978, p. 242).
149. V. Shankar, *My Reminiscence of Sardar Patel*, Vol. I (New Delhi: MacMillan, 1974, p. 195).
150. N.V. Gadgil, Government from Inside, *op. cit.*, p. 145.
151. *Bombay Chronicle*, 11 September, 1937.
152. P.N. Chopra (ed.), *The Collected Works of Sardar Vallabhbhai Patel*, Vol.VII, *op. cit.*, p. 112).
153. S. Gopal, in Rafiq Zakaria, *Sardar Patel and Indian Muslims, op. cit.*, p. 88.
154. Vallabhbhai Patel to Jawaharlal Nehruon 6 February, 1948, Patel Papers, Navajivan, Ahmedabad.
155. P.N. Chopra (ed.), *The Collected Works of Sardar Vallabhbhai Patel*, Vol. X, *op. cit.*, p. 156.
156. *The Hindustan Times*, 23 December, 1949.
157. Rajmohan Gandhi, *Sardar Patel: A Life*, *op. cit.*, p. 431.
158. Rafiq Zakaria, *Sardar Patel and Indian Muslims, op. cit.*, pp. 55-6.
159. P.N. Chopra (ed.), *The Collected Works of Sardar Vallabhbhai Patel*, Vol. III, 1998, *op. cit.*, p. 133.
160. Nehru-Liaquat Ali Pact was signed between the Prime Ministers of both India and Pakistan to protect the interests of the Minorities in the two countries. The Pact created a lot of controversies in India following which K.C. Neyogy and S.P. Mookerjee, Ministers in Nehru's cabinet tendered their resignation. For details, N.V. Gadgil, Government from Inside, *op. cit.*, pp. 90-1.
161. G.M. Nandurkar (ed), *Sardar's Letters: Mostly Unknown*, Vol. III (Ahmedabad: 1983, p. 83).
162. D. Pathak and P. Sheth, *Sardar Vallabhbhai Patel: From Civic to National Leadership*, *op. cit.*, p. 343.
163. *The Hindustan Times*, 6 March, 1949.
164. P.N. Chopra (ed.), *The Collected Works of Sardar Vallabhbhai Patel*, Vol. X, *op. cit.*, p. 322.

165. *Bombay Chronicle*, 28 August, 1939.
166. *The Hindustan Times*, 21 November, 1939.
167. P.N. Chopra (ed.), *The Collected Works of Sardar Vallabhbhai Patel*, Vol. XV, *op. cit.*, p. 157. *The Hindustan Times*, 15 May, 1950.
168. N.D. Parikh, *Sardar Vallabhbhai Patel*, Vol. 2, 1956, *op. cit.*, pp. 198-99.
169. *The Hindustan Times*, 5 November, 1948.
170. *Ibid.*, 15 May, 1950.
171. *Ibid.*, 16 January, 1950. P.N. Chopra (ed.), *The Collected Works of Sardar Vallabhbhai Patel*, Vol. XIV, *op. cit.*, p. 99.
172. Vallabhbhai Patel to Rajendra Prasad, 2 October 1937, Rajendra Prasad Papers, National Archives of India, New Delhi.
173. *The Hindustan Times*, 17 December, 1948.
174. *Bombay Chronicle*, 10 May, 1938.
175. Vallabhbhai Patel to Rajendra Prasad, 2 October, 1937, Rajendra Prasad Papers, National Archives of India, New Delhi.
176. P.N. Chopra (ed.), *The Collected Works of Sardar Vallabhbhai Patel*, Vol. XV, *op. cit.*, p. 66.
177. *Ibid.*, p. 248, *Ibid.*, Vol. XIV, p. 184, *Ibid.*, Vol. XII, p. 14, *Ibid.*, Vol. XV, p. 69.
178. *The Hindustan Times*, 6 March, 1949.
179. David Pocock, *Kanbis and Patidars, op. cit.*, pp. 12-3.
180. G.I. Patel, *Vithalbhai Patel: Life and Times* (Bombay: 1950, *op. cit.*, p. 19).
181. Navajivan, 12 June, 1922.
182. P.N. Chopra (ed.), *The Collected Works of Sardar Vallabhbhai Patel*, Vol. IV, *op. cit.*, p. 93.
183. *Ibid.*, p. 147.
184. Vallabhbhai Patel to Subash Bose, 1 June, 1938, AICC Papers, NMML, New Delhi.
185. Rajmohan Gandhi, *Patel: A Life, op. cit.*, p. 9.
186. David Pocock, *Kanbis and Patidars, op. cit.*, p. 155.
187. *Bombay Chronicle*, 25 February, 1935.

188. Narahari Parikh, *Sardar Vallabhbhai Patel,* Vol. I, *op. cit.*, p. 407.
189. Rajmohan Gandhi, *Patel: A Life, op. cit.,* p. 4.
190. P.N. Chopra (ed.), *The Collected Works of Sardar Vallabhbhai Patel,* Vol. X, *op. cit.*, p. 14.
191. D.N. Dhangare, *Peasant Movement in India*, 1920, 1950 (New Delhi: Oxford, 1991, p. 104).
192. P.N. Chopra (ed.), *The Collected Works of Sardar Vallabhbhai Patel,* Vol. VIII, *op. cit.*, p. 99.
193. *Bombay Chronicle*, 11 June, 1936.
194. *Ibid.*, 25 September, 1935.
195. P.N. Chopra, *The Sardar of India, op. cit.*, p. 274.
196. *Prajabandhu*, 8 May, 1938.
197. P.N. Chopra (ed.), *The Collected Works of Sardar Vallabhbhai Patel,* Vol. VIII, 1996, *op. cit.*, p. 201.
198. G.M. Nandurkar (ed.), *Sardar Patel: In Tune with the Millions,* Vol. II, Birth Centenary Series, Ahmedabad, 1978, p. 175.
199. P.N. Chopra (ed.), *The Collected Works of Sardar Vallabhbhai Patel,* Vol. V, 1994, *op. cit.*, p. 93.
200. *Ibid.*, Vol. I, *op. cit.*, p. 247.
201. *Prajabandhu*, 20 December, 1928.
202. *Ibid.*
203. P.N. Chopra (ed.), *The Collected Works of Sardar Vallabhbhai Patel,* Vol. X, 1997, *op. cit.*, p. 147.
204. P.N. Chopra (ed.), *Ibid.*, Vol. XII, *op. cit.*, p. 31.
205. Navajivan, July, 1930.
206. *Bombay Chronicle*, 23 March, 1928.
207. P.N. Chopra (ed.), *The Collected Works of Sardar Vallabhbhai Patel,* Vol.IV, *op. cit.*, p. 55. *Ibid.*, Vol. X, p. 44.
208. G.M. Nandurkar (ed.), *Sardar Mosly Unknown*, Birth Centenary Vol. IV (Ahmedabad: 1937, p. 302).
209. *Gujarat Samachar*, 3 October, 1934.
210. *Ibid.*, 25 June, 1936.

211. P.N. Chopra (ed.), *The Collected Works of Sardar Vallabhbhai Patel,* Vol. II, *op. cit.*, p. 131.

212. *The Hindustan Times*, 2 March, 1950. *Ibid.*, 21 May 1950.

213. P.N. Chopra (ed.), *The Collected Works of Sardar Vallabhbhai Patel,* Vol. II, 1991, *op. cit.*, pp. 256-7.

214. *The Hindustan Times*, 9 May, 1949.

215. N.D. Parikh, *Sardar Vallabhbhai Patel,* Vol. I, *op. cit.*, pp. 265-6.

216. D.V. Tahamankar, *Sardar Patel* (London: George Allen and Unwin, 1970, p. 125).

217. Navajivan, 28 December, 1931. *Bombay Chronicle*, 21 October 1937.

218. Prakashitlal Majumdar, "His Love for the Downtrodden" in G.M. Nandurkar (ed.), Birth Centenary Vol. (I), *op. cit.*, p. 186.

219. D. Pathak, and P. Sheth, *Sardar Vallabhbhai Patel: From Civic to National Leadership, op. cit.*, p. 354.

220. *Bombay Chronicle*, 21 November, 1936 *Ibid.*, 7 February 1937. Vallabhbhai Patel to G.B. Pant, 7 November 1945, Rajendra Prasad Papers, National Archives of India, New Delhi.

221. *The Hindustan Times*, 12 August, 1950.

222. P.N. Chopra (ed.), *The Collected Works of Sardar Vallabhbhai Patel,* Vol. XIV, *op. cit.*, pp. 147-8.

223. *The Hindustan Times*, 2 March, 1950.

224. P.N. Chopra (ed.), *The Collected Works of Sardar Vallabhbhai Patel,* Vol. XIV, *op. cit.*, p. 147-8.

225. P.N. Chopra (ed.), *Ibid.,* Vol. XII, *op. cit.*, p. 49.

226. *The Hindustan Times*, 21 January, 1948.

227. *The Hindustan Times*, 24 February, 1950.

228. Vallabhbhai Patel, *For a United India: Speeches of Sardar Patel* 1947-50, (New Delhi: Publication Division, 1967, p. 109).

229. *Bombay Chronicle*, 9 April, 1927.

230. *Gujarat Samachar*, 6 March, 1935.

231. *Bombay Chronicle*, 5 March, 1935.

232. R.K. Murthi, *The Man and His Contemporaries* (New Delhi: Sterling, 1976, p. 62).

233. D. Pathak and P. Sheth, *Sardar Vallabhbhai Patel: From Civic to National Leadership, op. cit.*, p. 352.
234. *Gujarat Samachar*, 1 October, 1935.
235. G.M. Nandurkar (ed.), *Sardar Patel: In Tune with the Millions* (I), *op. cit.*, p. 255.
236. *The Hindustan Times*, 7 May, 1949, Publication Division, For a United India, *op. cit.*, p. 133.
237. P.N. Chopra (ed.), *The Collected Works of Sardar Vallabhbhai Patel*, Vol. XIII, *op. cit.*, p. 2.
238. G.M. Nandurkar (ed.), *Sardar Patel: In Tune with the Millions* (I), *op. cit.*, p. 249.
239. *The Hindustan Times*, 18 May,1948.

4

The Concept of Nation-State

The state is the highest political organisation in the society and it is essentially characterised by the attribute of sovereignty that involves internal supremacy in its relationship with the people and external independence so far as the relationship with the other states is concerned. However, in reality the exercise of sovereignty by the state seems to be essentially affected by the level of unity and integration of its people and the level of their loyalty and commitment to the cause of the state. Therefore, the state is required to develop itself into the Nation–State, so that it may have stability and effectiveness within and may carve out a status of dignity and independence in its relationship with other states. It is because of this necessity of formation of the Nation–State that leaders and statesmen of Developing Politics tend to speculate on requisite techniques for the specific goal-attainment, keeping in view the history, culture, economy and politics of their respective societies and also the exigencies of time. Viewed in this perspective, Vallabhbhai as a distinguished leader of India was no exception. As he is very closely linked to the formation of the Indian state, his ideas particularly on the concept of Nation–State needs to be inquired and analysed.

Indian nationalism, as in case of most of the Afro-Asian countries was not a mere creation of the colonial power.[1] Though, developed initially to modernise the political set-up, it managed to bring about a comprehensive overhauling in the socio-economic and political field. The long duration of the struggle made it matured enough to resist all hurdles and to rely mostly upon the principles like peace, non-violence and humanism. Born during such times, Vallabhbhai obviously became part of the process.The pragmatic *Patidar* attitude influenced him to realise the possibility of a devil instinct in man which needs to be regulated by an indigenous political authority. Thus, Vallabhbhai believed in the ability of the state for the protection of the individual. His exposure to the Western secular values and the nineteenth century convention of social hierarchy helped him to monitor the growth of Indian nationalism and contribute to it in a distinct way. The family, community, educational institutions, profession and the leaders of his time influenced him to synthesise the networking of various horizontal and vertical linkages at various layers of the society and to shape the nationalistic fervour in a new way to provide a solid plural base to the Nation–State.

4.1 Growth of Nationalism

Vallabhbhai picked up all the essential qualities of a great leader like determination, dedication, discipline etc. in the family itself.[2] The impact of the Swami Narayana Cult upon the family helped him significantly in this process of acculturation. In fact, his middle class peasant background taught him to fight against adversities in a hostile environment. As the life sketch reveals the typical *Patidar* joint family structure infused in him a sense of reverence for the elders. It subsequently enabled him to extend his loyalty towards the nation. Vallabhbhai himself admitted: "The lessons of give and take, negotiations and compromise that one could learn in the family could come in very useful in dealing with the world outside."[3] If mother Ladba's religious attitude made him humble, duty-conscious and tolerant, father Jhaverbhai's ability to make quick decisions as the village headman instilled in him confidence and interest to look beyond the world of one's own existence. The typical *Patidar* boldness of his father got further refined in him with age and taught him to assert himself first in the family to get rid of the apparent sense of negligence of a 'middle child' and subsequently to refuse any form of humiliation.[4]

Vallabhbhai's nationalistic orientation was also deeply influenced by the prevailing environment. His inherent sense of independence got a further boost in his early casual, rustic *Patidar* style of living[5]. He was essentially part of the *Patidar* community known for its quest for upward mobility in the social hierarchy by virtue of its traits like solidarity, pragmatic outlook, independent mindset and hardworking ability. Vallabhbhai was exposed to the conservative approach of the Patidars, who, because of such traits had moved beyond the 'middle peasantry' status by the mid-nineteenth century.[6] Such pragmatism helped the community to cope with the challenges of the British policy and to redefine the patidarhood.[7] It had come a long way in influencing the political career of Vallabhbhai and encouraging him to look for solutions in the existing set-up. He was also influenced by the political awareness of the community. Such awareness among the influential Patidars was to some extent the result of their newly elevated status. It united the community and encouraged the upper section to take up the moral responsibility of protecting the lower.[8] Again, internally if the political consciousness of the community increased further as a result of the developments in Gujarat like the spread of English education and activities of the social reform organisations like the Arya Samaj, externally it was the result of the trade relationship established by the British particularly with Gujarat and contact of the Patidars with the far-off places like East Africa. The level of awareness created among the *Patidars* in the early part of the twentieth century could be assessed from the circulation of news papers like the *Patidar Hithechhu*, *Patel Bandhu*, *Kaira Niti Prakash*, *Kaira Vartamann,* etc. and the formation of semi-political associations like the *Patidar* Yuvak Mandal. All these helped the 'solidarity seeking' community to channelise its energy in the direction of political developments. It was evident from the key role played by the community in the Swadeshi movement and various peasant mobilisations against the British arbitrary policies in the early part of the twentieth century. Gandhi had recognised the potential of the community and said: "I have come to regard the *Patidar* Yuvak Mandal in high esteem ever since I was in Africa. I was said that I would get full cooperation of the *Patidar* Mandal on my return to India."[9] Thus, peasant protest in Gujarat could hardly be due to any outside intervention or because of mere peasant deprivation.[10] It was rooted well within the organised *Patidar* community. Vallabhbhai being part of such a well-knit community could hardly have remained immune from its influence. In fact, it must have shaped his inherent trait of resisting any undue encroachment in one's personal domain.

Vallabhbhai's exposure to education provided him with enough opportunities to assert himself particularly outside the family. His passion for 'captaincy' claimed to have been taken up for good causes,[11] enabled him to challenge any form of indiscipline and indifference on the part of the school authorities. He managed to organise a boycott of students against a particular teacher neglecting his duty.[12] In subsequent period, he utilised the technique at the political level by taking advantage of the communal bond and mechanical solidarity of the Indian society. His keen participation both in curricular and extra-curricular activities in the school developed his organisational ability. True to a Patidar's obsession for English education, his exposure to it not only broadened his outlook but also provided him with ample scope to make himself acquainted with nationalistic ideas imparted by the Petland English school.[13]

Though, Vallabhbhai soon after his school education decided to become a district pleader in order to support his family but in the long run it sharpened his independent attitude. The experience of the legal profession made him very much confident of himself. Later on, his trip to England and success in the examination of Bar-at-Law, particularly in an adverse condition strengthened his resolve to realise his goal. The very 'goal-directed nature' probably kept him focused in his studies and dissuaded him not to keep track of the developments going on in England, particularly in relation to India.[14] The exposure to the British jurisprudence strengthened his conservative mindset. He was struck by British nationalism and the prevalence of the rule of law in England. At the same time, he was equally disturbed by the colonial mentality of the same people in India. He observed: "As soon as the Englishmen crossed the Suez Canal, their mentality changed into that of world conquerors—a superiority complex which relied on brute force to maintain its supremacy. They assumed the role of custodian of the backward people of India, who they believed had been ordained by providence to be ruled by the British."[15] This realisation might have been responsible for changing his ideas on Western education and culture. Even while in England, Vallabhbhai always expressed his longing for his native place. In one of his writings he expressed: "I have completed my examination and have passed in the first class. It means that I shall be coming six months earlier than usual, which could be sometimes in January next. January is not far and God has been kind that He reduced the period of my stay here by six months."[16] In fact, he was exhibiting the typical traits of the Patidar, who managed to keep in touch with their native places despite being away in far off places like East Africa.[17] Such an attitude might have helped him extend his initial concern for the family especially in the capacity of a son, brother and father, towards the Nation later.

Vallabhbhai had to bear the pain of the death of his wife Jhaverba prior to leaving for England. He once acknowledged: "when I was in full vigour of youth, at the age of 32, my partner-in-life disappeared suddenly, leaving two young children – a son of two and daughter of the age of four."[18] Because of his additional responsibility he could not opt for any public career as in case of the elder brother Vithalbhai. Though, on his return from England he made a mutual understanding with his brother to look after the family during the latter's preoccupation in politics, yet he failed to conceal his fascination for all such activities. He said: "My brother gave up his flourishing practice and started on a career of public service, while I bore the burden of maintaining the household. I had thus to commit all the sins and he performed all the good deeds, but I reconciled myself by the thought that I could claim at least a share in his good work".[19] The political awareness of his own community and the success of Vithalbhai in politics prompted him to think on such lines. Undoubtedly, his involvement in politics might have compensated to some extent for the loneliness in his life.[20]

There was hardly any dividing line between the professional and public career of Vallabhbhai. Besides the factors mentioned above, he might have overcome his initial hesitation to join in politics because of his success in the legal field. It provided him with an opportunity to become a member of the Gujarat Club, which was then a venue for ventilation of views on public issues. He was persuaded by important members of the Club like Govind Rao Patil, Shivabhai Patel etc. to join in politics.[21] But, the real focus of attention was the declining administrative set-up of the Ahmedabad Municipality. His ability to counter independently the bureaucratic encroachment by British officials showed his courage to challenge any form of exploitation. During his two terms in the civic body, he took several measures which kindled the nationalistic fervour at the grass roots level. He gave priority to the appointment of efficient Indian candidates in order to indianise the set-up gradually. His use of horizontal and vertical mobilisation strategies to refuse the grant on education and to avoid unnecessary regulation of the authority had created a lot of political awareness among people. During the whole process, he was in touch with the Non-Cooperation Movement and was prepared to utilise the civic body as a venue for struggle against the British administration. Reinterpreting the role of the Municipality in this context, he said: "our Municipal outlook no longer remained restricted to cleaning of roads and privies, maintenance of drainage and water works and the ordinary routine work just for the convenience of the people. To us, Municipality really meant *Swaraj* with all its implications of national life."[22] The impact of the new strategy of Vallabhbhai was far-reaching. It was observed by *Prajabandhu*, a local daily: "Last Thursday the Municipal Board of our city passed the motion of Vallabhbhai, rejecting Educational grant from the Government amid scenes seldom witnessed within the precincts of Rippon Hall. A vast concourse of more than 1000 persons watched the heated discussion with breath and received final decisions with vociferous shouts of *Vande Mataram* and *Mahatma Gandhi ki Jai*."[23] In fact, during his presidentship (1924-1928), out of the 92 proposals approved 16 were meant to kindle nationalistic fervour.[24] Some of the prominent measures were cancellation of war celebration, defiance to the Government directives to observe the Victory Day (1919), giving honours to national leaders, hoisting of the National Flag, holding of condolence meetings to pay respect to the departed leaders, raising monuments after such great leaders, renaming Rippon Hall as the Gandhi Hall, demanding the recognition of the degree of the Gujarat Vidyapitha, opening national school in Ahmedabad and propagating the use of Swadeshi or indigenous products.[25] Thus, Vallabhbhai, managed to channelise his professional success in creating nationalistic ethos.

In the initial phase of its evolution, Vallabhbhai's nationalistic orientation was further shaped by the attitudes of many contemporary leaders. The most prominent of them was Gandhi with whom he had come in contact in 1918, during the Kheda agitation. Even prior to the arrival of Gandhi, he was exposed to the thinking of other Congress leaders like Dadabhai Naoroji and Bal Gangadhar Tilak who symbolised two contrasting lines of thinking within the organisation so far as negotiation with the British authority on political reform was concerned. He was inspired by Naoroji's 'drain theory' which exposed the British tactics of ruining India economically, and also by Tilak for his extremist tactics and demand for *Swaraj*. The impact of the second group appeared to be more decisive as it led to the emergence of 'radical nationalism' in Gujarat. Due to a number of factors like the partition of Bengal, influence of the Arya Samaj and contact with revolutionary leaders of Bengal like Aurobindo Ghosh who was then teaching in the Baroda College, the Gujarat province experienced an extreme form of emotional outburst against the authority.[26] The prevailing spirit in Gujarat was reflected in one of the pamphlets: "The new phase of development in the aspirations of the people of India is nothing but the expressions of the ground ideal of *Swaraj*. Its goal is absolute freedom so also its method of organisation and social work. While its motto is self-help, self-reliance and self-sacrifice."[27] Despite Vallabhbhai's differences with this line of radical thinking propagated in Gujarat by Mohanlal Pandya and Narasinghbhai Patel, he revered it for reviving India's past glory as done earlier by Shivaji and Dayananda Saraswati.[28] Reiterating Tilak's message on nationalism, he said: "When there were 35 crore of slaves, it is the duty of everyman to remove his slavery and it is the birthright of everyone to remove himself from the foreign yoke and if this is sedition, everyone must do it."[29]

Despite all these developments, Vallabhbhai's conservative but pragmatic mindset was not prepared to follow completely any of the existing lines of thinking. In this context, Gandhi's arrival with new ideas, acted like a catalyst in reshaping the nationalistic urge of Vallabhbhai. His defiance to the authority at Champaran in 1917 impressed every Indian. The use of *Satyagraha* by means of non-violence and penance infused moral strength among the Indians to counter the British authority. It might have reminded Vallabhbhai his own experience of boycott pursued during the school days. He was impressed by Gandhi's unique way of reorganising the Gujarat Sabha which insisted on having its regular annual session, use of colloquial language in its proceedings, and delinking the designation of the Imperial authority from its official deliberations. The new agitational politics of Gandhi conveyed the message that in a traditional society where pockets of influences were numerous, non-violence could bind all equally and create a base for a parallel power structure to meet the requirements of the people independent of the British authority. In this atmosphere, Vallabhbhai became very much realistic to realise the significance of such a message to confront the British power. Finally, the attraction of 'leaving a better legacy than money, motivated him to leave his roaring legal practice and join with Gandhi in various local agitations and all India level struggles.[30] Thus, a combination of several factors led to the evolution of a sense of nationalism in Vallabhbhai and he took the momentous decision to enter in to public life at the matured age of forty two.

4.2 Vision of Nation-State

Vallabhbhai had the unique distinction of operating against the British authority at the provincial and all-India levels simultaneously by following both the politics of 'confrontation' and 'participation'. Due to his command over the *Patidar* community in particular and the rural society of Gujarat in general, he could successfully transform the local grievances into all India issues and in the process strengthen the freedom struggle. In course of the long struggle, his vision of the Nation–State took a concrete shape.

Vallabhbhai got an opportunity to organise the people for the first time during the Kheda agitation. It was launched by Gandhi in 1918, under the banner of the Gujarat Sabha to demand tax relief for the farmers of the locality. He was chosen by Gandhi specifically for the purpose. The protest initiated at the local level, enabled him to realise its possible ramification over the rest of the country. He said: "By their courage the agriculturists of Kheda have drawn towards them the attention of the whole country. . . . We hope that they will develop their great qualities still further and bring credit to their motherland. The public of Kheda have rendered great service to themselves, to the struggle for independence and to the state."[31] Hence both the experiences of Kheda and the Ahmedabad civic body emboldened him to expand his activities to a larger scale. Vallabhbhai, who had started introducing reforms in the Ahmedabad Municipality, found no difficulty in demanding the same at the all-India level when the British authority promulgated the Rowlatt Act. In an attempt to protect the honour and dignity of the people of India, he said: "Can we really forget this attempt to dishonour India.... The coming generation have a claim on us, who are their trustees: If we leave them only a heritage of insults and dishonour, what use would all the wealth and all comforts be that we may leave to them. If we put up with the insult, would it be a matter of surprise if for all the time to come we are despised by civilised nations."[32] Subsequently, at the time of the Non-cooperation Movement, he introduced 'linkage politics' by joining the local civic body with the National struggle through Gandhian techniques[33]. It not only helped him to make the civic body at the grass roots level more effective but also to launch a more vigorous struggle against the British Government following the Jalianawala Bagh Massacre. This shift in approach reflected his nationalistic orientation. His cynic mind could detect the hypocrisy behind the so called universal British jurisprudence and attributed the pitiable conditions of the Indians to the blind faith they had reposed upon the prevailing system of law[34]. At this stage, his decision of not entering into the Council was to foil the British 'Policy of Cooptation', introduced to weaken the freedom struggle by associating only a few Indians in the administration. Vallabhbhai apprehended it and said: "What difference will it make if we merely replace some foreign officers by Indians? . . . . Even so, merely by throwing a few drops of Ganga water into the sewage one can scarcely hope to purify it. There must be a radical change of outlook in the administration. The Government of India must be run for the people of India."[35]

For Vallabhbhai, the process of articulation of *Swaraj* or independence unfolded slowly as he continued to mobilise people against the British on various sensitive issues concerning the people of Nagpur, Borsad and Bordoli. In all these mobilisations he made efforts to remind the people the significance of the Flag, the duty of the government to protect the life of the people and responsibility of the authority to honour the basic principles of governance that there should be no taxation without representation. His efforts created tremendous political awareness which was required for the realisation of a Nation–State. In fact Bordoli agitation made him an all-India figure. Assessing correctly his contribution particularly in Bordoli, Gandhi said: "Vallabhbhai had rightly distinguished the proposed *Satyagraha* from the *Swaraj Satyagraha*... But, though the object of the proposed Satyagaha is local and specific, it has an All India application. What is true of Bordoli, has also an indirect bearing on *Swaraj*. Whatever awakens people to a sense of their wrongs and whatever gives them strength for discipline and peaceful resistance and habituates them for corporate sufferings, brings them nearer to Swaraj."[36]

With such an impact of the movements on Vallabhbhai, it was but natural that he was never far away from the goal of independence. He was chosen to become the Party President to lead the Party for political activities. He supported the report of the Nehru Committee constituted in 1928 by the Congress to make suggestions on the upcoming constitutional reforms and to counter the Simon Commission Report. Given the well-entrenched position of the British authority in India, the conservative *Patidar* inclination in him might have motivated, him to appreciate the Committee's suggestion of 'Dominion Status' for India to prepare its people mentally before making the final claim for complete independence. In this regard, he appeared to have the same opinion as Gandhi but differed from Nehru. Though, in 1929 he supported Nehru's Lahore Resolution of 'complete independence' and extended full cooperation to the Civil Disobedience Movement yet, he had never hesitated earlier to criticise the same decision of the radical faction within the Congress as 'premature'. Criticising the young leadership under Nehru, he said: "if we old men are not in a hurry, would the younger man like you show haste? We wish to see India free before we quit this world. We are in a greater hurry than you are. Let us keep our sword sheathed, but let us keep them sharpened and shining. That is possible only if we continue to follow the programme of boycott of foreign clothes, encouragement of Khadi and self-purification."[37] Tahamankar argued that the apprehension of Vallabhbhai proved to be right as the Civil Disobedience Movement was not only crushed but also the strategy of non-cooperation denied the Congress the opportunity to participate in the First Round Table Conference especially at a time when the apparently pro-Indian Labour Government of Ramsay MacDonald was in power.[38]

The failure of the Civil Disobedience Movement led to dissension within the Congress Party. Vallabhbhai felt that it could pose threat to the goal of independence. Guided by a strong sense of realism, he always gave priority to the cause than any individual. So he supported Gandhi's decision to withdraw from active politics as it would enable the Congress to switch over to electoral politics and in the process gain greater effectiveness to negotiate with the British.[39] As a perfect Patidar, who attached more importance to ends than means,[40] he took advantage of the opportunities offered by the authority. In the process he deviated from the paths followed by Gandhi and Subash Chandra Bose, the leader of the radical faction of the Congress. As Bose did not agree to his Council-entry programme and insisted on launching a Civil Disobedience Movement, Vallabhbhai adopted a ruthless strategy of sidelining him within the party. On this aspect of his nature, Gandhi once said, "Heaven will help those who cross Sardar's path.[41] In the changed situation, Vallabhbhai defended his decision of Council-entry and office-acceptance. As he said, "We have not accepted office in order to carry out a few reforms. We have accepted office with a view to moving on towards a far greater thing, complete independence. If by accepting office, our ability to move towards that goal is increased, well and good. But, if we find that our final goal is jeopardised, we must immediately give up office."[42] In reality, he did it in 1939, when the Government forced the people of India to join the War which was contradictory to the policies of the Congress. If, in the past the goal of independence had motivated Vallabhbhai to assume office, it was the same consideration which influenced him to return to the Gandhian fold to pursue the struggle even in a vacuum created after the resignation of the provincial Congress Ministries. He returned to agitational path to use it as a defensive mechanism, in order to lead the people of India who were quite disillusioned by the half-hearted approach of the Cripps Mission over constitutional reform and were skeptical about the sincerity of the authority in protecting them from the likely Japanese aggression. Arguing in favour of independence, he said: "India has nothing to choose between British imperialism and German Nazism. If these powers are fighting to strengthen the foundations of their empires and thereby give permanence to India's slavery, there is then no basis for us to side with either."[43] Hence, he supported Gandhi's Quit India Movement, though he did not hesitate to go beyond non-violence by urging the people to resort to violence in case of necessity to challenge the British authority effectively.[44] In subsequent period, the decision was hailed by Nehru who had earlier expressed reservation over it.[45] But Vallabhbhai was too realistic to foresee the side-effects of the reversal of the Council-entry programme. It provided space to the Muslim League to move ahead with its agenda for Pakistan. This realisation might have made Vallabhbhai apprehensive of his goal and influenced him in the subsequent period to keep the option of dialogue with the authority open.

Be it participation or defiance, Vallabhbhai never deviated from his goal of creating a stable Nation–State. A man with perfect command over facts, he could synthesise the national and international developments in the post-Second World War period to develop a strategy to the advantage of the people of India. He was helped by certain external developments such as the growing influence of the USA, changing stand of Russia and the declining economic condition of England. At the same time he was inspired by the sense of unity created within the country by the Indian National Army's trial and the Royal Naval Mutiny. As it became evident that the British Government would leave the country after the War, he decided to use each and every opportunity to negotiate with the authority. He became confident of his stand due to the party support behind him, which was reflected during the election for the post of the Party President in 1946. But he could not ignore the growing stature of the Muslim League. In fact, by the mid-forties, Jinnah the Muslim League Leader, who was sidelined by his own party after the Khilafat agitation and overshadowed by the charismatic leadership of Gandhi, had transformed himself from a Nationalist leader into a self-styled spokesperson of the Muslim Community. During the process, he was helped by the authority's divisive strategies such as the formation of the League governments in Sind, Assam, Bengal and the North-West Frontier Province after the resignation of the Congress Ministries, recognition of the minorities through the Cripps Mision plan and the representation of the League in the Shimla Conference as the sole spokesperson of the Muslim community. Jinnah's strategy of supporting the authority during the Quit India Movement paid off and he emerged as a key player in the political scene.

Thus, by the time the Cabinet Mission arrived with a comprehensive scheme on the formation of the Interim Government and the Constituent Assembly, Vallabhbhai was matured enough to realise that it was the best opportunity to tide over the advantages given to the League by the authority as part of the strategy to balkanise India. He took full advantage of the indecisive mood of the League which was denied parity of status in the proposed Interim Government. He prevailed upon the Congress to accept the proposal on the formation of the Constituent Assembly and extended full support to the 16 May Plan of the Cabinet Mission to claim the sole right to form the government. Thereby, he ignored the 'group clause' over which he had deep reservation as it had the potential to create Pakistan. He was confident of getting it changed after the Congress assumed power and formed the Interim Government. The decision had isolated the League for a while at least and put a question mark on the viability of Pakistan. Realising Vallabhbhai's strategy, Wavell observed: "This section had no interest in the framing of a final Constitution; all it wants is power; complete power and power at once. The leader of this section of the Congress Working Committee is of course Patel."[46] In fact, till the mid 40s Vallabhbhai was firm on liberation of the country as a whole. He argued: "Individual members of our committee while expressing their personal views may have laid emphasis or one on the other parts of the Congress resolution. But, I can assure that all of us are united on the one question that the Congress as a whole stands for the unity of India and it cannot agree to any division"[47]. But during the process of negotiations, he faced many challenges both within and outside the Congress. The authority's initiative to include the League within the Interim government, despite the latter's involvement in the ongoing communal violence and lack of faith in the Cabinet Mission Plan itself, enhanced the morale of the League which had entrenched its position due to its victory over a contiguous zone in the 1946 election. The die was cast when the British authority through the London Declaration conceded that no transfer of power would take place bypassing the Muslims. Churchill, the leader of the Conservative Party in England, propagated that any attempt to establish the reign of a Hindu numerical majority would never be without a civil war and motivated the British leadership against the Congress.[48] Lastly, the role played by Mountbatten, the last Governor-General in ensuring a hurried settlement in favour of the outgoing authority, left little option before the Congress leaders.[49] Besides the external factors, Vallabhbhai had to encounter internal division within the Congress leadership.

In this backdrop of chaos and confusion, the ultimatum given by Prime Minister Atlee in February 1947 to leave India by June 1948, encouraged leaders like Vallabhbhai to extract the maximum advantages. Though, partition became the ultimate reality in view of the communal animosity, he managed to foil the dream of Jinnah from having the 'Greater Pakistan' with provinces such as Bengal, Punjab, Sind, NWFP, Assam and Baluchistan as a whole. He was instrumental in foiling the dream of 'sovereign Bengal' visualised by the Muslim League premiere Suhrawady who was strongly supported by Jinnah. As communal violence continued to rise unabated, like many others Vallabhbhai had to reconcile with the partition of the country. He had to accept the separation of the North-West Frontier Province which played a crucial role during the freedom struggle. But his initiative succeeded to a large extent to dilute the 'group clause' of the Cabinet Mission Plan to snatch Assam and limit the partition process within the Muslim dominated areas of Bengal and the Punjab. He argued: "Nobody likes the division of India and my heart is heavy. But, the division is between one division and many divisions, we must face facts, we cannot give way to emotionalism and sentimentality."[50] Vallabhbhai's logic convinced most of the party members. The resolution on partition was approved by the Working Committee of the Congress Party by 127 votes to 27 with 32 remaining neutral. Thus, the firm and crucial role played by him led to a large extent the creation of India as an independent state.

4.3 Bases of Nationalism

Vallabhbhai became a national leader mainly because of his role within the Gujarat Province. The involvement in the peasant politics of Gujarat in general and the Bordoli agitation in particular won him recognition at the all-India level. But he did not have a parochial attitude. It was substantiated by Gandhi, who after the Kheda agitation had started depending on Vallabhbhai for his understanding and command over the grass roots conditions.[51] Vallabhbhai's skillful utilisation of his nexus with the local influential *Patidar* community paid off in his struggle. He understood its psychology properly and tried to accommodate it in the Gandhian agitational strategy. Vallabhbhai's association with Gujarat developed partly because of his legal profession[52] and partly the attitude of a Patidar, who always considered the province as his private property.[53] In subsequent periods, he depended upon his native place to get a stable support base to counter the British policies which normally affected the national politics more than that of the provinces. Anyhow, his activities like reforming the civic body through the Non-Cooperation Movement and mobilisation of people in Kheda, Nagpur, Borsad and Bordoli had national ramifications. Thus, he became a national leader using provincial politics as a launching pad.

Vallabhbhai's concern for India as a whole could be inferred from the way he criticised the education system even at a point of time, when he was yet to establish himself as a national leader. He attacked the British for interfering with Indian culture through education. At the time of the Non-cooperation Movement, he argued: "Some are propagandists of the Western way of life; they see in the spinning wheel a sign that the country is going back a hundred and fifty years; but they fail to realise that Western advancement is really the cause of the unsettled state of world today . . . . India alone prefers to stand out against it in the process to save not only itself but the world . . . . As India which believes in the strength of the soul cannot be attracted by a shallow demonical culture."[54] He tried to expose the British hypocrisy of entering in to the First World War in the name of protecting the self-determination status of smaller states while denying the same to India[55]. Even in course of organising the peasant protests in the provinces, Vallabhbhai's concern was much beyond the *Patidar* community for which he took initiatives to preside over the conferences of the Raniparaj (backward) communities in 1922 and 1929 and organised the Borsad struggle with the help of some of them. In fact, he had learnt the technique of leaning upon the 'outside help' since 1923, from the time of the Flag *Satyagraha.*[56] Then he took the help of the provinces such as Bihar, Sind, Punjab, Bengal, Karnataka, UP, Hyderabad, etc. to get the support of the required volunteers. He also drew the attention of the Congress at the all-India level to pressurise the government to bring an early end to the Bordoli struggle.[57] After the agitation, his extensive tour into various parts of the country such as Poona, Madras, Karnataka, Bihar, etc. proved his anxiety to understand the problems beyond the provinces of Gujarat. Taking advantage of his experience of organising people in Bordoli, he addressed the people of Tamilnadu and Bihar to get rid of caste exploitation and peasant oppression. During these years, his aversion towards the Simon Commission for having no Indian representative and his refusal to celebrate the king's birthday showed his strong nationalistic orientation.[58]

In the early thirties, during his tenure as the Congress President, Vallabhbhai was criticised by some Congress leaders like Subash Bose for allegedly remaining aloof towards the problems of provinces like that of Bengal.[59] But it was rejected by many leaders from the province itself who wholeheartedly supported Vallabhbhai's impartial role played during the Hijli-Chittagong police atrocities.[60]

His broad outlook was revealed as he reacted against Rabindranath Tagore, a prominent votary of the freedom struggle, who demanded extra favour for the Bengali Mills against others and recommended the boycott of the non-Bengali Mills by the Bengalis.[61] As the Party President, he also tried to widen the base of the Congress. He not only criticised the policy of Communal Award of the British Government, but also impressed upon the Party to accommodate the interests of the minorities to make it a national organisation in true sense of the term and foil the plan of the authority to divide the social base of the country.[62] He never allowed the party to attend to any personal problems of the members. When P.A. Pereira approached the organisation to settle his personal rift with the Bengal Mercantile Life Insurance Company, he refused to intervene and said: "I agree that you should have so much difficulties in getting your dues, but I am afraid I was not within my jurisdiction as President to go into the private affairs of the members of the Congress.[63] The approval of the Party resolution finalising the shape, design and colour of the National Flag and proclaiming it as the symbol of national aspiration and communal harmony substantiated his nationalistic orientation. Vallabhbhai was not only concerned for the people of his province but also for every Indian living in far-off places like South and East Africa.[64] His advocacy of self-determination status for nations reflected his mental horizon which could hardly be categorised as provincial. Commenting on the case of Burma, as Party President he said: "Whether Burma separates from India or remains a part of independent India, it is for the people of Burma to decide. But, it is our duty and that of the whole world to ensure that all parties get an opportunity to present their case."[65] The *Patidar* trait of keeping oneself abreast of the surroundings motivated Vallabhbhai to develop interests beyond the province.[66] While in Jail, he once said: "I may make it clear that I did not want a Gujarati daily for its views or information. I am getting all possible information regarding political events in the country from the generous supply of English dailies, allowed to me in jail and I am sure no body will think for a moment that any vernacular paper will influence my political views in any manner."[67] He appeared to be quite anxious for the dissemination of the Hindi language and its association with other provincial languages in order to develop a future national language for the country.[68] His thrust upon the popularisation of Hindi to carry forward the National Education since the days of the Non-cooperation Movement revealed his commitment which could hardly be categorised as provincial or parochial.[69]

During the freedom struggle, Vallabhbhai was pragmatic enough to assume that unity referred to coming together of like-minded people for the achievement of independence. He developed a calculated strategy to motivate many of the reluctant rulers in the Princely states to join the freedom struggle. The threat of the Socialist movement helped him convince the rulers and it provided a wider base to the upcoming nation state. He appeared ruthless against party functionaries who differed from his ideas. He gave priority to the cause of independence. So he wanted to keep the party united in order to carry on an effective struggle against the British. Hence, he convinced his party members to support the resolution on Quit India. It was in pursuance of his realisation that the essential condition of the Hindu-Muslim unity would not be possible in the presence of a third force. Despite all his ideological differences his acknowledgement of the role of the Bhagat Singh and his associates and Indian National Army (INA) in the liberation of the country indicated his sincerity towards the same goal. In fact, his effort to help the authority in ending the Naval Mutiny was intended to create a conducive atmosphere for the impending transfer of power.[70]

The partition of the country evoked extreme reactions from different sections of people. Some argue that it could have been avoided had the Congress leadership dealt with Jinnah more carefully. Even Azad, a prominent Congress leader admitted that Nehru's decision of not involving the League in Bombay and U.P. where it secured some votes in the provincial elections (1937) created conditions for the alienation of Jinnah. Further, he argued that Nehru's emotional outburst as the Vice-president of the Interim Government about the intention of the party to tamper with the 'Group Clause' of the Cabinet Mission Plan created suspicion in the minds of Jinnah. He also blamed Vallabhbhai for his insistence on the Home Portfolio in the Interim Government which the League wanted. Some others argue that Vallabhbhai's rejection of Gandhi's advocacy for a National Government with the Congress and the League as partners, acted as a catalyst for Jinnah's demand of Pakistan. Another section believes that the Muslim League was able to form Government in some border states in 1946 taking advantage of the Patel–Azad differences, which gave opportunities to the League to consolidate its position.[71] But people like K.M. Munshi denounced the logic of pacifying Jinnah by involving the League in the provincial set-up.[72] Rafiq Zakaria made it further clear by arguing that the post-war scenario influenced the authority to pursue the balkanisation plan in connivance with Jinnah, who being neglected sufficiently from all sides not only ignored any possible settlement, but also started propagating the irreconcilable differences between the Hindus and Muslims by taking advantage of the backwardness of his community.[73] The Muslim League due to the adamant attitude of Jinnah did not cooperate in the functioning of the Interim Government and the Constituent Assembly. In fact, Ram Manohar Lohia, who blamed the Congress leadership largely for the partition, did not miss to point out the British chicanery, conservative Muslim mindset, Hindu chauvinism, etc., as the vital factors behind the creation of Pakistan.[74] In the aforesaid situation, it was obviously beyond the control of any individual to influence the course of political development. As partition seemed inevitable, Vallabhbhai a diehard realist accepted it as the only available option at that point of time. His sincerity in creating a stable Nation–State became mere apparent as he convinced and motivated Nehru to agree upon the 'Dominion Status' to get through the Indian Independence Act in the British Parliament.[75]

Vallabhbhai continued to show concern for the stability of the Nation–State, even after independence. He was very critical of the Prince of Bhopal for his hobnobbing with the Political Department to disintegrate India. During the sensitive period of partition, he criticised the Muslims for showing disloyalty to India.[76] He also attacked the Hindu Mahasabha for claiming to be the sole custodian of the Hindu community.[77] He believed that religious fanaticism was against nationalism. He condemned all those who indulged in activities inimical to the interest of the country. Mavalankar observed: "Having a strong mind, combined with sentiment, his likes and dislikes are also strong—sometimes strong to a fault, but the greatest merit is that he never has any personal motive to grind, not even obliging a friend or hurting a foe. He measures everything and moulds his attitude and conduct to achieve what he considers to be the best interest of the country.[78] Vallabhbhai's commitment in this regard was evident from the fact that he accommodated many ambitious princes and politicians like C.F. Nariman, the President of the Bombay Congress unit against whom he had taken harsh steps for showing disloyalty to the Party during the freedom struggle. Further, his nationalistic orientation becomes clearer soon after independence from the fact that soon after independence he opposed regionalism purely on linguistic basis as it could have encouraged narrow provincialism. He argued, "We should cease thinking in terms of different states or provinces. Instead, we should think that we are Indians and that we should develop a sense of unity.[79]

4.4 Strategies for the Nation-State

In his effort to realise the goal of the Nation-State, Vallabhbhai devised different strategies like rearrangement of social relations, confrontation and electoral participation. In this regard, he was influenced by the conservative approach of a *Patidar* and was inclined more in favour of synthesising the existing variables than going in favour of any radical solution.

4.4.1 Rearrangement of Social Relations

Vallabhbhai felt the need for unifying the society segmented on the line of caste, language, religion, etc. He emphasised upon the value of mutual harmony which he had learnt in his childhood within the family.[80] To achieve his objective, he tried to integrate the society by giving importance to caste emancipation, women participation and Hindu-Muslim unity.

Caste Emancipation

Vallabhbhai in his attempt to reorganise the society, tried to uplift the lower caste people (the Kaliparajas) who were languishing because of abject poverty and low morale. In fact, the withdrawal of the Non-cooperation Movement in 1922 unveiled the structural weakness of the Gandhian strategy as it failed to mobilise the lower section of the society.[81] The inability to get consistent support of the *Patidar* community of the upper strata (the Ujaliparajas) further weakened the struggle.[82] So Vallabhbhai was compelled to rope in the Kaliparajas and make it more broad based. During the 36th session of the Congress (1921) he attacked the practice of untouchability as a psychological one and emphasised upon removing such segregation in course of time.[83] The extensive tours he undertook with Gandhi, particularly in the Kutch province, made him aware of the inhumane existence of the untouchables. During the Borsad struggle (1923) he broadened the base of the agitation by involving the lower caste groups like the *Patanavidyas* and *Barayias*. During this period, he was actively associated with the Antyaj Seva Mandal, formed for the untouchables. He also appreciated the report of the Raniparaj (*Kaliparaja*) Enquiry Committee constituted by the Congress in 1927, which suggested for the implementation of the policies of prohibition and spinning of *Khadi* to enhance the self-respect of the community.[84] Though he was not a diehard advocate of Khadi,[85] yet he was keen to popularise it to legitimise the status of the Dhed untouchables who were professional weavers. He argued: "when the *Charkha* goes into a hut, liquor and tadi are automatically expelled. Those who ply *charkha*, have rid themselves of their fears. They make their own cotton, spin it into yarn and then weave it into cloth. Thus, they have become minor industrialists."[86] He also suggested empowering the village *Panchayat* to implement the policy of prohibition.[87] He did not hesitate to remind the administration of the Princely States of their responsibility towards the downtrodden. He argued: "The untouchables in Kathiawar are a harassed lot. They suffer great inconvenience when they travel by rail. It is the duty of the state to protect the weak . . . . The untouchables must be given the right to study in public schools, draw water from public wells and tanks and seek shelter in public buildings. Arrangement should be made to see that they are not treated as untouchables in the royal court."[88] As the President of the 46th session of the Congress (1931), he again highlighted the need of removing untouchability to make the Civil Disobedience Movement more effective. He argued: "If the Hindus had removed untouchability, the struggle which we waged for the past twelve months would have been thousand times more successful. One thing is certain and that is without completing this task through self-purification and without removing the stigma from the face of the Hindu community, Swarajya even if it comes, would be as empty as it would be without boycott of foreign cloth."[89] Subsequently, in another Raniparaj Conference (1935), he urged for the integration of the low caste people in the society.[90]

Apart from all his efforts to uplift the lower section of the society, Vallabhbhai because of his knowledge of social realities at the grass root level could visualise the integrative value of caste. He realised the significance of the convergence of caste with class in the rural society of Gujarat. The lower castes (*Kaliparajas*) looked forward to the upper castes (*Ujaliparajas*) for their survival, while the latter thought it was their moral responsibility to protect the former. An inherent pragmatist, he did not hesitate to depend on the upper castes in general and the *Patidars* in particular to use them as instruments in the struggle against the British authority. He advised the people: "Go on strengthening your caste organisation. No one can have anything to say against it. These handful of men who came over here from a land 6,000 miles away, rule over us because they have a caste organisation of their own. Their close cooperation is devised to protect even the wrong doers amongst them . . . . Their cooperation always relying on brute strength has as its object the exploitation of the weak, ours has the only objective of self-preservation[91]. Thus, in course of reposing confidence in the higher section, he appealed to the non-Brahmins of the Tamil Province to have faith upon the former to ensure unity. He asked them: "Why are you so envious of Brahmins? ... Do you know what harms those other 'Brahmins' (the British) have done both to you and to these Brahmins? . . . . Let us assume that your own Brahmins have done harm to you; have they however, done you so much harm as these other Brahmins"[92]. Thus, it is evident that he highlighted social integration for the cause of independence.

Given this inclination for unity, it was quite natural for Vallabhbhai to lean heavily in favour of the *Patidar* community known for its solidarity seeking habit[93] to organise people during any *Satyagraha*. Observing advantage of the community over others he said: "The *Patidar* community had a closely knit organisation, but others had not . . . . The *Raniparaj*, the meekest of the meek were likely to bend under the first blow. The *Vanias*, some of whom had heavy stakes, holding as they did hundred acres of land, might not hold out until the last. Some of them had intimate social relations with Government officials, and there was evident fear of their being shamed into submission . . . . The *Anavils*, proud and defiant were still sitting on the fence and their calculating nature made them hesitate to join the fray. . . .[94] Because of these advantages of the community, Vallabhbhai had earlier recommended to Gandhi to change the venue of the Civil Disobedience Movement (1922) from Anand to a *Patidar* dominated area like Bordoli. The British Government Report also subsequently corroborated this trait.[95] Thus, while the *Patidars* were basically mobilised on the issue of the exploitative 'land tax', the Banias another faction of the *Ujaliparajas*, were made part of the struggle to ensure financial assistance for them. The conviction that the caste organisation provided strength to the weak and a member of caste became weak before the caste decision,[96] encouraged him to use it to infuse discipline in the public during the struggle against the British. He found that the traditional caste councils played the primary role in motivating the people. He appreciated the efforts of the local leaders in ostracising their fellow members who cooperated with the Government by way of paying taxes. During the Bordoli struggle, he acknowledged and commended the role played by the *Patidar* Caste Councils.[97] Due to his pragmatism, he gave emphasis upon minimising the losses of the participants of the freedom struggle. During the no-tax campaigns, he always assured the peasants regarding return of their confiscated lands. He used caste pressure to deter the *Dharlas* and *Parsees*, from buying the lands of the *Patidars* confiscated by the authority. He argued: "I shall see that every inch of the confiscated land goes back to the rightful owner. There can not be any alternative proposed in this regard. The land will and shall be restored to the man who owns it…"[98] He also came forward to help the *Vaniyas* (traders) for their assistance. As the Gandhian programme of boycott of foreign clothes caused heavy losses for the *Vanias* during the *Satyagrahas*, he assured them of support. He advised them to have an inventory of their stocks to prevent the selling of foreign cloths and assured them of compensation after the formation of the National Government.[99]

Women Participation

Vallabhbhai emphasised upon the participation of women in the freedom struggle as they comprised almost half of the population[100]. His experience in the Kheda agitation influenced him to involve this sizeable section to prevent people from paying tax at the time of confiscation of land. He also wanted to utilise their religious bent of mind to infuse moral strength in their menfolk.[101] Realising the economic and social significance of *Khadi*,[102] he tried to motivate them for *Khadi*-spinning emphasising upon the effeminate character of the weaving profession.[103] While dissuading them from using foreign cloth, he said: "I call upon the ladies of Gujarat not to wear foreign cloth... we are being rendered cowardly by wearing foreign made cloth."[104] During the Bordoli struggle he mobilised the womenfolk with the help of the women leaders like Maniben, Bhaktiba, Sharda Mehta, etc.

Hindu–Muslim Unity

Vallabhbhai realised that religion played an extremely important role in a dissension ridden traditional society like India as it generated a sense of unity among people. He mobilised the people of Dwarka in 1917 against the unwarranted arrest of Bharati Krishna, a contender for the post of *Shankaracharya*, citing it as encroachment upon the Hindu religion. He appealed to the people: "How can a man who eats cow flesh, drinks liquor and who is a Yavana and mlech (lesser mortal), understand who is *Shankaracharya*?[105] He criticised the removal of the *Khalifa*, the religious head of the Muslim community and supported the Non-cooperation Movement of Gandhi. He argued: "The Turkish Empire was divided in spite of Britain's promise . . . . Even the Viceroy admitted that some of the conditions of peace could not but offends the Muslim community. It was as a matter of fact a heart-breaking episode for the Indian Muslims and how can Hindus stand by unaffected when they see their fellow countrymen, thus in distress"?[106] In the 36th session of the Congress (1921), he described Hindu-Muslim unity as an evidence of fruitful cooperation which was then the need of the hour to take the nation forward[107]. He warned against the habit of suspecting each other and reminded the Hindus that it was their duty "to help protect Islam by rendering every possible assistance to the Muslims by expressing full faith in the goodness of the community."[108] He was always cautious about the possible division of the Congress which could obviously dilute the strength of the freedom struggle. The Congress saw the emergence of the 'no-changer' and 'pro-changer' groups within its fold in the early twenties in response to the Montegu–Chelmford Report. In contrast to the 'pro-changer' group which wanted to enter the Legislative Assemblies, the 'no-changers' under the leadership of Gandhi and Vallabhbhai stuck to the existing policy of agitation. Anyhow Vallabhbhai did not hesitate to extend support to the compromise formula of Maulana Mohammed Ali, the Congress Muslim leader. He wanted to prevent the internal division going out of control. He admitted, "I have thought a great deal and I see that I can help the *Maulana* best by withdrawing my opposition... Today, we look upon each other with suspicion and without love. This is an attempt to re-establish affection."[109] His quest for Hindu-Muslim unity was further revealed during Bordoli struggle as he took initiative for the recitation of both the Gita and Quran.[110] Influenced by him the leaders of the Central Khilafat Committee like Maulana Shafi Daoodi, Mir Mohammed Baloch, Sheikh Abdul Majeed, Maulana Saukat Ali, etc. came forward to criticise the obstinacy of the authority in Bordoli. Later on, as the President of the All-India Congress (1931) he reiterated the need for communal harmony and assured all the minorities including the Muslims, to take care of their representation in any future political set-up only based on their consent.[111] He appeared to be quite consistent in opposing the communal representation from the very beginning of his political career in the Ahmedabad Municipality.[112] Moreover, he not only criticised the British policy of communal award but also suggested to introduce joint electorate system to create Hindu-Muslim unity.[113]

4.4.2 Creation of Awareness

During the whole span of his struggle for an independent state, Vallabhbhai was aggrieved to see people languishing under the imperial rule. He thought of using education and press and developing a well-framed intelligence network in order to create awareness among the people.

Education

Vallabhbhai rightly visualised the significance of education in creating consciousness among the people. It was through the manipulation of this medium that the British authority had legitimised itself.[114] Vallabhbhai was highly critical of the prevailing education system. He believed: "The greatest defect of modern education is that children are neither loyal to their motherland nor behave like Indians. Their life is in doldrums. So weak are they rendered, as if they are devoured by white ants and they roam helter-skelter in search of jobs. They turn averse to their family, country as well parents. The chief malady is the foreign power and unstable politics."[115] Hence, he tried to motivate the civic body of Ahmedabad to reform the system of education. He thought of devising a national policy on education which gave equal thrust upon both moral and physical education.[116] He was keen to inculcate a sense of self-reliance by reforming the education system. In order to give a definite shape to his ideas, he took several initiatives to groom institutions like the Gujarat Vidyapitha. He even raised donations for its maintenance.[117] During the Civil Disobedience Movement (1930), when the authority took over its control, he not only sought for its retrieval, but also monitored *Rastriya Shalas* at various places as its substitutes.[118] His genuine interest to nurture such public institutions became more pronounced as he appealed to the Provincial Congress Government in Bombay to accord due recognition to the degrees of Gujarat Vidyapitha.[119]

Press

Time and again Vallabhbhai used to take the help of the Press to generate public awareness. He was actively involved in the regular publications of the '*Satyagraha Akhbar*' and the '*Young India*' during the Non-cooperation Movement and the Civil Disobedience Movement respectively. During the *Flag Satyagraha*, he appreciated the effects of local dailies like the 'Udaya' and

'Lokmat' which created positive opinion regarding the ability of the Swarajists or the 'pro-changer' faction within the Congress[120]. Vallabhbhai also set-up a publication bureau at the time of the Bordoli Satyagraha to publish the '*Bordoli Satyagraha Patrika*' to make people aware of the details of the Land Revenue Code and the Civil Procedure Code. Time and again, he utilised the services of the dailies like the *Bombay Chronicle*, the *Statesman* and the *Pioneer* to mobilise people against the authority.[121] The use of the *Borsad Satyagraha Patrika* by him at the time of the Civil Disobedience Movement made people aware of the coercive ability of the *Patidar* community and hence motivated them.[122]

Intelligence

Vallabhbhai managed to create awareness through a well nurtured intelligence network, which he could develop because of his knowledge of the realities at the grass roots level. In fact, during all the *Satyagrahas* it was his developed communication network which unified the rural and urban areas and enabled the villages to prepare themselves in advance to counter the retaliatory measures of the authority. Even the British authority admitted effectiveness of his strategy. As Leslie Wilson the Governor of Bombay wrote: 'The agitators have got a very well organised scheme of campaign. Everyone, who is suspected of willing to pay his own tax is shadowed every hour of the day and night"[123]. During the Borsad agitation, he managed to procure a secret circular of the Government, which instructed the lower officials to turn a blind eye towards the dacoit menace. He utilised it against the authority to counter the punitive tax imposed upon the people of the area to set right the law and order situation.[124] In order to strengthen his attack against the imposition of extra tax he succeeded in procuring evidence showing the lower officials' recommendations against any such measure.[125]

4.4.3 Strategy of Confrontation

Vallabhbhai driven by the self-pride of a *Patidar* never shied away from raising voice against injustice. He had the courage to confront the authority in various stages of his life to seek redressal.

He boycotted a schoolteacher, for defying the code of conduct of the institution.[126] During the first stint in the civic body of Ahmedabad, he frequently resorted to such strategy. He adopted the technique to counter the domination of the nominated members, groupism of the elected members and arrogance of the corrupt British officials. He also dragged the Municipality to the Court of law for supplying water to the cantonment area at the expense of the tax-payers. He skillfully used many local factors like the Gujarati tradition of social discipline and public spirit in order to make his strategy of confrontation effective. Later on, the Gandhian *Satyagraha* at Champaran motivated him further to revive the technique of boycott and use it on a wider scale. Hence, Vallabhbhai was able to redefine the dimension of politics and expand the jurisdiction of the civic body. During the Non-Cooperation Movement, he convinced its members to boycott the Government grant for education. In his attempt to make the strategy effective, he took certain steps like monitoring the operation of the local schools (Kelavani Mandal) and raising taxes to withstand retaliatory measures like the retrenchment of employees, and blocking of grants other than education and suspension of the civic body. His experience as a successful criminal lawyer equipped him with a sixth sense to foresee and anticipate the movement of the authority. As an ace Bridge player, he successfully gauged the moves of the opponents to make timely and appropriate counter-moves like introduction of the people-oriented policies, harnessing of talents of colleagues and eliciting the cooperation of the authority.

Vallabhbhai could pursue a successful strategy of confrontation with the British because of his familiarity with rural social realities. He realised that the local problems could paralyse administration more effectively than any all-India issue. His association with various no-tax campaigns in general and protest against land-tax in particular created huge political awareness. He tried to encash the influence of the dominant landholder *Patidar* community upon the landless people. He rightly anticipated that such boycott had not only political and economic ramifications, but also seemed to have a moral dimension, as it held the government accountable for any lapses.[127] It was even admitted by Lord Irwin who said: "Land revenue payers are bound to develop a political self-consciousness and as they do so, are likely to scrutinise more jealously any enhancement of revenue, they may be called upon to pay. There is here an obvious field for the political agitator, who will certainly not be slow to avail himself of any opportunity that offers for the organisation of a mass movement, on an issue of immediate interest to large number of persons, which may embarrass Government."[128] In fact, during the Civil Disobedience Movement, Vallabhbhai was quite skeptical about Gandhi's decision to boycott salt.[129] So, when the latter was imprisoned he retrieved the programme of boycotting the land tax. Its impact was so decisive that the then Home Secretary too admitted: "A widespread extension of revenue refusal would probably cause more embarrassment than any other feature of the Civil Disobedience Movement."[130] Vallabhbhai achieved great success in Kheda, Bordoli as well as the Civil Disobedience Movement due to the effective use of the issue of land tax. Besides land, he also organised the public on the issue of punitive tax in Borsad and demanding the right to hoist National Flag in Nagpur. During all these struggles, he adopted measures like picketing, Khadi spinning, prohibition and boycott of public institutions which were perceived as strategies to help in the effective confrontation of the authority directly or indirectly. He used his command over the colloquial language to influence the people of all strata. K.M. Munshi, believed: "Vallabhbhai can attack, appeal, ridicule and make an audience cry. Above all, he is a master of winged words which like shafts pierce the heart."[131] He also emphasised upon discipline to make the struggle against the authority more effective. He appealed to his followers: "I do not allow anybody to speak and you won't have time to suggest any change or put forward any suggestion. The orders I give whether it involves violence or non-violence, you may discuss it with Gandhi after the struggle is over. Like Gandhiji, I would not sit to discuss or show love and affection when the struggle is going on . . . . although I may not continue to be a leader for all the time to come."[132] Despite his emphasis upon non-violence, he allowed the use of violence sparingly.[133] He expected retaliatory measures by the British authority. So he thought of pre-emptive strategies and he raised donations for the political campaigns. He also helped create Vinaya Mandirs for the education of the children of the affected peasants apart from providing moral support to them to withstand such pressure.[134]

Vallabhbhai's uncanny ability to withdraw from the scene of confrontation at the right moment always provided him great dividends. He used to keep his eyes and ears open and never missed an opportunity to arrive at a just compromise even while pursuing the path of confrontation. In his fight, he was fully aware of the essential and non-essential, to grasp the opportunity at the right moment. Keeping with the pragmatic approach of a *Patidar* he argued: "Why should you be anxious for a settlement prematurely? You know that to expect, if you pluck an unripe mango, it will simply set your teeth on edge. On the other hand, if you allow it to ripen, it will drop itself and the patience will be rewarded."[135] Hence, Suman Mehta rightly observed "Vallabhbhai knew when to negotiate and on what terms."[136] He always took advantage of the compulsions of the authority and tried to create the ground of withdrawal at the opportune moment. He had decided to withdraw from the *Flag Satyagraha*, when the Government in the Central Province was keen to end it.[137] Similarly, he ended the Bordoli agitation at a point of time when the authority was eager to cover up its administrative loopholes before the Simon Commission.[138] He never hesitated to take the help of the 'pro-changer' factions or the Swarajists despite his ideological differences with them. He skillfully utilised their eagerness for ending the agitation early, to get the support of the members of the legislative Assembly for the smooth passage of the small Land Holding Bill and Land Revenue Code Amendment Bill.[139] Thus, he had the ability to use even the weakness of the Congress and turn them into advantages by properly timing the withdrawals of the agitations.

4.4.4 Strategy of Electoral Participation

Vallabhbhai's inclination for withdrawal from any ongoing agitations indicated a conscious strategy to carve out space for negotiation. In fact, the very presence of the Imperial set-up enabled him to adopt the strategies of confrontation and participation simultaneously. For this very reason, he constantly remained in close touch with grass roots politics. His experience in Ahmedabad Municipality provided the perfect background and the mental climate for building a party. The All India Congress Committee session of 1920 and 1921 gave a new direction to the country's politics in the light of which the Ahmedabad Municipality launched the Non-Cooperation Movement. The need for generating confidence in the people through a parallel political set-up broadened the dimension of politics. The Municipality not only looked after the civic amenities of the people but also took up the challenge of countering the British authority. All these developments made the party an indispensable part of the political structure. Hence, Vallahbhai argued: "We want to send our representatives into the municipality because it is impossible to carryout any programme of work without the agreement of a majority . . . . The Municipality has already suffered enough in the past. No improvement was made for a number of years until the Swarajya party under my presidentship took up into its hands the work of constructing gutters and many other works of public good. But, that Swarajya Party did not consist of members pledged to a vow nor were there any rules and regulations of their programme of work. A great difficulty was therefore, experienced many a time when the question-affecting persons of influence came for consideration. A party is therefore, required to work on the basis of common principles for the speedy betterment of the city."[140]

Vallabhbhai seemed to have followed the British system to reorient the political party with a hierarchy of province, district, *taluka* and village Congress committees. But, in reality, he emphasised more on the grass roots workers for their command over the local conditions than upon the upper section leaders who appeared to be quite sophisticated and aloof from their surroundings. Vallabhbhai differed from Gandhi who was least bothered about the day-to-day organisational activities of the Congress Party and also from the grass roots workers like Mohanlal Pandya, Ravishankar Maharaj, etc. who were known for their commitment to social service. In the initial stage besides harping upon the organisation, he thought of ways for its maintenance. So, he followed business etiquettes like keeping accounts, showing concern for the people having financial interests and invoking the historic tradition of public spirit to ensure easy finance for the organisation. *The London Times* observed: "In all his dealings with big business, his personal integrity was not questioned; he was the master not servant of those who provided the Congress with its funds. Because he knew their strength and weakness, he could shape men to his purpose. That purpose was Indian freedom."[141] He was also interested in ensuring regular enrolment of members into the party. In an attempt to reorganise the party even when it was declared illegal by the authority in the early thirties, he influenced Gandhi to drop the condition of *Khadi*-wearing as a mandatory provision for the recruitment of its members.[142] He appealed to the people: "I want every single man, woman and child in each province, district and town to feel that he or she should take up the burden of carrying on the national fight, if the Congress organisation is declared unlawful and all recognised leaders are put to jail. Each Congressman then becomes a Congress Committee for the purpose of the fight."[143]

The changed scenario in the thirties influenced Vallabhbhai to give more thrust upon electoral participation than confrontation. It motivated him further to seek reorganisation of the political party. During the given period, the Labour Government's policies like the publication of the Simon Commission Report, initiation for the Round Table Conference, announcement of the Communal Award and release of the White Paper and the proceedings of the Joint Committee on the Constitutional Reform transformed politics into an autonomous activity. But all these also created disagreement within the Congress which was then declared unlawful by the authority for its role in the Civil Disobedience Movement. The period in between January 1930 to July 1934 was perfectly described by the Government as the 'phase of drift'. The imprisonment of Gandhi put the unity of the party at stake. His charismatic presence managed to hold divergent strands of thinking within the organisation under one belt. The emergence of groups like the Hindu Mahasabha, the scheduled caste faction of B.R. Ambedkar, the non-Brahmin lobby of Madras and Maharastra and over and above the revival of the Swarajist Party under the leadership of A.S. Aney, questioned the continuation of the agitational method of Gandhi. The forthcoming election for the Central Legislature and the subsequent revocation of the suspension order of the Congress allured many in the Party to think of an alternative, to counter the vested interest of the authority which was clearly revealed in the Communal Award and the 1935 Act. Besides the internal change, the growing influence of the Socialist group challenged the basic agenda of the Congress. All these factors influenced Vallabhbhai to take a firm and concrete stand like revival of the Council-entry programme to keep the party united before the internal and external challenges and to confront the authority successfully. Hence he argued: "Let me remind the public that the Congress enters into the field of legislature with the sole object of demonstrating two things. Firstly, that the country, as I said earlier thoroughly condemns the stark repressive policy carried out by the Government during the last four years. And secondly, we reject in to the reactionary proposal of reforms clothed in the White Paper. Any single role that will be recorded in favour of the non-Congressman, however eminent he may be, will be a vote for the government and therefore the approval of the Government's dual policy."[144]

The switching over of the strategy from confrontation to participation by the Congress compelled Vallabhbhai in 1934 to reconcile finally with the withdrawal of Gandhi from active politics. He correctly assessed the dilemma of Gandhi whose utopian ideals appeared to be of less relevance particularly in the age of practical politics. He said: ". . . . If Mahatma is outside the Congress it would be more efficient and he would be more helpful to it. If he remains in the organisation, he would only impede the organisation and make it weak."[145] Expressing his inability to face the new situation, Gandhi also admitted: "I have not the slightest idea how elections are fought."[146] But, Vallabhbhai thought of using him skillfully to enhance the base of the Party in the rural areas in order to make up the deficiency of horizontal and vertical mobilisation of the people. Such policy of ruralisation pursued with the help of leaders like Mavalankar, Shankarlal Banker, Narahari Parikh, etc. helped him to counter the influence of the Socialists and hold on to the Council-entry programme.

Besides the policy of ruralisation, Vallabhbhai also sincerely implemented the policy of centralisation to streamline the Party required by the strategy of electoral participation. He took measures to sideline the opponents and also to enforce discipline upon the party members. With this backdrop, he monitored the formation of the Central Parliamentary Board in 1934 to supervise the election of 1934 and 1936. He shrewdly supported the candidature of Nehru as the Party President in 1936 for both the sessions of Lucknow and Faizpur. The strategy paid off as it alienated Nehru from the Socialist influence and motivated him to accept the Council-entry programme. After the election, it cleared the way for office-acceptance which was vehemently opposed by the radical factions or the people with Socialist line of thinking. Though, Vallabhbhai made Nehru the President of the Party, he hardly allowed him to monitor any agenda without consensus. He admitted: "My withdrawal should not be taken to mean that I endorse all the views Jawaharlal stands for."[147] The new guidelines set by him in the Faizpur session restricted the powers of the Party President. He reiterated the view of Motilal Nehru and tried to define its authority. He held: "The Congress President has no dictatorial powers. He is the Chairman of a well-knit organisation . . . . The Congress does not part with its ample powers by electing any individual no matter who he is."[148] Further, in the Haripura session (1938) he obstructed the collective affiliation of the trade unions and peasant leagues with the Congress to neutralise the impact of the Socialists within the Party. Vallabhbhai allowed Subash Chandra Bose, a man of Socialist orientation to preside over the session. But he did not agree with Bose's attempt to revive the Civil Disobedience Movement and obstruct the already approved Council-entry programme. Hence, in the Tripuri Congress (1939) he tried to highlight the position of the Congress Parliamentary Board by asking its members to tender resignation en masse. He also isolated Subash Bose the President-elect, further by successfully canvassing in favour of the 'Pant Resolution' which reiterated faith in the Council-entry programme and demanded accountability of the provincial Congress committee to the Parliamentary Board. In view of all these developments Subash Chandra Bose claimed that Vallabhbhai wanted a President who would be mearly a figure-head and a tool in the hands of the Working Committee.[149] But it hardly affected Vallabhbhai who as the Chairman of the Congress Parliamentary Sub-Committee took these measures to protect the strategy of electoral participation.

While adopting measures like sidelining the Socialist members, Vallabhbhai thought of regulating the party members to prepare them to face the challenges of election. So he brought Bulabhai Desai, a man with a long parliamentary record into the Central Parliamentary Board. Under his direct supervision, candidates were chosen for the coming central and provincial legislative elections, manifestoes were drafted, disciplinary rules were formulated, plural constituencies were monitored and donations were raised. Looking at his involvement, K.M. Munshi comments: "I saw him arranging election, fixing up candidates, setting up ministries, controlling them, giving to diverse centrifugal forces a harmonious direction. I saw him arranging, organising, directing men and forces all over the country breaking through hostile combinations and aligning new forces."[150] His close supervision enabled the Congress to become part of the political set-up in eight out of the eleven provinces. His success led the British authority to recognise him as a 'figure of growing importance.'[151] Such recognition made him a key player in the subsequent constitutional dialogues. Vallabhbhai felt the necessity of enforcing discipline to enable the inexperienced party members to cope with the challenges of power politics. Under his supervision B.G. Kher was chosen as the Premier of Bombay and the name of the influential K.F. Nariman, the President of the Provincial Congress unit was dropped for the latter's alleged involvement in anti-party activities during the 1934 election and just after the 1936 poll. Vallabhbhai also replaced the Premier of the Central Province and suggested the name of R.S. Shukla in place of N.B. Khare for violating the 'Panchmari Resolution' and thereby sidelining the Congress Parliamentary Board and hobnobbing with the Governor of the Province to dissolve the legislative assembly. Such decisions were criticised by people like Rafi Ahmed Kidwai, the President of the UP Provincial Congress Committee who accused Vallabhbhai of leading a 'Grand Fascist Council'.[152] Some others allege that he violated constitutional propriety in the name of discipline.[153] Vallabhbhai justified his decision and said: "Yes, I am called a Fascist… I checkmated Nariman and at my instance the Working Committee deposed a provincial premier. But, we had good grounds. Is it Fascism to carry out disciplinary measures, which are subjected to the scrutiny of the Working Committee?"[154] He hinted about the moral responsibility of the Congress when there was alien authority at the Centre, represented by a Governor in the province and public awareness appeared to be low. In the absence of any other alternatives he was compelled to be harsh in order to streamline the Congress and implement the promises made in the electrical manifesto. Gandhi also supported the measure to enforce discipline.[155] *The Statesman* justified the stand of the Congress Parliamentary Board for playing the supervisory role only in the absence of a legitimate authority at the all-India level. It said: "As a party the Congress worked for its policy all over India and has remarkable success in having seven governments to carry out its policies. In those provinces, we must assume, the ministries are where they are because of the situation, they must look to the Congress High Command for directives."[156] It was believed that the measure was taken to mitigate the self-interest, trying to prop up in the cloak of joint responsibility, thereby going against the much approved policy resolutions and affecting the long cherished goal of independence[157]. When the retreat of the British authority became almost imminent in the forties, the constitutional developments became faster. It had reminded Vallabhbhai further the significance of the Party as an alternative to the outgoing authority. He actively supervised the election for the Central and Provincial Assemblies in 1946. He was on the stage again playing the familiar role of choosing and firing party men, raising donations and making alliances. With most of the Congress leaders behind bar and the absence of an updated electoral list, Vallabhbhai found the task tougher. Last but not the least, the simmering internal division within the Congress compounded the problem further. All these hindrances limited the success of the Congress in the Muslim- dominated areas. Anyhow, the Congress under him secured 91 per cent of the general seats in the Central Assembly and clear majority in eight provinces. The unique achievement compelled the British authority to admit: "Sardar Patel is the recognised 'tough' of the Congress Working Committee and by far the most forcible character amongst them. He is probably the only one of them capable of standing upto Gandhi."[158] In subsequent period, this success gave him further legitimacy and made him a force to reckon with during the final negotiation for the liberation of the country.

4.5 The Emerging Pattern

Vallabhbhai's longing for a Nation–State was rooted in the *Patidar* self-pride and its sense of independence. This inherent trait bloomed into a full-fledged nationalistic orientation in course of his gradual association with the family, community, educational institutions, professional and political associations. He acquired further maturity and confidence due to his exposure to the West. He could understand the hidden agenda of the colonial authority which was following a double standard towards the Indians. His early anglophile outlook and attachment towards his native province, transformed into a broad consensual sense of nationalism in course of his association with various grasroot struggles. His contact with Gandhi seemed to have acted like a catalyst in shaping his nationalist orientation.

The quest for a stable Nation–State inspired Vallabhbhai to think of a comprehensive strategy to drive out the mighty British Empire. A pragmatic Patidar, he skillfully synthesised the strategies of confrontation and electoral participation in his struggle against the colonial power. As the success of both the strategies depended on social unity, he relied upon caste emancipation, women participation and Hindu–Muslim unity. Even while advocating for caste emancipation, Vallabhbhai did not forget to utilise its integrative values by highlighting the cause of the upper castes. As he realised that political awareness was necessary for the success of these strategies, he gave due attention to Press, Intelligence network and the Education Policy. The changed political landscape in the 1930's encouraged him to groom the Party as an election machinery, which was till then utilised to mobilise people against the authority. He reoriented the party through various programmes of ruralisation and centralisation and transformed it into an alternative to the British power. Thus, the vertical and horizontal mobilisation of the people through the party and caste helped create a broad basis of Indian nationalism. The long association of Vallabhbhai with the freedom struggle provided him with the opportunities to expand the nationalist domain by linking regional issues with their national counterparts. It created political awareness in the periphery and made the base of the upcoming nation-state more democratic ad plural. Vallabhbhai utilised it to lay the foundation of the Indian Nation–State. Even in the post-independence period, he took steps, though hard, ruthless or unpleasant for many, for the purpose of the stabilisation of the nascent Nation–State. A staunch nationalist, Vallabhbhai wanted to set the highest standard in public life. He always put the cause of the Nation first. He believed it was the duty of every citizen to render self-less service to the nation and expect nothing in return from the state. In this context, he appreciated the role of the mutineers of the 1857 Mutiny but condemned their heirs who demanded compensation. Thus, nationalism seems to be the sole motivating factor for Vallabhbhai.

Notes and References

1. Rajni Kothari, *Politics in India* (New Delhi: Orient Longman, 1970, p. 21).
2. N.D. Parikh, *Sardar Vallabhbhai Patel*, Vol. I (Ahmedabad: Navajivan, 1953, p. 6).
3. *Vallabhbhai Patel to Maniben*, 24 October 1923, Patel Papers, Navajivan, Ahmedabad.
4. *Vallabhbhai Patel*, 'When I was a Child' in G.M. Nandurkar (ed.), Birth Centenary Vol. I (Ahmedabad: 1974, p. 167).
5. *Ibid*., p. 168.
6. Eric Wolf, *Peasant Rebellion in Teodar Shanin* (ed.), Peasant and Peasant Societies, Select Reading (London: 1971).
7. David Hardiman, *Peasant Nationalists of Gujarat: Kheda District (1917-34)* (London: Oxford, 1981, p. 42).
8. *Ibid*., p. 250.
9. Kalyani Meheta (ed., *Suvarna Jayanti Ank*, Section II (Surat: Vallabh Vidyarthi Ashram, 1970, p. 15).
10. Michael H. Lyon, *Sardar Patel and Indian Independence* (New Delhi: Konark Pvt. Ltd., 1996, p. 8).
11. *Vallabhbhai Patel*, 'When I was a Child', in G.M. Nandurkar (ed.) Birth Centenary Volume, *op. cit*., p. 167.
12. Devarat Pathak and Pravin Sheth, *Sardar Vallabhbhai Patel: From Civic to National Leadership* (Ahmedabad: 1918, p. 19).
13. David Hardiman, *Peasant Nationalists of Gujarat, op. cit*., p. 69.
14. Howard Spodek, *Sardar Vallabhbhai Patel at 100*, in Verinder Grover, (ed.), *Political Thinkers of Modern India*, Vol. 18 (New Delhi: Deep and Deep Publications, 1992, p. 356).

15. K.L. Panjabi, *The Indomitable Sardar* (Bombay: Bharatiya Vidya Bhavan, 1969, p. 17).
16. G.M. Nandurkar, (ed.) *Sardarshri Na Patro,* Vol. III (Ahmedabad: 1976).
17. K.L. Panjabi, *The Indomitable Sardar, op. cit.*, p. 17.
18. G.M. Nandurkar, (ed.) *Sardar's Letters Mostly Unknown*, Vol. I, (Ahmedabad, 1977, p. 301).
19. N.D. Parikh, *Sardar Vallabhbhai Patel,* Vol. I, *op. cit.*, p. 22.
20. G.M. Nandurkar, (ed.) *Sardar's Letters Mostly Unknown*, Vol. IV, *op. cit.*, p. 302.
21. N.D. Parikh, *Sardar Vallabhbhai Patel,* Vol. I, *op. cit.*, p. 27.
22. Devavrat Pathak and Pravin Sheth, *Sardar Vallabhbhai Patel From Civic to National Leadership, op. cit.*, p. 86.
23. *Prajabandhu*, 6 February 1921.
24. Devavrat Pathak and Pravin Sheth, *Sardar Vallabhbhai Patel: From Civic to National Leadership, op. cit.*, p. 352.
25. *Ibid.*, p. 348.
26. David Hardiman, *Peasant Nationalists of Gujarat, op. cit.*, p. 60.
27. F.B. Shah and C.N. Desai, *The Indian National Songs* (Nadiad: 1909).
28. Home Department, Special E/1928, 30 July, 1928. *Gujarat Samachar*, 9 January, 1935.
29. Home Department, Special, MSA, 2 January, 1935.
30. Raojibhai Patel, *Hind Ke Sardar* (Ahmedabad: Navajivan, 1972, p. 39).
31. *Prajabandhu*, 4 June, 1918.
32. N.D. Parikh, *Sardar Vallabhbhai Patel,* Vol. I, *op. cit.*, p. 115.
33. Devavrat Pathak and Pravin Sheth, *Sardar Vallabhbhai Patel From Civic to National Leadership, op. cit.*, p. 378.
34. *Ibid.*, p. 114.
35. *Ibid.*, p. 117.
36. *Young India*, 8 March, 1928.
37. *Navajivan*, 5 April, 1931.

38. D.V. Tahamankar, *Sardar Patel* (London: George Allen Unwin Ltd., 1970, p. 112).
39. *Bombay Chronicle*, 29 October, 1934.
40. Rani Dhavan Shankardass, *Vallabhbhai Patel: Power and Organisation in Indian Politics* (New Delhi: Orient Longman, 1988, p. 53).
41. K.L. Panjabi, *The Indomitable Sardar, op. cit.*, p. 254.
42. N.D. Parikh, *Sardar Vallabhbhai Patel*, Vol. 2, 1956, *op. cit.*, p. 270.
43. B. Krishna, *Sardar Vallabhbhai Patel: India's Iron Man* (New Delhi: Indus, 1995, p. 197).
44. P.N. Chopra (ed.), *Collected Works of Sardar Vallabhbhai Patel*, Vol. X (New Delhi: Konark Pvt. Ltd., 1997, p. 129).
45. Michael Brecher, *Nehru* (London: Oxford, 1959, p. 294).
46. Wavell to Henderson on 21 May 1946 Transfer of Power, VII, No. 350, India Office Record, NMML, New Delhi.
47. D.N. Banerjee, "Sardar Vallabhbhai Patel and the Partition of India", in V. Grover, (ed.), *Modern Indian Political Thinkers (18), op. cit.*, p. 336.
48. Stanley Wolpert, *Jinnah of Pakistan* (New York: 1984, pp. 303-4).
49. Rafiq Zakaria, *The Man Who Divided India*, (New Delhi: Popular Prakashan, 2001, p. 137).
50. V.P. Menon, *The Transfer of Power* (New Delhi: Orient Longman, 1957, p. 385).
51. David Hardiman, *Peasant Nationalists of Gujarat, op. cit.*, p. 128.
52. Rani Dhavan Shankardass, *Sardar Vallabhbhai Patel: Power and Organisation in Indian Politics, op. cit.*, p. 18.
53. David Pocock, *Kanbis and Patidars* (London: Oxford, 1972, p. 53).
54. N.D. Parikh, *Sardar Vallabhbhai Patel*, Vol. I, *op. cit.*, p. 124.
55. *Ibid.*, p. 113.
56. Vallabhbhai Patel to Nehru on 1 August 1923, Nehru Papers, Nehru Memorial Museum Library, New Delhi.
57. Shirin Mehta, *The Peasants and Nationalism: A Study of the Bordoli Satyagraha* (New Delhi: Manohar, 1984, p. 136).

58. Home Department (Special), F. 321/165, 3 February 1929. Home Department (Political), 20 March, 1935, National Archives of India, New Delhi.
59. Vallabhbhai Patel to Jawaharlal Nehru, 7 October, 1931, AICC Papers, NMML, New Delhi.
60. Jawaharlal Nehru to Vallabhbhai, 12 October, 1931, AICC Papers, NMML, New Delhi. Bombay Chronicle, 19 October, 1931.
61. Vallabhbhai to Jawaharlal Nehru, 25 November, 1931, AICC Papers, NMML, New Delhi.
62. *Times of India,* 24 August, 1934. *Bombay Chronicle*, 28 September, 1934.
63. AICC File No. 17 of 1931, NMML, New Delhi,
64. Navajivan, 5 April, 1931.
65. *Ibid.*
66. David Pocock, *Kanbis and Patidars, op. cit.*, p. 17.
67. Home Department (Special), MSA, 14 January 1934,
68. Home Department (Special), F.584 E(Ptv) 1929, *Gujarat Samachar*, 6 January 1933.
69. *Gujarat Samachar*, 31 October, 1935.
70. P.N. Chopra (ed.), *The Collected Works of Sardar Vallabhbhai Patel*, Vol. X, 1997, *op. cit.*, p. 197.
71. For a comprehensive analysis on Partition, see Frank Moraes, *Witness to An Era* (London: 1973, p. 56). Abul Kalam Azad, *India Wins Freedom* (Calcutta: Orient Longman, 1958, p. 131, 170). Ram Manohar Lohia, *Guiltymen of India's Partition* (Hyderabad: 1970, pp. 9-11).
72. K.M. Munshi, *Pilgrimage to Freedom* (Bombay: 1967, pp. 47-8).
73. Rafiq Zakaria, *The Man Who Divided India, op. cit.*, p. 81.
74. Rammanohar Lohia, *Guiltymen of India's Partition, op. cit.*, p. 1.
75. B. Krishna, *Sardar Vallabhbhai Patel: India's Iron Man, op. cit.*, p. 290.
76. S. Heredia, *A Patriot For Me* (New Delhi: Orient Longman, p. 195).
77. *Ibid.*, p. 194.
78. B.K. Ahluwalia, *Sardar Patel: A Life* (New Delhi: Sagar Publications, 1974, p. 235).

79. S.R. Bakshi, *Sardar Patel: His Political Ideology* (New Delhi: Anmol Publications, 1990, p. 119).
80. Vallabhbhai Patel to Dayabhai, 15 October, 1929, Patel Papers, Navajivan, Ahmedabad.
81. Shirin Mehta, *The Peasantry and Nationalism*, *op. cit.*, p. 87.
82. David Hardiman, *Peasant Nationalists of Gujarat*, *op. cit.*, p. 108.
83. *Navajivan*, 28 December 1921.
84. *Young India*, 16 June 1927.
85. Jagat Ram Dave, "Was He A Blind Follower?" in G.M. Nandurkar (ed.), *Birth Centenary Series*, Vol. I, *op. cit.*, p. 190.
86. *Navajivan*, 7 April, 1929.
87. *Indian Review*, September, 1927.
88. *Navajivan*, 7 April, 1929.
89. *Navajivan*, 5 April, 1931.
90. *Harijan Bandhu*, 3 March, 1935.
91. Mahadev Desai, *The Story of Bordoli* (Ahmedabad: Navajivan, 1957, p. 82).
92. N.D. Parikh, *Sardar Vallabhbhai Patel*,Vol. I, *op. cit.*, pp. 400-1.
93. I. Catanaoh, *Rural Credit in Western India: 1875-1930* (California: 1970, p. 108).
94. Mahadev Desai, *The Story of Bordoli*, *op. cit.*, pp. 36-7.
95. Report on Civil Disobedience, 4 May-6 June, 1935, H. Pol. 1931, File No. 116, p. 4, National Archives of India, New Delhi.
96. Ishwarlal Desai, *Bordoli Satyagraha* (Surat: 1970, pp. 209, 320).
97. *Bordoli Satyagraha Patrika,* 4 April, 1928.
98. *Bombay Chronicle*, 13 March, 1931.
99. Narahari Parikh, Vol. I, *op. cit.*, p. 95.
100. Stray Bulletin, *Bordoli Satyagraha*, 9 March, 1928
101. *Ibid.*, 30 May, 1928
102. Navajivan, 8 April, 1931.
103. David Hardiman, *Peasant Nationalists of Gujarat*, *op. cit.*, p. 126.
104. Navajivan, July, 1930.

105. Bombay Secret Abstract, 1921, p. 1091.
106. N.D. Parikh, *Sardar Vallabhbhai Patel*, Vol. I, *op. cit.*, pp. 112-3.
107. P.N. Chopra, *The Sardar of India*, *op. cit.*, p. 19.
108. B. Krishna, *Sardar Vallabhbhai Patel: India's Iron Man*, *op. cit.*, pp. 458-9.
109. N.D. Parikh, *Sardar Vallabhbhai Patel*, Vol. I, *op. cit.*, p. 186.
110. Shirin Mehta, *The Peasantry and Nationalism*, *op. cit.*, p. 112.
111. Navajivan 5 April, 1931.
112. Devavrat Pathak and Pravin Sheth, *Sardar Vallabhbhai Patel: From Civic to National Leadership*, *op. cit.*, p. 343. *Bombay Chronicle*, 25 February 1931.
113. *Times of India*, 24 August, 1934, *Bombay Chronicle*, 20 November, 1934.
114. N.D. Parikh, *Sardar Vallabhbhai Patel*, Vol. I, *op. cit.*, p. 11.
115. *Gujarat Samachar*, 24 October, 1935.
116. *Gujarat Samachar*, 9 January, 1935.
117. *Bombay Chronicle*, 11 April, 1931.
118. P.N. Chopra (ed.), *The Collected Works of Sardar Vallabhbhai Patel*, Vol. IV 1994, *op. cit.*, p. 185. *Gujarat Samachar*, 6 January, 1935.
119. Vallabhbhai to Bala Saheb, B.G. Kher, Papers 5 July, 1938, NMML, New Delhi.
120. Rani Dhavan Shankardass, *Sardar Vallabhbhai Patel: Power and Organisation in Indian Politics*, *op. cit.*, p. 45-6.
121. *Pioneer*, 11 July, 1928.
122. Leslie Wilson, *Governor of Bombay to Lord Irwin*, Irwin Papers, No. 41A-547, National Archives of India, New Delhi.
123. *Borsad Satyagraha*, Patrika, 5 November, 1930.
124. David Hardiman, *Peasant Nationalists of Gujarat*, *op. cit.*, p. 165.
125. Rani Dhavan Shankardass, *Vallabhbhai Patel: Power and Organisation in Indian Politics*, *op. cit.*, p. 50.
126. Devavrat Pathak and Pravin Sheth, *Vallabhbhai Patel: From Civic to National Leadership*, *op. cit.*, p. 19. Michael Lyon, *Sardar Patel and India Independence*, *op. cit.*, p. 18.

127. David Hardiman, *Peasant Nationalists of Gujarat, op. cit.*, p. 55.
128. *Ibid.*, p. 3.
129. *Young India*, 12 March, 1930.
130. Emerson on 27 June 1930, Home, Political Department File, 214, p. 30, National Archives of India, New Delhi.
131. K.M. Munshi, "The Indomitable Sardar", in P.D. Saggi, (ed.), *Life and Works of Sardar Vallabhbhai Patel* (Bombay, 1951, p. 5).
132. *Prajabandhu*, 16 January, 1930.
133. P.N. Chopra (ed.), *The Collected Works of Sardar Vallabhbhai Patel*, Vol. IX, 1997, *op. cit.*, p. 129.
134. *Bombay Chronicle*, 18 April, 1918, *Ibid.*, 1 May, 1928.
135. *Bombay Chronicle*, 3 July, 1928.
136. Suman Meheta, "Bordoli *Satyagraha*", *Bombay Chronicle*, 8 June 1928.
137. Rani Dhavan Shankardass, *Vallabhbhai Patel: Power and Organisation in Indian Politics, op. cit.*, p. 47.
138. *Ibid.*, p. 81.
139. *Ibid.*, 77.
140. Bombay Criminal Investigation Department, Records 2/INC 136(8).
141. *The London Times*, 16 January, 1950.
142. *Gujarat Samachar*, 2 October, 1934.
143. *Bombay Chronicle*, 3 July, 1930.
144. *Ibid.*, 28 October, 1934
145. *Mumbai Samachar*, 21 September, 1934.
146. Gandhi to Vallabhbhai, 20 August 1934, in Rani Dhavan Shankardass, *Vallabhbhai Patel: Power and Organisation in Indian Politics, op. cit.*, p. 128.
147. N.D. Parikh, *Sardar Vallabhbhai Patel*, Vol. 2, *op. cit.*, p. 220.
148. *Ibid.*
149. Subash Bose, *Crossroad (1938-1940)* (Bombay: 1962, p. 135).
150. Rajula Jain, *Vallabhbhai Patel, And the Indian National Congress: A Study (1934-39)*, (New Delhi, Gyan Sagar Publication, 1997, p. 158.

151. L.N. Sarin, *Sardar Patel* (New Delhi: S. Chand & Co. Ltd., 1972, p. 61).
152. *The Hindu*, 5 March, 1937.
153 L.N. Sarin, *Sardar Patel*, *op. cit.*, p. 65.
154. Rajmohan Gandhi, *Patel: A Life* (Ahmedabad: 1991, p. 271).
155. B. Krishna, *Sardar Vallabhbhai Patel: India's Iron man*, *op. cit.*, p. 189.
156. Abdul Majid Khan, *A Leader by Merit* (Lahore: 1946, p. 227).
157. V.B. Kulkarni, *The Indian Triumvirate* (Bombay: 1969, p. 357).
158. Panderel Moon (ed.), Wavell: *The Viceroy's Journal* (London: Oxford, 1973, p. 495).

5

Role as Nation Builder

Every Nation–State after its creation faces the inevitable problems of nation building and hence must strive to address those for the sake of stability and development. It became all the more important for India, as the long spell of colonialism left in its trail a host of problems including that of integration and administration. Its very creation through a process of physical division and the consequent emotional trauma not only complicated the problem of unification but also put a question mark upon the loyalty and commitment of the people. Hence after independence, maintenance of unity became the most crucial challenge for the Indian leaders.

Vallabhbhai, the Minister of Home and States, entrusted with the onerous task of securing the unity of India realised the tough task lying ahead. He argued: "What we have is not *Swaraj*, abolish distinctions of caste and creeds, banish untouchability, improve the lots of hungry masses and live as one joint family, in short to create a new way of life and bring about a change of heart and a change of culture."[1] He set his goal to guard the freedom of the country against dangers from both within and without. The role of Vallabhbhai in the post-independence period needs to be examined to assess his contribution towards the realisation of this goal. Here his role has been analysed in the context of framing of the Constitution of India, integration of states and restructuring of the administrative machineries to unveil the extent of political obligation towards the nascent nation state.

5.1 Framing of the Constitution

Long before independence, Vallabhbhai had articulated the need for a uniform procedural framework to define the relationship between the ruler and the ruled, which would strengthen the bond of unity. His mindset was influenced by the *Patidar* convention of the 'rule by the chosen meritorious few' and by the British Constitutionalism.[2]

Vallabhbhai had thought of developing a universal regulation for the people of India for the first time in 1929.[3] It was even before the open declaration of the Congress in 1936 to have a Constitution of India. Vallabhbhai abandoned the Gandhian path of agitation and adopted new strategies in the mid-thirties, to foil the British design of imposing regulation of its own making. Regarding the demand for an elected Constituent Assembly he argued: "The Constituent Assembly demanded by the Congress was the elected tribune of the people of the country. The Congress did not claim the right to frame the Constitution exclusively. This right belonged to the people of the country, who would entrust the task to their representatives."[4] But when the Cripps Mission came to India in 1942 to formally initiate the constitutional development process, he criticised it as a 'false coin.'[5] It deferred the formation of a National Government allowing the Princes to nominate members and at the same contained sufficient scopes for the creation of Pakistan. His desire to create a genuine representative body for the framing of the Constitution was revealed from the way he supported the long-term plan of the Cabinet Mission irrespective of its loopholes like the incorporation of the 'group clause' for the provinces and return of paramountcy to the Princely States and played an active role for the election of the Constituent Assembly. He argued: "Undoubtedly, there are defects in the scheme, but such defects are inherent in any scheme of compromise."[6] His support to the plan was based on the hope that the controversial provisions could be got rid of once the Congress became part of the Interim Government. His shrewd and swift decision compelled the Muslim League, another contender for power to accept the plan and thus initiated the process of drafting of the Constitution.

Vallabhbhai played a significant role in the smooth functioning of the Constituent Assembly. His emphasis to infuse discipline and a non-partisan character enabled it to overcome the obstructive stand of the Muslim League and the ideological differences within the Congress. It was due to his initiative that Bhimrao Ramji Ambedkar, a non-Congressman but a brilliant lawyer, was made the Chairman of the Drafting Committee and given the onerous responsibility of preparing the Constitution for the country. Ambedkar himself acknowledged the significant role played by Vallabhbhai in this regard[7]. In fact, M.V. Kamath, another member of the Constituent Assembly too expressed the same opinion about Vallabhbhai in the following way: "I am sure that without his firm grasp of the realities of real politics and his statesman like intervention on crucial occasions, even on the pilot of the Constitution Bill, Ambedkar might have found it hard to carry conviction to members of the Assembly. I am equally certain that in the Provincial Parliament, Prime Minister Jawaharlal Nehru might have often found himself in a quandary, without Vallabhbhai Patel, the Deputy Prime Minister by his side".[8] During the whole process of the framing of the Constitution, Vallabhbhai played a decisive role. He headed the Fundamental Rights Sub-committee, Provincial Constitution Sub-committee and the Minorities sub-committee in the Constituent Assembly and provided valuable inputs in the process of drafting of the Constitution.

5.1.1 Chairman of the Fundamental Rights Sub-committee

Vallabhbhai as the Chairman of the Fundamental Right Sub-committee gave a distinct shape to the spirit of constitutionalism. As the President of the party, he had introduced the concept of Fundamental Rights and Duties in the Karachi Session of the Congress in 1931. The document recognised rights of people under the sections such as the Fundamental Rights and Duties, Labour and Socio-economic Programmes. These rights were claimed for the individual in an absolute manner against the Imperial authority. But after assumption of power by the Congress in the provinces in the mid-thirties, Vallabhbhai rationalised the imposition of restrictions by an elected Government to ensure peaceful coexistence. Further, at the time of independence, the impending problems of refugees and a war with Pakistan made him more cautious about the grant of absolute Fundamental Rights, to the people. Hence during the deliberations in the Constituent Assembly, he preferred to divide the Fundamental Rights into justiciable and non-justiciable categories and kept most of the socio-economic rights in the latter categories. As he revealed: "There were two schools of thought in the committee of Fundamental Rights . . . . Those two schools viewed the matter from two different angles, while one school considered it advisable to include as many rights as possible in this Report . . . . rights in regard to which a citizen may without difficulty go straightaway to a court of law and get his rights enforced. The other school of thought considered it advisable to restrict Fundamental Rights to a very few essential things that may be considered fundamental. Between the two schools there was a considerable amount of discussion and finally a mean was drawn which was considered to be a very good mean."[9]

Thus, Vallabhbhai as the Chairman of the Fundamental Rights Sub-committee, introduced rights like the Right to Equality, Right to Freedom (including the Right against Exploitation), Rights relating to Religion, Cultural and Educational Rights and certain other miscellaneous Rights covering the Right to Property and Right to Constitutional Remedies. But, he was in favour of imposition of conditions and due restrictions on all of them. In fact, the Government had been empowered to introduce measures in the form of protective discrimination and reasonable restrictions to regulate the Right to Equality and Freedom of Speech and Expression to ensure public decency and just order.[10] Further, it was allowed to restrict the Right against Exploitation to get the compulsory requisition of public service, the Right to Religion to avoid conversion and the Right to Property with due compensation to make adequate socio-economic reforms. The move to allow restrictions on Fundamental Rights elicited strong response from members like Somanath Lahiri, who thought that Vallabhbhai's approach was even more autocratic than that of the British Government.[11] But, Vallabhbhai was firm on introducing the Fundamental Rights in a 'reasonable way'. He criticised those who believed that under the Fundamental Rights, "there should be no police, there should be no jail, there should be no restrictions on the press, the bastion, the lathi or the bullet."[12] He justified imposition of reasonable restrictions on those who threatened peace and security of the state. He considered the restrictions essential as they ensured proper enjoyment of freedom by the majority.[13] His view was supported by members like N.G. Ranga, who argued: "We are told that this document is prepared from the view point of a policeman. I do not know where the policeman comes in except by way of our attempt to keep him out of the exercise of our Fundamental Rights.... we have had such a bitter experience of policemen in this country that the authors of the document have had to formulate these clauses in such a way to have the least possible interference of policemen."[14]

Though Vallabhbhai made the Fundamental Rights conditional, he was determined to make them effective in every possible way. The introduction of the 'enforceable' clause with the due involvement of the independent judiciary was the first step in this regard. He argued: "This is a clause which provides a judicial remedy. If we provide for Fundamental Rights, it is necessary that we must provide also for a remedy. But, it does not mean that this excludes or appropriates the jurisdiction of other Courts or High Court."[15] He overruled the apprehension of K. Sanathanam that the Right to Constitutional Remedy could be the exclusive prerogative of the Supreme Court.[16] Besides the advocacy for judicial review, his emphasis upon the uniform implementation of the Rights within the union and states, and abrogation of all the existing legislations, notifications, customs etc. for being inconsistent with the Fundamental Rights, proved his sincerity to protect the rights of an individual.

After laying down the Fundamental Rights, Vallabhbhai in accordance with the Objective Resolution presented before the House certain principles of governance that would take care of other basic necessities of people in the long run. This section, heavily loaded with the obligations of the Government in making economic reforms, resembled with the second and third sections of the original Draft on Fundamental Rights, proposed in the Karachi Congress. But given the imbalanced economic growth and partition complications, Vallabhbhai proposed to keep the section in the form of instructions which would no doubt put moral pressures upon any elected Government for being 'fundamental' in governance, but need not be construed as mandatory upon it[17]. Thus, he tried to ally the apprehension of certain members regarding the effectiveness of this provision to look after the poor.

5.1.2 Chairman of the Minorities Sub-committee

The problem of Minorities in India was the result of the Imperial policy of 'divide and rule'. It posed major challenge to the unity and integrity of the country. In fact, it was one of the key factors behind the creation of Pakistan. Vallabhbhai rightly realised his responsibility for bridging the gap between the minorities and the majority. He acknowledged, "When I was first appointed as the Chairman of the Advisory Committee on minorities, I was really trembling and I took up the job with a heavy heart because I felt the task was immensely difficult owing to the history of the past of so many years of foreign rule."[18]

Vallabhbhai took certain positive measures to instill a sense of confidence in the minorities. He assured them protection of their scripts, culture, language, religion and an impartial attitude in providing them financial assistance and non-interference in the maintenance of their educational institutions. He favoured reservations for the Anglo-Indians in public services and educational institutions. He also insisted on the abolition of the practice of untouchability affecting the Harijans or the Scheduled Castes. He fought for giving the Hindu religious institutions a public character to enable all to have a free entry and supported state initiative for social welfare.[19] He strove to make all these provisions part of the Fundamental Rights in order to be claimed effectively against the state with the due intervention of the judiciary.

Vallabhbhai was against the policy of communal representation introduced by the British authority through the Morley–Minto Reform (1909), to divide the people of the country on the basis of religion.[20] In an attempt to ensure secular democracy mentioned in the Objective Resolution of the Constitution, he argued, "I am against separate electorate. Can you show me one free country where there are separate electorates? But, in this unfortunate country, if this separate electorate is going to be persisted in even after the division of the country, woe betide the country: it is not worth living in."[21] He succeeded in his effort and got the motion approved to replace the policy on communal representation with joint electorate system.[22] As the post-partition conditions turned fluid especially in provinces like the Punjab and Bengal, Vallabhbhai wanted to assure the minorities by giving certain political safeguards. He was instrumental in the introduction of specific measures like the proportional representation of the communities through a joint electorate system, and the right of their participation both from the reserved and unreserved seats.[23] He supported reservation for certain religious minorities in the legislatures in proportion to their population. He initiated certain other regulatory mechanisms like the appointment of an officer by the President at the Centre and the Governor in the States to monitor the effective implementation of the safeguards. He further helped introduce a provision to set up a statutory commission to investigate into the condition of the socially and educationally backward classes. Despite opposition from members like H.C. Mookerjee and Rajkumari Amrit Kaur, who insisted on economic measures for the minorities he was able to get the proposals on political safeguards approved on the ground of providing security to the minorities in an atmosphere surcharged with communal tension.

While introducing the positive measures for the safety and security of the minorities, Vallabhbhai was careful against its misuse. With a firm conviction in the retrieval of a healthy relationship between the minorities and the majority, he was in favour of introducing certain safety valves. Hence he wanted the Right to Religion to be regulated to check the ongoing process of conversion.[24] He also cautioned not to overlook the efficiency of the administration while making reservation for the disadvantaged section. He argued: "It is well known that since this departure has been introduced in the matter of services, our administration has suffered considerably. Now, that we begin afresh, we must see that where we have to fill some administrative posts of a higher level, these posts have to be filled by competition such as competitive examinations and tests."[25] He did not want an indiscreet use of the safeguards. He appreciated the gestures of some of the minorities like the Parsees who came forward to forego any such concessions. He shared with their convictions that in the long run reservation would cause more harm than good. He acknowledged: "Either in the legislature or in the services they stand so high in the general standard of the nation that they have disclaimed any concessions and I congratulate them on their decisions.[26] He dissuaded the Muslims and Sikhs from claiming such benefits for being the most organised and brave communities. He was apprehensive of mass scale conversion as fallout of such reservation. He supported reservation for only the Scheduled Castes and the Anglo-Indians for bearing the brunt of caste segregation and the sudden withdrawal of the British authority respectively. Subsequently, after much hesitation, he agreed to extend it to the Scheduled Castes in the Sikh community as these people were compelled to migrate from the fold of Hinduism out of humiliation and failed to upgrade themselves even after accepting a new faith. Finally, with the easing of communal tension in 1949, he demanded abolition of some of the political safeguards like statutory reservation of seats in the legislature for the religious minorities.[27]

Besides working for the implementation of these measures, Vallabhbhai tried to develop mutual understanding between the minority and the majority communities to bridge the gap between them. He argued: "So, the future of a minority, any minority is to trust the majority. If the majority misbehaves, it will suffer. It will be a misfortune to this country if the majority does not realise its own responsibility. In the long run, it would be in the interest of all to forget that there is anything like majority or minority in this country and feel that in India there is only one community."[28]

5.1.3 Chairman of the Provincial Constitution Sub-committee

As the Chairman of the Provincial Constitution Sub-Committee Vallabhbhai was entrusted with the job of drafting the Constitution for the provinces. India was divided in to the British India Provinces and Princely States due to the lapse of the policy of annexation pursued by the colonial power. Initially, the Provincial Constitution Sub-committee was given the responsibility of devising the modalities of administrations for the provinces governed directly by the British authority. The Cabinet Mission Plan had made the return of paramountcy to the Princely States mandatory thereby putting a question mark on the merger of such units into the Indian Union. The subsequent acceptance of the Mountbatten Plan which divided India, nullified the provision of return of paramountcy and left the Princes with no option but to join either of the two Unions. Vallabhbhai, as the Minister of States was entrusted with the responsibility of motivating the Princes to join with the Indian Union. Hence, as the Chairman of the Provincial Constitution Sub-committee he tried his best to accommodate their interests. Though, during the freedom struggle he adopted different strategies to motivate both the British India provinces and the Princely States, yet he was quite sure of their cultural affinities and ability of co-existence and held them at par with each other.[29]

It strengthened his belief in the need for a united India which could be possible with the help of an integrated, uniform constitutional framework. He argued: "As however, the states come closer to the centre, it was realised that the idea of a separate Constitution being framed for the different constituent units of the Indian Union was a legacy from the Ruler's polity and that in a people's polity there was no scope for variegated constitutional pattern. We, therefore, discussed the matter with the premiers of the various unions and decided with their concurrence that the Constitution of the states should form an integral part of the Constitution of India."[30] In fact, he was aware of the necessity of such integration while presenting the report of his committee, much ahead of the Union Power Committee headed by Nehru, entrusted to formulate the provisions for the Union Government in the Constitution of India. He argued: "The real point is whether it is better to stand on the legs or on the head and we prefer to stand on the legs. We start with the provinces and we will come to the top, but, some people occasionally try acrobatic feats and it is open to them to do so."[31] He remained in touch with the Union Power Committee throughout, to avoid any inconsistencies with the Objective Resolution of the Constitution.

As the Chairman of the Provincial Constitution Sub-Committee, Vallabhbhai tried to ensure the uniform implementation of rule of law in the provinces especially through the provisions like the supremacy of legislature, collective responsibility and integrated judiciary. Initially, he tried to protect the identity of the states envisaged by the Cabinet Mission Plan and persuaded the Union Power Committee to involve the provinces in the election for the President of India. But subsequent developments such as the orgy of violence perpetuated by communal organisations changed his perception on the centre-state relationship. It forced him to advocate in favour of a strong centre. The compulsion of introducing parliamentary set-up in the provinces and the partition complications influenced him to recast the role of Governors in the states as the head of the

Constituent Units. In the changed situation, Vallabhbhai felt the need for making the centre effective enough to override the states in order to protect the unity and integrity of the country and maintain the spirit of Parliamentary democracy. He advocated the use of the emergency power as safety valve in order to empower the Parliament to take over the law and order situation of the states with the help of the Governor.[32] In this context, he advised the premiers of the Provinces to repose faith in the Governors appointed by the Centre, as the trusted Congressmen.[33] Reiterating the need for such provisions, he said, "There is no doubt that an encroachment of this kind on the power of the ministry is bound to be resented and is bound to create difficulties also and in a democratic Constitution it does not fit in properly . . . . On the other side, others feel that in the present condition of the country, it is a dangerous thing not to provide for emergency of such nature as it mentioned or as is contemplated namely, when there is a complete breakdown of the machinery of law and order . . . . if such a situation arises, it would not be enough for a machinery in the province to report to the centre, but there would be something more effective."[34]

Vallabhbhai's emphasis on an independent and integrated judiciary was part of the process to ensure the rule of law at the provincial levels and protect the dignity of the individual. In a suggestion to the Government of Hyderabad he said: "We should scrupulously safeguard the independence and integrity of the judiciary and nothing shall be done to give the impression that the judiciary is being subjected to ministerial interference."[35] It was proved further when as the Home Minister, he urged Nehru not to seek the resignation of Justice Kania, the then Chief Justice of India who objected to the Government proposal on making Basir Ahmed as the Justice of the Madras High Court. He cautioned the Prime Minister that such action on the part of the Government might be dubbed as interference with the judiciary.[36] He moved the Judicial Commissioner Court Bill (1950) to upgrade the status of the lower Courts in states to bring uniformity. He insisted on appointment of the High Court judges in line with that of Supreme Court. He suggested a fixed service condition for the judges of the High Court which included a regulated salary scale, restriction on the right to practice and a fixed age limit.[37]

Thus, Vallabhbhai as the Chairman of the Provincial Constitution Sub-Committee contributed significantly to the evolution of a uniform and integrated procedural framework for the governance of the whole country.

5.2 Integration of States

Vallabhbhai's commitment towards the Nation–State was revealed from his keen interest to provide stability through the process of integration. One of the founding fathers of the Constitution of India he was equally concerned about the creation of a united India. He realised its significance much before the independence and his apprehension was based on the British antagonistic policies aimed at the balkanisation of India.

The emergence of India as a politico-territorial unit had a link with the native Princely States. True to its pluralist traditions the country had multiple centres of power with varieties of cultural frameworks. Prior to the arrival of the British, the centralised Mughal dynasty had failed to unify them completely because of its one-man rule and lack of adequate administrative structure. Ironically, it was during the colonial period, the use of modern infrastructure introduced for the benefit of the British trade, initiated the process to integrate the country. It was further strengthened by the policy of annexation, pursued by the East India Company in between 1765-57. It changed the equation between the states and authority from a position of equality to that of superiority.[38] The shifting of administration from the Company to the British Parliament found little change in the relationship because of the challenges of nationalist upsurge, economic advancement and the First World War. The Butler Committee (1928) reiterated the unequal relationship and argued that states in India were not sovereign as defined by the International Law. After the Second World War, the realisation of leaving India compelled the British authority to abandon its big brother attitude towards the Princely States in order to balkanise the country at the time of its final departure. Hence, the Political Department which was then in charge of the Princely States, conveniently ignored the claim of the Congress Party regarding the existing religious, cultural and economic affinities of the Princely States and advocated the logic of granting them paramountcy to recognise them as sovereign entities.

With this self-motivated changing stand of the Imperial power, it was not possible on the part of the Indian leadership to ignore the 'group clause' in the proposal of the Cabinet Mission. Vallabhbhai Patel because of his long intimate association with the Princes was in the most advantageous position to meet the challenge. He was in touch with the politics of the Princely States with the formation of the States People's Conference (1927). He was hesitant of any form of their direct involvement in the freedom struggle till the late thirties as it would have failed in the absence of active help of their rulers and adequate awareness of the people. It could hardly be denied that he was sympathetic towards the Princes as they were a humiliated lot under colonialism.[39] But the rise of the Prajamandal Movements in the mid thirties motivated Vallabhbhai to change his earlier policy of the indirect involvement in the states into a direct one[40]. In the Tripura Congress (1938), he came forward with a plan to involve the Provinces and the Princely States in the freedom struggle. He emphatically declared: "The red and yellow colours on India's map have to be made one. Unless that is done, we cannot have *Swaraj.*"[41] The *Rajkot Satyagraha* (1939) reflected the changed mood, where Vallabhbhai on behalf of the Congress played a key role in bringing about an amicable settlement between the ruler and the ruled. He wanted to encash the rising political consciousness of the people and make them stand up against the British authority. With such political experiences, Vallabhbhai became the obvious choice for the Department of States, created at the time of independence to monitor the process of integration. Mountbatten, the last Governor General of India even went to the extent of advising him to get rid of other portfolios to take charge of the onerous responsibility. He advised him: "The one portfolio you must not give up is the states. For the princes have come to trust you in a quite remarkable way and so long as you have got V.P. Menon to carry out your policy so loyally, the Ministry of States will continue to be the mainstay of the Dominion."[42] No doubt, in course of discharging his responsibilities, Vallabhbhai was challenged by the Princely States, particularly because of their demographic composition and economic viability. He observed that these states had been emboldened by the declaration of Atlee, the Prime Minister of England, regarding the withdrawal of the British power from India. He also encountered the defying mood of the ambitious Princes of Hyderabad, Bhopal, Travancore, etc. who were encouraged by Jinnah and Cornard Corfield, the Secretary of the Political Department to form the 'third force'. They moved the Bombay Resolution in January 1947 on behalf of the Chamber of Princes to put terms and conditions for protecting their identities. But, Vallabhbhai relied upon his association with the princes and seized the opportunities to resolve the past conflicts between the people and rulers to establish a united India. He had sensed the divisive strategy of the British much earlier. So he wanted the Home portfolio even at the cost of incurring displeasure of many party members. It proved to be of great help in solving the complex and intricate problems of state integration[43].

Vallabhbhai started wooing the princes since May 1947, though the Department of States was constituted formally two months later. During the process, he followed different techniques to tackle the princes who had their own unique problems. But, basically he relied upon the age old policy of Chanakya, the architect of the Mauryan empire, which included *Sama* (persuasion), *daam* (money), *danda* (punishment) and *bheda* (division). Many also compared him with Bismarck the architect of modern United Germany.[44] The whole process of integration began at the time of independence and virtually coincided with the formulation of the Constitution of India. It came to a close by the end of 1949. The arduous task was carried out in three stages of accession, reconstitution and centralisation.

5.2.1 Policy of Accession

The formal process of integration started with the Cabinet Mission Plan, Vallabhbhai wanted all the 554 Princely States to sign the twin documents of the Instrument of Accession and the Standstill Agreement in order to make them part of the Indian Union gradually. The much articulated, well drafted proposals on the integration was prepared by Vallabhbhai with the help of V.P. Menon, the Secretary of the Department of States. It first demanded the states to surrender subjects like Defence, External Affairs and Communication to the Government of India under the Instrument of Accession with the assurance that it would lead to the Standstill Agreement simultaneously in between the Union and States by virtue of which the Princes would have status quo so far as the other earlier administrative and economic agreements were concerned. Vallabhbhai was reminded of the policy of 'Crown Paramountcy' of the erstwhile Viceroy Reading and Linlithgow, who advocated for surrendering the ultimate power to the British authority in the matter of Defence. The twin documents were applied differently to suit the varying economic requirements and political scenarios of the states. The first 140 states, whose rulers had full powers, were simply asked to part with these three subjects in favour of the Union Government. The second category of 300 states situated mostly in Kathiawar, Orissa, Central Province etc were attached to the adjoining bigger states under the attachment scheme of 1943. In these states the crown used to exercise only certain powers and was asked to surrender all the residuary powers including the three original subjects. Lastly, the 70 odd states which were bigger than the second category and smaller than the first one, were instructed not to exercise powers higher than they had prior to 15th August 1947. But in all the cases the Standstill agreement remained common thereby allowing all the administrative arrangements to remain effective between the crown and the States till new alternatives were devised.

Vallabhbhai employed techniques like conciliation, persuasion, good offices, diplomacy from the position of strength and lastly force in order to convince the rulers to sign the agreements. Using these techniques, he evolved his own variants of these conventional techniques to suit the purpose of tackling the feudal Princely Rulers of India with due courtesy, minimum injury and maximum accommodation. Though there was an element of coercion behind the process of negotiation, he tried to be persuasive as far as possible to invoke least resentment.

Conciliation

In the absence of an independent fact finding body, Vallabhbhai initially used the Department of States to accumulate information and formulate proposals required by the policy of integration. He wanted the Princes to have sufficient information and to take right decision regarding merger. With the approval of the Cabinet Mission Plan, he made it clear to the rulers that though the plan permitted them to secede from India, it would not be possible prior to the completion of the formulation of the Constitution. So he made them realise the necessity of joining the Constituent Assembly by signing the Instrument of Accession.[45] His argument succeeded in motivating the Princes of Baroda, Bikaner, Cochin, Jaipur, Patiala and Rewa etc. to come forward to participate in the constitutional proceedings. It weakened the 'third force', constituted under the leadership of the Nawab of Bhopal and helped Vallabhbhai to tackle each individual ruler firmly. No doubt, Mountbatten's June 3rd Plan on partition replaced the original clause on the right to secede and allowed the rulers to have paramountcy even prior to the finalisation of the Constitution, but Vallabhbhai apprised the rulers that it was hardly possible in reality. The acceptance of the status of twin dominions weakened the position of the states by preventing them to become independent members of the Commonwealth group of Nations and thereby compelling them to take side with either Dominions.[46] In this regard, Vallabhbhai also reminded Sir Corfield, the Secretary of the Political Department, the earlier stand of the Imperial authority which refused to recognise the status of Paramountcy of States. He referred to Viceroy Readings who was reported to have said, in 1926: ". . . . the sovereignty to the British crown is supreme in India, and therefore, no ruler of an Indian state can justifiably claim to negotiate with the British Government on equal footing."[47] The revelation, exposed the dual standard adopted by the colonial power to balkanise India. Again, he apprised the rulers regarding the limitations of their demand on paramountcy which in the changed situation lay with the people.[48]

Persuasion

Vallabhbhai also used his persuasive skill to convince the rulers in favour of merger. His command over facts sharpened this trait, which he had been nurturing since the beginning of his legal career. His long association with the states convinced him about the equality of status between the British India provinces and the Princely States for having the same culture and character. He tried to invoke the sense of patriotism of the rulers to persuade them to remain within the Indian Union. He reminded them of their past follies which many invaders took advantage of and appealed to them not to get trapped again by the lure of Paramountcy. He urged: "we are at a momentous stage in the history of India . . . . I hope that the Indian states will bear in mind that alternative to cooperation in the general interest is anarchy and chaos, which will overwhelm great and small in a common ruin, if we are unable to get together minimum of common tasks."[49] He assured them of the least interference in their internal matter on behalf of the Government of India. He categorically told them, "They (the Congress) are no enemies of the princely order, but, on the other hand, they wish them and the people under their aegis all prosperity, contentment and happiness. Nor would it be my policy to conduct the relations of the new department with the states in any manner which savours of the domination of one over the other, if there would be any domination it would be that of our mutual interests and welfare."[50] He tried to placate the Princes by giving them a definite role in the making of the Constitution in order to be recognised as contributors of peace. While negotiating, he appealed to them to make the Nation proud by utilising their bravery and intelligence in the army and various diplomatic assignments.[51]

Good Offices

In course of his negotiations with the rulers, Vallabhbhai skillfully used the good offices of many influential people. It was quite easy on his part to use this strategy as he was known for his ability to choose the right man for the right work in the right situation[52]. He decided to utilise the services of Jam Saheb, the ruler of Nawanagar and his brother and Queen for the integration of the states of Kathiawar and the formation of the Saurastra Union. He was also helped by the initiative of Rajkumari Amrit Kaur for the accession of Indore, Patiala and Baroda. He did not forget to encash the patriotic feelings of the state *Diwans* such as V.T. Krishnamachari (Jaipur), B.L. Mitter (Baroda), K.M. Panikkar (Bikaner), M.A. Srinivasan (Gwalior), etc. He acknowledged that these people had "worked like *Tarjons* in the great cause of bringing the two sides together and averting the dreaded balkanaisation of India."[53] Last but not the least, Vallabhbhai took advantage of his good rapport with Mountbatten. As the Crown's Representative Mountbatten was indispensable for the process of integration. He was the only official link between the rulers and the Government of India. He played a decisive role in the weakening of the Karachi-Jodhpur-Bhopal axis, nurtured by Jinnah in connivance with Bhopal to disintegrate India. Mountbatten apprised the reality to the ruler of Bhopal. He wrote: "I pointed out to His Highness that no amount of friendship would enable me to protect either himself or his state or the new ruler of the state, if the future Government of India thought that he was acting in a manner hostile to the Government by trying to induce an all Hindu state to join

Pakistan."[54] He also pressurised the young ruler of Jodhpur to honour his father's decision to accede to India.[55] It gave a rude shock to the ruler and made the task of Vallabhbhai easier. Bhopal which was earlier weakened for parting ways with Bikaner, became isolated further due to the weaning away of Jodhpur and decided to go in favour of the Union of India. Fall of Bhopal led to the merger of Indore, one of its closest ally whose leader was given a "dressing down of painful severity" by Mountbatten.[56] He tried to motivate the Nizam of Hyderabad to sign the Standstill Agreement. While paying tribute to his decisive role, Vallabhbhai acknowledged: ". . . . it is as such that I am bold to say that when the history of the six months of your Viceroyalty comes to be written, it cannot but accord you the major share of the credit for the manner in which the manifold difficult tasks have been accomplished."[57]

Diplomacy from the Position of Strength

Vallabhbhai as the Minister of States and Home, used his position skillfully to convince many ambitious Princes. He warned the Princes who were adopting dilatory tactics and unduly delaying the integration process which was needed to be over by the 15th of August, 1947. He did not mind warning the young ruler of Jodhpur, the son of one of his friends, about a possible intervention. It subdued the ruler, who was already isolated by the joining of Udaipur and Jaisalmer in the Constituent Assembly. Vallabhbhai also cautioned the ruler of Baroda for the latter's indecisiveness even after joining the Constituent Assembly. He warned the ruler of Bhopal even after the merger of the state against involvement with divisive forces.[58] Thus, by the stipulated day of independence almost all the states except Hyderabad, Kashmir and Junagarh had acceded into the Indian Union under the guidance of the Department of States.

Force

The recalcitrant attitude of a few states compelled Vallabhbhai to take drastic action against them. The non-adherence of the Instrument of Accession by the states like Junagarh, Kashmir and Hyderabad on different grounds challenged the authority of the Government of India. The sudden and surreptitious accession of Junagarh into Pakistan, coinciding with the time of the partition of the country, had a lot of ramifications. It not only violated the norms of cultural affinity, economic prospect and demographic composition, but also adversely affected the ongoing negotiations with Hyderabad and Kashmir and undermined the legitimacy of the Government of India. Junagarh's forcible annexation of two of its erstwhile feudatories such as Babariawad and Mangrol, which had already consented to go with India, violated all international norms. Vallabhbhai apprehended a threat from the decision of Junagarh as it had the potential of spreading communal tension and disintegrating the whole Kathiawar region, which was thinking of forming a confederation under the leadership of Jam Saheb of Nawanagar. At this hour, Mountbatten's recognition of accession of Junagarh to Pakistan and suggestion to refer India's claim over Babariawad and Mangrol to the United Nations for an independent arbitration complicated the situation further. Besides Junagarh, the claim of independent status by Hyderabad was also against the basic principles of geographic contiguity and cultural homogeneity as adopted for the process of integration. It was situated at the belly of India, with a sizeable Hindu population and a rich reserve of natural resources. Vallabhbhai anticipated fissiparous tendencies from the decision of the Nizam to form the 'Third Dominion'. In fact, the idea had been articulated in the form of a demand for internal sovereignty since 1925, but it was rejected by the British. It started surfacing again during the unfolding of the constitutional development, with due support from the Political Department of the outgoing authority. Hence, the Nizam dared to violate the spirit of the Standstill Agreement, signed between Hyderabad and the Government of India as the first step towards accession. The defiance was further revealed as he influenced the minor ruler of Bastar to mortgage its mineral resources, extended financial help to Pakistan, banned Indian currency and the export of precious stones from the state, employed Mir Laik Ali a Muslim League member as his Dewan, made an arms deal with the Birmingham Small Arms Company, attempted to buy Goa from the Government of Portugal and encouraged the Razakars of the Ittehad-ul-Mussalmaan to spread communal violence in the state. The British authority, which recognised Hyderabad as one of its 'trusted ally', for its role in the First World War, complicated the situation further. It chose delaying tactics as a way of helping him. The Nizam also wanted the same thing as it suited his interests. It was evident from the observation of Walter Monckton, the Constitutional Advisor to the Nizam who was trying to take advantage of the keen interest of Mountbatten and Nehru to solve the problem amicably. While Mountbatten was eager to create a lasting image for himself before his departure, Nehru was worried about the fate of the Muslims in Hyderabad. Monckton acknowledged: "I wanted the negotiation to continue for Hyderabad as long as possible after 15th August . . . . the longer they continue, the better for us . . . . We have a breathing space to get ready for the economic and political conflict if it comes... I know that Patel was and is against any extension of time to Hyderabad and that the Governor General prevailed over the Cabinet of the Dominion to allow him personally two months time to see whether he and I, who had known each other intimately for many years publicly and privately could find a compromise satisfactory to both sides."[59] Vallabhbhai was equally concerned about the problem of Kashmir though he never approved the 'Quit Kashmir Movement'(1946) launched to demand autonomy for the state yet he had little hesitation for its accession into Pakistan. He was aware of its demographic composition and the lack of direct link with India. He said, "If the ruler felt that his and his state's interest lay in accession to Pakistan, he could not stand in his way."[60] However, the linking of Jammu with the rest of India due to the division of Gurdaspur by the Redcliffe Commission changed the geographic scenario. Later the tacit support of Pakistan given for the Junagarh accession and the tribal aggression in Kashmir made him realise the strategic importance of the area.[61]

Thus, Vallabhbhai was forced to take drastic action. His intention was to foil the plan of annexation of Babariawad and Mangrol by Junagarh, to prevent communal tension in Hyderabad and to counter the tribal aggression in Kashmir. Even while using force, he tried his best to keep it at the minimum level. In case of Junagarh, he first imposed an economic blockade and then deployed the regional force under the supervision of the Kathiawar Defence Force, that too only in the nearby Babariawad and Mangrol area to prevent undue resistance. In Hyderabad prior to the Army operation, he tried for around one year to resolve the issue through negotiation. He argued, "But, consistent with the policy to secure agreement, not by coercion, but so far as possible with the minimum degree of goodwill on both sides and with due regard to the overall position, we felt that an agreement of this nature, even for a limited period, would have considerable advantages, in the absence of any agreement what so ever"[62]. Accordingly, he first allowed the Nizam of Hyderabad two months of time for negotiation, and then under the supervision of Mountbatten, he persuaded the state to sign the Standstill Agreement, without going through any formalities and lastly agreed with the outgoing Governor General to give more privileges to the province which were not given to others. But support of the *Razakars* and the Political Department made Nizam intransigent. Vallabhbhai encashed skillfully the departure of Mountbatten and death of Jinnah in Pakistan and convinced his Cabinet colleagues to agree to an army operation in Hyderabad. In contrast to Hyderabad and Junagarh the provocation in Kashmir was more blatant. The tribal aggression which could have affected the sovereignty of India motivated Vallabhbhai to convince the Government to take immediate measures in the province in terms of ensuring the supply of adequate military assistance, protecting the life of the ruler and by taking initiative to connect it with rest of India by road. But prior to it, he had ensured the accession of Raja Hari Singh into India in lieu of Indian guarantee of security to the valley. All these concrete steps no doubt stalled the inward march of the enemy and initiated the democratisation process in the state but could hardly bring permanent solution as in case of Junagarh and Hyderabad. The emotional obsession of Nehru for Kashmir, ambition of the National Conference leader Sheikh Abdullah and the anxieties of Mountbatten to avoid an open clash between India and Pakistan at the time of the British withdrawal were not conducive to find an early resolution to the Kashmir problem. A Kashmiri Pandit by birth, Nehru was strongly attached to Kashmir and wanted a lasting solution for the Province. In this context, he took certain initiatives like shifting of Jammu and Kashmir from the Ministry of States to the Ministry of External Affairs, placing Kashmir under Gopalaswamy Ayyangar, Minister without Portfolio, beginning a democratisation process in the state by sending the ruler into exile, recognising Sheikh Abdullah as the Prime Minister of Kashmir and ensuring a special status for the state in the Constitution of India. But all these measures only fuelled the aspiration of the regional leader and made him bold enough to declare an "independent Kashmir."[63] The tribal aggression changed the scenario of the state. It forced the native ruler to seek the help of the Government of India. Even Sheikh Abdullah,the undisputed leader of the muslims of Kashmir who had a strained relation with Jinnah agreed to accession of Kashmir. Ironically Nehru's sense of idealism was then swayed away by the advice of Mountbatten and made the merger of Kashmir unilaterally conditional. Mountbatten's success in influencing Nehru to refer the matter to the United Nation further complicated the situation as it led to a hasty ceasefire. It was admitted by General S.P.P. Throat the Officer heading the Indian Army in Kashmir: "Our forces might have succeeded in evicting the invaders, if the Prime Minister had not held them in check and later ordered the cease fire . . . . Obviously great pressure must have been brought to bear on him by the Governor General . . . ."[64] Looking at all these constraints Vallabhbhai confided: "If Jawaharlal and Gopal Swamy Ayyanger had not made Kashmir their close reserve, separating it from my portfolio of Home and states, I would have tackled the problem as purposefully as I had done in Hydeerabad."[65]

5.2.2 Policy of Reconstitution

After securing the accession of almost all the states by 15th August, 1947, Vallabhbhai entered into the second stage of integration. His aim was to bring administrative uniformity as it was by accident that some parts were in the British India and others were in the Princely States. He was very much keen to counter the restive Prajamandal Movements in various backward states launched to have progressive reforms as in case of the states like Mysore, Travancore, Cochin etc. He was also cautious about the inability of the small states to exploit the rich reserve of natural resources necessary for the development of the country. Hence, he offered two different schemes both for the small and big Princely States for their reorganisation. He approached first the smaller states to avoid undue resistance and urged them to merge themselves in the nearby provinces where sound administrative system was already in existence. Here it can be pointed out that a number of similar principles had been applied elsewhere in the past. Those were the schemes of the East India Company applied in India in between 1774 to 1815, recommendation of the Simon Commission (1930), the Attachment Scheme of Linlithgow (1943) and the Godbhole Plan of the Diwan of Poona. But for bigger units like the conglomeration of states as existed in Kathiawar and Rajputana, he suggested them to form independent union instead of simple merger. Last but not the least, he intended to create some centrally administered territories to fulfill the strategic requirement of the country. Thus, keeping an eye on economic upliftment, strategic consideration, national unity, cultural homogeneity, administrative viability, and the process of democratisation, Vallabhbhai managed to merge 219 states, involving a total area of 84,774 square miles and a population of 120.18 lakhs with adjacent provinces of Orissa, the Central Province, Bihar, Madras, East Punjab and Bombay. This was followed by consolidation of 22 states, into units like Himachal Pradesh and Kutch, covering a total area of 19,061 square miles with a population of 14.37 lakhs. Then came territorial integrartion of 294 states to create new viable unions of Saurastra, Matsya Union, Vindhya Pradesh, Rajasthan, Madhya Bharata and the Patiala and East Punjab States Union (PEPSU), involving a total area of 1,500 square miles and a population of 277.64 lakhs. Finally, the creation of still larger unions like Kathiawar, Cochin-Travancore Union and Greater Rajasthan completed the process and eliminated the threat of assertion by the Princes in any form.

To achieve the whole process smoothly, Vallabhbhai, in the second stage utilised the techniques of persuasion, bargaining and lastly coercion.

Persuasion

Vallabhbhai utilised his persuasive skill again to convince the rulers about the benefits of complete merger through a process of reconstitution. He exploited their limitations like small size, little resource at disposal, limited manpower and finally the feudal mentality of the rulers leading to stiff resistance from the people. Citing the example of the ongoing reform process, taking place in the nearby provinces, he urged them: "In the world of today, where distances are fast shrinking and masses are gradually brought into touch with the latest administrative amenities, it is impossible to postpone for any day longer than necessary the introduction of the measures which would make the people realise that their progress is also proceeding at least in the line of their neighbouring areas. Delays inevitably lead to discontent which in turn result in lawlessness. In such circumstance there was no alternative to integration and democratisation."[66] He tried to convince the Princes that their future lay in the service of the people, not in the continued assertion of their autocracy. He assured them of least interference in case of merger and guaranteed them of assuming only the charge of central subjects by the Government of India, leaving all the provincial subject in the hands of the local authorities. In course of the formation of Union, he pursued the strategy of 'encirclement'. It was followed not only to secure administrative and economic efficiency, but also to counter the nefarious designs of states like Alwar, Bikaner,

Jaipur, Jodhpur, etc. who wanted to resist the process of integration. He reminded the rulers: "the history of the world in the last two centuries amply demonstrate that it is only by coming together that smaller states can retain their distinctive culture, safeguard their economic interest and take their due share in the political life of the country."[67] He invoked the patriotic feelings of the people of Rajsthan, Malwa, Kathiawar and the Punjab and reminded them the dangers of disunity. His intention to form greater Unions was in line with this strategy.

Bargaining

With a strong distaste for radical change, Vallabhbhai relied upon the strategy of bargaining in the second stage of integration. He believed: "It is better to secure a half rupee from the rulers without a fight, if it could be avoided than fight to get a whole rupee. But, the people should take care to see that half rupee coin given to the subjects is a sound coin and not a counterfeit."[68] As the merger demanded from the rulers surrendering of all their powers for all times to come, he found it was only elementary justice to compensate them for it. He was influenced by the precedents followed in Mysore, Baroda, Travancore, etc., and the suggestion of the Political Department and the Godbole Plan and agreed upon guaranteeing 'Privy Purse' to the rulers through the provisions of the Constitution.[69] He argued "The minimum which we could offer to them as *quid pro quo* for parting with their ruling powers was to guarantee Privy Purse and certain other privileges on a reasonable and defined basis. The Privy Purse settlements are, therefore, in the nature of consideration for the surrender by the rulers of their ruling powers and also for this dissolution of the states as separate units."[70] Though, initially the Privy Purse was to be charged from the state exchequer, with the extinction of the states and sharing of financial resources between the Centre and the provinces, it was to be shared by both. The success of the bargaining policy was based on mutual understanding. One of the rulers admitted: "Ever since you (Vallabhbhai) took over the charge of the Ministry of States, you have shown greatest consideration towards us . . . . Indeed hardly to assure that we will be prepared to do our best for the cause of our motherland."[71] Besides offering Privy Purse, Vallabhbhai provided them the scope to be part of the administrative process. The erstwhile rulers were offered to become the *Rajpramukhas* or the Constitutional heads in various states. Accordingly, the ruler of Nawanagar was made the Rajpramukh for the Saurastra Union, the ruler of Gwalior for the Madhya Bharata, the Maharaja of Udaipur for the Union of Rajasthan and the Maharaja of Patiala for the Punjab and East Punjab States Union.

Coercion

Lastly, Vallabhbhai cautiously used coercion against the states who were not keen on merger. He found that their attempt was to keep alive the spirit of assertion and threaten the unity of the country. During the merger of the Orissa state on which the fate of Chhattishgarh state was dependent, the *Maharaja* of Patna was told, "the Government of India are almost anxious to maintain law and order. We cannot allow your state to create problems for the Government of Orissa and if you had not signed the agreement, we should have been compelled to take over administration of your state."[72] In fact, he appeared to be quite firm and swift on the issue of merger as he did not want to allow any scope for the rulers to be indecisive. He even ignored the view Rajendra Prasad one of his close colleagues, who suggested referendum to decide on the claims of some Princely States in Bihar and Orissa.[73] He used the same technique for the *Maharaja* of Swantawadi and Nawab of Janjira[74] and applied it for the Deccan states to enable them to merge with the Bombay Province. He did not mind warning the states of Alwar and Bharatpur for showing reluctance to be part of the Matsya Union.[75] He threatened the Akalis for showing lack of cooperation in the formation of the Patiala and Eastern Punjab States Union. He cautioned them: "The doctor operates only when the boil is fully ripe, so that bleeding is the minimum and the patient suffers as less pain as possible . . . . It has come to my hearing that our Sikh brethren wish to set up a Khalistan.... But, I want to tell them that Hyderabad showed its teeth and we had pulled them out. If our Sikh brethren wish to do the same, they would meet with same fate. The Government of India has enough strength to face the situation."[76] In the second stage of integration, Vallabhbhai initiated the formation of several bigger units like the Rajasthan Union, Matsya Union, Malwa Union, Union of Vindhya Pradesh, Union of Kathiawar, Patiala and Eastern Punjab States Union etc. by using threats wherever required to bring administrative uniformity and stability. In subsequent period, Greater Rajasthan, Madhya Bharata and Cochin–Travancore Union were formed as part of the same strategy.

5.2.3. Policy of Centralisation

Vallabhbhai was aware of the centralising tendency in most countries[77] and harped upon it in the third stage of the integration process. In fact, the formation of the big federal unions and centrally administered territories were part of such strategy for consolidation. To pursue the plan further, he made a sincere attempt to bring the states at par with the provinces and devised a common framework of governance through the Constitution of India. He put some states in Part I and some other in Part II in because of the differences in their administrative development. He incorporated the provision of emergency in it as a 'safety valve' to cope with the challenges in a transition period.[78] He envisaged a 'recombination plan' to make the civil servants more competent particularly in the less developed states. He also felt the necessity of an integrated armed service for the protection of the country. The armed Central Reserve Police Force was created to root out indiscipline appearing during the process of integration. The Indian States Finance Inquiry Committee was constituted for the proper financial integration which first involved the functional partition of the composite state governments and then the merger of the partitioned federal portions with the Government of India. During the process, he was very much keen to ensure equality in the treatment of states especially in the sharing of divisible federal taxes, grants-in-aid, subsidies and dues of the 'Privy Purse'.

Thus, within the shortest possible time, Vallabhbhai managed to foil the balkanisation plan of the British authority with the least reliance upon force and integrated the whole country in to one Union.

5.3 Restructuring of Administrative and Socio-economic Machineries

Vallabhbhai's obsession for a stable Nation–State encouraged him to look beyond the attainment of independence. The effort to integrate it and provide it with a definite procedural format of governance was part of the larger goal. At the same time, he could hardly ignore the myriad administrative challenges that the nascent state was grappling with. It was his experience of fighting against the realities of life in a hostile environment that enabled him to identify such challenges and also find solution.

5.3.1 Administrative Challenges

Vallabhbhai observed that the day-to-day administration was affected by internal factors like dissension within the cabinet, declining hold of the bureaucracy, weak provincial political set-up and by external factors such as the aggressive attitude of the neighbouring countries.

Dissension in the Cabinet

As a key member of the Government Vallabhbhai observed that dissension in the political set-up was affecting its efficiency. Though cabinet in the true sense of the term was virtually non-existent in the Interim Government, its functioning was obstructed by the long cherished goal of the Muslim League, nurtured in connivance with the outgoing British authority.[79] Subsequently, in the post-independence period, lack of homogeneity in the political set-up and ego clashes among the members of the cabinet put a question mark on the ability and efficiency of the political system to take on the challenges.

The Interim Government was created based on the Cabinet Mission Plan in September 1946. It had an ominious beginning. It had to bear the brunt of the Direct Action Day observed by the Muslim League as a pressure tactics to demand for a parity of status with the Congress. But subsequently, the League's entry into the Government with the help of the Imperial authority, emboldened it to create dissension within it and then strive for partition. It was substantiated by the revelation of one of the League members, who claimed that the party was participating in the Interim Government to create a launching pad for Pakistan.[80] This mindset of the League members encouraged communal animosity. It provided enough opportunities to the British authority to pass on its responsibility to the beleaguered provincial units in the name of devolution of power. It thereby created more problems for the Interim Government as the administrative arrangement kept the provinces out of its purview.

In this stage of transition, the performance of the Government was bound to be affected because of the dismissive attitude of the Congress towards its partner and also the intransigent attitude of the League. Nehru's emphatic declaration on the ability of his party to change the 'group clause' and his subsequent visit to the North West Frontier Province created apprehension in the mind of the League Members.[81] In response, Jinnah replaced many of the League nominees with people of hawkish nature.[82] It was rightly observed: "That choice itself indicates a desire to have conflict rather than cooperation. The Muslim League has taken the plan to send their most suitable men."[83] The London Declaration (1946) announced by the British authority in a haste recognised the Muslim League as a key player in the ensuing transfer of power. True to apprehension of Vallabhbhai, it further legitimised the League and widened the rift between the partners in the Government. The League defied the collective spirit of working and refused to attend the meeting convened by Nehru as the Deputy President of the council. It criticised the Congress members openly in the Assembly and obstructed the appointments of foreign representatives. It utilised the services of A.S. Bukhari, the Director of All India Radio in giving undue importance to Urdu at the cost of Hindi[84]. Last but not the least, the budget presented by its member Liaquat Ali Khan was alleged to be communal and to have upset the base of the Congress by bringing permanent damage to commerce and industry[85]. Ironically, the Minister did not follow the same strategy while presenting the first budget in Pakistan. Thus, with the League in charge of portfolios like Finance, Communication, Commerce, Health and Law, the Congress members of the Coalition Government laboured under several handicaps in maintaining secrecy of their communication, getting their grants sanctioned and in securing satisfactory internal departmental coordination. As regards the state of affairs in the Government, Vallabhbhai described: "My experience in office during the past year showed that it was impossible to do anything constructive with the Muslim League. The League representatives during their continuance in office did nothing but create deadlocks and their attitude was entirely an obstructionist one."[86] The dissension in the Government had its ramifications upon the bureaucracy already divided on communal line and it was skillfully utilised by the press to its own advantage.[87]

The internal dissension within the Government became more apparent after independence and hampered its efficiency. Though the League ceased to exist, yet the withdrawal of the British presence from India opened up the Pandora's box in the form of ideological differences within the Congress, which was skillfully synthesised by Gandhi during the freedom struggle. The decline in Gandhi's role particularly after the acceptance of the Cabinet Mission Plan widened the rift further. In the Meerut Session of the Congress (1946), the existence of various factions such as the Socialists, the advocates of the underground movements and the erstwhile Indian National Army exposed the ideological differences within the party. It was further witnessed at the time of the elections for the Party President. The functioning of the Government was also affected by its heterogeneous character.

The conglomeration of fourteen representatives from the Congress, the Hindu Mahasabha, the Sikhs, the Christians and the Scheduled Caste groups could not present unified views on various policies including the policy of secularism. The problem of the Government was also compounded by the absence of proper communication among the leaders and leakage of information by certain section of the press.[88]

Because of all these constraints, the state of affairs in the first Cabinet was anything but a smooth one. The spell of resignations tendered by Ministers confirms it. It was only C.H. Bhabha, the Minister of Commerce who had to quit office on personal grounds. In fact, the resignation of S. Chetty, the first Finance Minister apparently on the basis of lapses in punishing the defaulters of Income Tax created a lot of ripples.[89] Over and above reservations were expressed by other Cabinet members like John Mathai on the formation of the Planning Commission; S.P. Mookerjee and K.C. Neyogy on the Nehru-Liaquat Ali Pact and N.V. Gadgil on the sharing of river water with Pakistan, presentation of the 1949 Budget, the appointment of ambassadors and refugee rehabilitation.[90] Last but not the least, the differences between the Prime Minister Nehru and Vallabhbhai especially on the issues of refugee resettlement, Kashmir and the economic policy divided the Cabinet[91]. The difference in their perceptions might be because of their different upbringings. It led to different ideological approaches which polarised the party rank and file. Regarding his withdrawal from the race of Presidentship in the Lucknow Session of the Congress (1936) Vallabhbhai declared: "My withdrawal should not be taken to mean that I endorse all the views of Jawaharlalji... For instance I do not believe in the inevitability of classwar.... Whilst the Congress holds non-violence and truth as indispensable means for the attainment of independence, the Congressmen must believe in the possibility of weaning those who are mercilessly exploiting the masses from what is a crime against humanity."[92] The withdrawal of the British authority increased the difference in their approaches on many vital issues which affected the nation building activities.

The commanding stature of Vallabhbhai due to his hold over the Party, influence in the first Cabinet, position of the Deputy Prime Minister and the success in the integration of the states made Nehru apprehensive of him. Further, the communication gap between the two leaders, mainly because of the ill health of Vallabhbhai and the change of residence by Nehru,[93] was fully exploited by the latter's associates like Mridula Sarabhai, the General Secretary of the Party and Rafi Ahmed Kidwai, the President of the Uttar Pradesh Congress Unit.[94] Maniben, daughter of Vallabhbhai, claimed that Abdul Kalam Azad was also playing a vital role in widening the gap between the leaders.[95]

In this backdrop, the performance of the Government was affected while dealing with the important problems like refugee influx and communal violence. In fact, both the problems were interlinked. The inflow of the refugees caught by the partition, provided a fertile ground for the communal uprisings. But the top leadership was divided on these issues. Though, both Nehru and Vallabhbhai wanted to make India a secular state,[96] Nehru's idealistic vision aimed at showing sympathy for the Muslims partly to protect the international image of India, while the pragmatic outlook of a *Patidar* in Vallabhbhai taught him to be firm enough to counter the nefarious designs of certain communal bodies. The latter could hardly ignore the shifting loyalties of prominent Muslim leaders, divided allegiance of the army and bureaucracy, and the hostile approach of Pakistan towards its Hindu minorities. Hence, as the Home Minister, he was determined to deal with the Muslims firmly. He argued: "I believe in plain speaking. I do not know how to mince matters. I want to tell them frankly that mere declarations of loyalty to the Indian Union will not help them at this critical juncture. They (Muslims) must give practical proof of their declarations."[97] He wanted to adopt strong measures against the Muslims showing disloyalty in view of the Pakistan-sponsored tribal invasion in Kashmir. Much against the wishes of Nehru, he brought several legislations in the Parliament to control communal uprisings and refugee influx.[98] However, he appeared to have adopted a softer line than Nehru towards the Hindu organisations[99]. He urged Nehru to accommodate S.P. Mookerjee, a Hindu Mahasabha Member in the first Cabinet for his role in foiling the dream of a sovereign Bengal by Suhrawady, the then Bengal Premier. He appeared to be lenient on the Rastriya Swayamsewak Sangha while advocating to lift the ban order on it imposed immediately after the assassination of Gandhi. He justified his soft corner for the organisation for its contribution to restore peace at the time of partition. Nehru and Vallabhbhai also differed on the issue of integration of states. If Nehru was highly cautious of using force for the merger of sensitive states like Junagarh, Kashmir and Hyderabad, Vallabhbhai apprehended external interferences while referring such issues to any international organisations and demanded quick solutions.[100] Differences in ideological backgrounds influenced both the leaders to develop different economic visions. If for Nehru profit should be replaced with a sprit of social service, to Vallabhbhai it was a great stimulant to shape human conduct.[101] As a result, while Nehru wanted land reform with immediate effect, Vallabhbhai demanded a gradual process for it with due provision for compensation.[102] Moreover, a true socialist, Nehru emphasised upon planning and distribution of resources, while Vallabhbhai had scant regards for these and instead harped upon maximisation of production.[103]

Thus, the Cabinet dissension in general and the Nehru-Vallabhbhai differences in particular affected the administrative process of the country. The frequent resignation of ministers, repeated reconstitution of the Cabinet and the formation of several Cabinet committees reflected the state of affairs. Even Nehru in a rather curt manner reminded Vallabhbhai about the position of the Prime Minister in a Cabinet: "As I conceive it, the Prime Minister's role is and should be an important role. He is not only a figure-head, but a person who should be more responsible than any one else in the general trend of the policy and for the coordination of the work of various Departments."[104] This assertion of Nehru revealed dissension and the lack of collective spirit within the Cabinet.

Declining Bureaucracy

Vallabhbhai observed that the declining hold of the bureaucracy was lowering the efficiency of the Government especially in terms of meeting the challenges of partition. During colonial period, the necessity of spreading the messages of Pax-Britanica through the policy of constitutionalism demanded a semi-hegemonic foundation. Such a structure was based upon the bureaucracy, the erstwhile 'steel framework' of the British administration. It was rightly observed "At the centre of the benevolent despotism that British rule in the sub-continent adopted, the steel frame of the Indian civil service and in particular the figure of the district officer himself, the physical embodiment of Government along the Indian countryside."[105]

At the critical hour of partition the bureaucratic structure was severely crippled by deficiency in manpower strength. In the changed circumstances of the post Second World War, the Labour Government giving an indication of its final retreat, decided to stop all recruitments. In fact, ever since the end of the First World War, it had started reducing the recruitment of bureaucrats keeping in mind the ongoing reform process.

Besides the problem of depletion, efficiency of the bureaucracy was hampered by the sense of demoralisation creeping into it. The carrot and stick policy of the authority, adopted to counter the non-violent struggle of the nationalist force confused it a lot. The two-pronged policy wavering in between repression and conciliation lacked clear-cut direction. It created problems especially when the same set of bureaucrats had to implement both the policies. Such a dilemma had also arisen in the mid-thirties, when the officials who organised repression against the Civil Disobedience Movement, had to supervise the implementation of measures like the Gandhi-Irwin Pact (1931) and the Government of India Act (1935). It faced the apprehension of serving under those men, leading the provincial ministries. The likelihood of the return of the Congress to power continued to haunt the officials and weakened their morale. The then Governor of UP observed: "During the Congress regime officers were brought in contact with the Congress workers and possibly became friendly with them; it is only natural that they would be reluctant to take action against their former friends. But, apart from this, there is the fear of what their position will be if Congress returns to power."[106] The bureaucrats encountered a similar situation in 1945 when they faced the prospect of the Congress coming back to power against whom they had adopted severe repressive measures during the Quit India Movement. The structure deteriorated further during the war years and the long absence of its personnel from home. In fact, in the post-war situation, the slow and invidious decline of the Imperial authority made the bureaucrats apprehensive of their future. Vallabhbhai narrated the psychology: "But in the changed circumstance, Government machinery has become loose. Up till now, it was said that the Britishers will rule here forever, so bureaucracy used to work most sincerely. But the Sun of the British empire is setting, so the officers have now became slack"... I do not say that there are wrong persons, but officers think that they should not involve themselves in dispute."[107] Further, the replacement of the Oxford graduates and Second Officers in the Army with the grammar school and polytechnic boys not only changed the composition of the administrative structure but also reduced its influence. The policy of parity of the British officers with the Indians reached to such an extent that by 1945 the latter started outnumbering the former. It encouraged the permeation of emotionalism into the service and divided it on the issue of trial of the Indian National Army (INA), suppression of the Naval Mutiny, etc. Such a division put a question mark on its loyalty and reliability.

By the time of independence, the administrative wing of the Government had lost its unity of purpose. It had the British element which was keen on holding on to its position, the Muslims who did not want to remain in united India and considered that it was his religious duty and inviolable obligation to prepare the ground for Pakistan and the others who shared with the Congress the dream of a united India, but found themselves in a helpless situation. The apathetic attitude that the British officials adopted was basically to encash the political impasse. It emboldened the League a lot and converted the divided organisation into a pro-League one. The then Secretary of States and the Viceroy, admitted that it had become "more and more openly as if they were allied with the Muslim League."[108] In an atmosphere, surcharged with the effects of partition, the communal leanings on both the sides became quite obvious. Just prior to independence, in Bengal where the League Ministry was functioning, the Police appeared to be communally biased[109]. Even during the tenure of the Interim Government, Sir Gurunath Bewoor, a senior ICS Member in the Viceroy's Council revealed about the secret meetings of the Muslim ICS officials with the League members.[110] Over and above, the controversial stand adopted by A.S. Bokhari, the Director General of All India Radio, corroborated such leaning.[111] The trend was more apparent in provinces like the Punjab and UP

Weak Provincial Political Set-up

Vallabhbhai was challenged by the prevailing weak provincial political apparatus. In India, unlike the Princely States, the provincial set-up had started evolving since 1857. The policy of diarchy introduced in 1919 gave it a distinct shape. But the process of its indianisation began in the mid-thirties only after the assumption of office by the Congress. Yet Vallabhbhai found its growth to be inadequate due to the challenges posed by the British and the Muslim League prior to independence. The rising ambitions of the leaders and lowering of morale among the Congress workers further affected its performance after the liberation of the country.

Initially, the British administration tried to obstruct the elected provincial administration through the office of the Governor constituted under the 1935 Act for devolution of power. Central intervention became easy due to the non-implementation of the federal part of the Act and the non-committal attitude of the authority towards the assurance demanded by the Congress on non-interference. As anticipated, the Governors obstructed functioning of the government by trying to attend the Cabinet meetings, making contact with individual ministers and using veto power frequently. During this period, the role of Francis Wylie, the Governor of the Central Province, became controversial as he made alliance with the premiere N.B. Khare and helped him to dismiss three of his colleagues while deliberately keeping the Party High-Command in dark.[112] On other occasions, the Governors of Bengal, the Punjab, UP and Bihar, interfered in the release of political prisoners in order to embarrass the Provincial Congress Governments.[113] It was further confirmed when J.R. Dain, an I.C.S. Officer was appointed as the Governor of Orissa without consulting the provincial administration[114]. Vallabhbhai, tried to expose the strategy of the authority. He declared: "we had not lost anything by deciding to accept office as an experiment. We wanted to show that no transfer of real power has been made"[115]. Besides Central interference, efficiency of the Provincial political set-up was also hampered by the radical thinking of the Kishan Sabhas and Trade Unions.[116] Vallabhbhai found that overambitions on the part of the Congress workers in the provinces like the United Provinces threw a great challenge before the administration.[117] He observed: "There is no doubt that ambitions for personal position, squabbling for position of power have resulted in lowering the standard of our public office after acceptance of office".[118]

The Provincial Governments were also affected by the allegation of communal bias levelled by the Muslim League against the ruling Congress Party. Even though the allegation was denied by the authority, it put a question mark on the reliability of the Government.[119] The provincial units continued to be paralysed by the hawkish and biased attitude of the League Ministries. These governments were formed in 1942 in Sind, Assam, Bengal and North-West Frontier Province taking advantage of the vacuum created by the resignation of the Congress in 1939. Their intransigence became a potential threat to the Interim

Government. The situation further aggravated with the Muslim League gaining legitimacy in the election of 1946 and its subsequent entry into the Interim Government with the tacit support of the British authority. The provincial units remaining outside the purview of the Central Government became a headache for the Congress in the interim political set-up.[120] The virtual communalisation of the administrative machinery in the sensitive border states also posed major challenge to it. Moreover when Bihar was affected by communal riots in 1946, there was total disruption of the relief machinery in the Provincial Government.[121]

The provincial administration continued to be affected even after independence by the growing radical thinking in some parts of the country and the indiscipline within the ruling Congress party, manifested in the form of corruption and groupism. In states like West Bengal and Hyderabad, the immediate socio-economic transformation expected by the Communist party, created challenges for the administrative apparatus, still grappling with the problems of refugee influx, unemployment and the divisive elements like the *Razakars*. In the absence of effective administrative structures, the provincial units failed to cope with the challenges precipitated by the leaders raising strike phobia and spreading rumours. Besides violence, corruption too exposed the weakness of the provincial set-up in states like Bihar. The intervention of the Central Government in both the Molasses scandal and Bettiah Estate cases embarrassed the local administration a lot. Lastly, the resignation of Kripalani from the post of Congress President indicated the shifting of power equation from the party High Command to the Central Government. It weakened the grip of the Party over the Provinces and encouraged groupism in states like Uttar Pradesh and the Punjab. Observing the trend S.K. Patil, the member of the Bombay Legislature remarked: "It is very unfortunate that the Central Parliamentary Committee is not actively working. If that machinery were active, most of the things which happen in the Provinces and against which people have got a legitimate grievance, could have been avoided. In the absence of any direction from the Central Parliamentary Committee or the Working Committee, the Provincial Ministries everywhere are getting more and more autocratic[122]. Uttar Pradesh was the worst victim of it as the situation here became more complicated with the percolation of Nehru-Vallabhbhai ideological differences which led to the rift between GB Pant and Rafi Ahmed Kidwai, two prominent provincial Congress leaders. Subsequently induction of Kidwai from the province into the Central Cabinet polarised the party rank and file. Vallabhbhai found such groupism within the Congress a threat both to the Nation and the Provinces. In the Nasik Session (1950), he observed: "Organisationally, the Congress today is up against many dangers, but the greatest danger comes from within rather than from without. Sometime ago, some of our friends, with whom we had practically no ideological differences, parted company with us and chose to strike a different path. Today, we are threatened with what can be best described as group mentality constituting an actual or potential menace of disruption. Narrow parochial consideration of personal loyalty seems to rule out attachment and devolution to the sacred organisation to which we all have the honour to belong . . . . Adjustment between ministries and party organisation has been lacking. We do not seem to appreciate and understand that discipline is the very essence of democracy and mutual trust and confidence constitute the very life blood of a democratic organisation."[123] Vallabhbhai also found inter-provincial jealousies to be detrimental to the growth of Provinces. He criticised the narrow provincialism of Bengal and Hyderabad and warned them not to lose sight of the fact that all were parts of India.[124]

5.3.1.4 Threats of Aggressive Neighbours

Vallabhbhai found that the administrative set-up facing challenges from a set of aggressive neighbours like Pakistan, China, Nepal, Burma, etc. The planned tribal invasion, refugee influx, arms trading etc. put a lot of strain on the administration of the nascent state in particular and its very existence in general.

The very basis of partition had created a lot of tension in between India and Pakistan. The Government of India was upset over the lack of cooperation by Pakistan in the rehabilitation of refugees. The eviction of the Hindus from the West Punjab and East Bengal created law and order situations particularly in Delhi. It also put pressure on the overall public distribution system of the country. The delay in payment of 55 crore of rupees to Pakistan due to the latter's apparent involvement in the tribal invasion of Kashmir, widened the rift between the two countries. The report of the Defence Minister on the military preparation of Pakistan made Vallabhbhai highly critical of its intention.[125] Indo-Pak relation further deteriorated over the sharing of river water. The prospect of reduction of water supply due to the construction of the Bakhra and Harike dams adversely affected relations between the two countries. Over and above, the unilateral devaluation of rupee hastily done by India to overcome the currency imbalance with England was not reciprocated by Pakisthan. It caused heavy financial loss to India. It led to immediate price rise of essential commodities in India at a crucial point of time when after partition its industries were deprived of the smooth supply of raw materials from areas falling under the jurisdiction of Pakistan. It also compelled the country to bear a loss of 90 crores of the 300 crores dues from Pakistan. India's scarce resources were further strained because of the deployment of army in Hyderabad and Junagarh to suppress the divisive forces, operating under the Pakistani guidance. The complicity of Pakistan became clear with the fleeing away of Mir Laik Ali, the erstwhile Prime Minister of Hyderabad and the Nawab of Junagarh from India to that country. It clearly established the latter's involvement in India's internal matter and generated a lot tension between the two countries. Vallabhbhai was also quite perturbed over the aloof attitude of the Government of Sri Lanka, towards the Indians living there.[126]

Though, Vallabhbhai was very often criticised for being unable to think internationally,[127] yet he was the first to apprehend the Chinese ambition in 1950. The annexation of Tibet, a peace loving buffer zone, situated in between India and China made him weary of the latter. Expressing his concern he said: "The political ambition of the Chinese by themselves might not have mattered so much: but when they are combined with discontent in these areas, absence of close contact with Indians and Communist ideology, the difficulty of the position increases manifold."[128] Vallabhbhai expressed his displeasure over India's hasty recognition of the Government of Mao-Tse-Tung and the invasion of North Korea over the South Korea. He found the Chinese aggression in Tibet was part of a calculated strategy for the emergence of a determined, and ruthless power. In this given situation, he observed the fluid condition in Nepal, Sikkim and Bhutan to be highly dangerous. These countries which were traditionally supporters of India were getting alienated from it due to the latter's push for democratisation.[129] Vallabhbhai found that the instability in the border areas led to rise in refugee influx and arms trade which threatened the already vulnerable law and order situation of the country.

5.3.2 Remedial Measures

Administrative effectiveness is dependent largely upon the close interaction between politics and administration. Despite his lack of any formal administrative training, Vallabhbhai tried to establish relationship between the two. Hence, it was rightly observed: "What made Vallabhbhai a great political administrator, ...was his study of details, his knowledge of facts, combined with a deep insight, width of outlook and long range of vision."[130] Truly speaking, the *Patidar* sense of pragmatism, Vaishnovite humanism, sturdy peasant upbringing and exposure to legal intricacies enabled him to be a natural administrator.[131] So, he was recognised by Nehru as the 'strongest pillar' in the Cabinet.[132] V.P. Menon, his assistant in the Department of States said: "When he (Vallabhbhai) took over the Home Ministry in 1946, he had no experience even as a Provincial Minister. Yet he showed at once a clear grasp of the essentials of administration. He knew how to exercise power and how to deal with men. He would have each problem fully discussed hearing all sides and would then take his decision. Once taken, everybody knew, it was final. He assigned a man his responsibility and then left his job to him and everybody did his best because he could count on him being upheld"[133]. During his short tenure as a Minister, he faced a number of administrative challenges threatening the survival of the Nation–State. But he met them successfully and created conditions for the political system to work smoothly and efficiently. He envisaged some important remedial measures such as reorientation of the Cabinet, reconstitution of the bureaucracy and police, reorganisation of the provincial wing of the Congress Party, reshaping the Army and rejuvenating the socio-economic groups of the society.

5.3.2.1 Reorientation of the Cabinet

Vallabhbhai was deeply aggrieved over the dissensions in the cabinet in general and on his own differences with Jawaharlal Nehru, the Prime Minister in particular. Given his bitter experience in the Interim Government, he was very much keen to restore team spirit in the new Cabinet formed after independence. Born and brought up in a joint family, the spirit of mutual understanding was very much in his blood. Once advising his children Maniben and Dayabhai to give space to others both inside and outside the family, he had advised that it was natural to be disunited, but to expose disunity to the outside world was a blunder.[134] Such faith in expediency enabled him to give way to Nehru to become the Party President in 1929, 1936, 1939 and 1946, though he had enough strength at the party level to assume the office. His decision, which was appreciated by Gandhi as a reflection of least 'Parliamentary ambition,[135] helped the party to a large extent to unite itself against the rising influence of the Socialist wing. This was subsequently adhered to by him in the Interim Government for the smooth running of the coalition ministry. Liaquat Ali Khan, the First Finance Member admitted: "He (Vallabhbhai) always meant what he said and said what he meant."[136] In fact, it was this trait in him which prevented many communication gaps between him and the Muslim League.

Vallabhbhai's accommodative approach also helped him to contribute to the smooth management of the Government in independent India. He was instrumental in bringing the Cabinet proclamation on joint responsibility. He argued: "History will not say that a particular minister failed. It will say that the Government as a whole has failed.... Therefore, every one of us must exert himself to the utmost and give the best of him freely to the cause."[137] Despite his differences with Nehru on issues such as the economic policy, refugee rehabilitation, state integration etc., he extended whole-hearted support to the latter at the time of any national crises. He reposed full confidence in Nehru at the time of the assassination of Gandhi and said: "We have been life long comrades in a common cause. The paramount interest of the country and our mutual love and regard, transcending such differences of outlook and temperaments as existed have held us together. Both of us have stuck passionately to our respective point of views, of methods of work; still we have always sustained a unity of heart, which has stood many a stress and strain and which has enabled us to function jointly both in the Congress and in the Government."[138] It was the same approach which encouraged him to stand like a rock behind Nehru when rows of ministers tendered resignation on the issue of the Nehru-Liaquat pact, signed for the rehabilitation of refugees. He also supported the Government to cope with the food crisis, created partly due to the separation of Burma and Pakistan and partly for the profit motive of the business class trying to take advantage of the newly introduced policy of decontrol. In an attempt to find solution, he not only suggested restoring the public distribution system but also took initiative to influence Nehru to sign an agreement with the United States to obtain a loan for India to enable it to import wheat.

Vallabhbhai's concern for collective responsibility made him cautious with regard to his role as the Deputy Prime Minister of India. He was quite candid to admit: "I have been referred to as the Deputy Prime Minister. I never think in those terms. Our own leader is Jawaharlal Nehru. Bapu has appointed him as his successor . . . . It is the duty of all to carry out his request".[139] In the absence of Nehru, he managed the office of the Prime Minister at ease. However, he was in constant touch to avoid any communication gap. He assured Nehru: "You need not be in a hurry to come back. We shall arrange that the first few days of the Assembly are devoted to comparatively unimportant business, so that the business of the Assembly need not worry you at all".[140] During this period, he justified his warnings given to colleagues such as John Mathai, the Railway Minister on lapses in supplies to the refugees. He argued: "I have sufficient sense of responsibility to realise that as such I have no business save in my capacity as the Prime Minister of the Cabinet with a joint responsibility to express myself in relation to the duties and functions of another Ministry. But as Deputy Prime Minister, it has fallen to me, in the absence of the Prime Minister to coordinate in Delhi the various measures being taken for the evacuation and relief of refugees."[141] Even Mathai himself appreciated Vallabhbhai's sincerity. He admitted: ". . . . The only time when the Indian Cabinet really functioned was when Nehru away in Washington for a few weeks, towards the end of October 1948 and when Sardar Patel was acting as the Prime Minister. For the first time, the Cabinet functioned with joint responsibility and the acting Prime Minister conducted the meetings as the British Prime Minister would have."[142] It was further confirmed by N.V. Gadgil, another Cabinet colleague who revealed that Vallabhbhai even in his death bed sought assurance on joint responsibility from him so as to enable the Government a smooth sailing even after his death.[143]

Vallabhbhai recognised the individual contribution for the success of a team. He never emphasised upon collective responsibility at the cost of individual initiative. In fact, he did not hesitate to define the authority of the Prime Minister. He emphatically argued: "The Prime Minister's position, according to my conception is certainly pre-eminent; he is first among equals. But, he has no over-riding power over his colleagues; if he had any, a cabinet and cabinet responsibility would be superfluous. In my view, the Prime Minister as the leader of the party and head of the whole administration is inevitably concerned that Cabinet decisions are effective and that there is no conflict between one ministry and another. But the entire responsibility for implementing the policy of Government rests upon the ministers and ministries under them which are concerned with the subject matter of the Cabinet decisions . . . . I feel sure that this position of the Prime Minister not only safeguards his pre-eminence and makes him effective head of administration, but is also fully in accord with the democratic principles and rules of ministerial and Cabinet responsibility."[144] He felt it was his obligation as a Cabinet Minister to restrain the Prime Minister wherever required. He reacted against various decisions of Nehru on issues such as the deployment of H.V.R. Iengar the Home Secretary to review the law and order situation in Ajmer without due consultation with the Home Minister and the initiative to constitute a Cabinet coordination Committee.[145] He resisted the appointment of Mirza Ismail as an Ambassador as the Cabinet was kept in dark.[146] He convinced Nehru against inclusion of the controversial reservation provisions for Muslims in the Nehru-Liaquat Ali Pact.[147] He countered when Nehru asserted that "Cabinet or no Cabinet so long as I am the Prime Minister, I will carry out my policy."[148] He differed from Nehru and supported N.V. Gadgil in referring the taxation proposal (1949) to a sub-committee for reconsideration.[149] Vallabhbhai's efforts made the first Cabinet adhere to the principle of collective responsibility to a large extent. In fact, Gadgil confirms, "My five years of experience in the Cabinet is that no one would say a word against Nehru. While Vallabhbhai was alive, he (Nehru) used to consult him. After his death the Maulana and myself were the only senior colleagues of Nehru left and it is an accepted practice in Parliamentary democracy to consult senior colleagues. I do not think Nehru consulted any one.[150] It was corroborated by Geofrey Tyson who held Vallabhbhai to be responsible for restraining Nehru and infusing the spirit of collective responsibility which started waning after the death of the latter.[151]

5.3.2.2 Reconstitution of the Bureaucracy and the Police

The challenges of communal tension, disintegration and refugee rehabilitation put a lot of strain on the law and order situation of the country. Vallabhbhai preferred strengthening the existing administrative structures like the Bureaucracy and police more instead of creating a new one. It was rightly observed: "Though revolutionary in his fight against the foreign rule, Sardar Patel was no believer in abrupt change; progress by evolution was really his motto. And so, although in August 1947, power changed hand and with it the spirit of administration, the machinery of Government was preserved. As the Home Minister and Minister of States, Sardar had a double task; conservative in the good sense of the word in what had been the provinces in the old India creative in the Indian states."[152] Keeping in view the prevailing chaotic condition of the country he preferred the continuation of the bureaucracy even with its earlier image. He felt the need for its restructuring due to its tailor-made colonial character, growing depletion and large scale migration. As the Home Minister, he adopted both short and long term measures to create an efficient and dependable administrative set-up.

Vallabhbhai's conviction in making the bureaucracy a 'permanent machinery' especially at the time of crisis encouraged him to work for its revival and indianisation. In fact, he had started realising it since 1920 to make it an instrument to check the high-handedness of the British officials. He observed: "If certain British posts are replaced with Indian posts in the administrative machine, it is not going to make any difference... So long as the whole system is not changed and the Government of India is not run for the benefit of the Indians, no improvement is possible.[153] In line with this conviction, Vallabhbhai as the Chairman of the Parliamentary Board and subsequently as an important member of the Interim Government gave top priority to absorb the Indians in the services.[154] He became firm on it with the complete withdrawal of the British power. He argued:

"Unlike the Indian Civil Service, which was neither Indian nor Civil, the Indian Administrative Service marks the beginning of an all India service, officered entirely by Indians and subject completely to Indian control and the service will now be free to or will have to adopt its true role of national service without being trammeled by traditions and habits of the past."[155] Accordingly, the employees keen on leaving India, were offered the option to retire with proportionate pension and compensation for the loss of career. Though he approved the appointment of Sir Bertie Staig, as the Auditor General of India, yet he urged John Mathai, the Railway Minister to absorb only those Europeans, interested to serve the country without any extra incentives.[156] Thus, he tried to bring a sense of commitment in the services. Concerned about the apparently communal composition of the service,[157] he asked the employees to leave who had no loyalty towards the country. But, he did not give such liberty to any Indian employees as he believed: "I do not see any individual officer should expect or ask for an appeal from one to render to the country what they owe to it."[158] A system of over-age recruitment process was followed as per the recommendation of the Gorwala Committee to fill up the vacuum in the services and to avoid the gap which might crop up after the beginning of the regular process of appointment. Priority was given to the personnel of demobilised armed forces, known for their tremendous loyalty to the country.

Vallabhbhai's faith in the service was further enhanced because of its efficiency, shown at a time when the country was passing through a tough period of transition. He confessed: "I am speaking with a sense of heavy responsibility and I must confess that in point of patriotism, in point of loyalty, in point of sincerity and in point of ability one can not have a substitute... I want to place on record that if during the last two or three years most of the members of the services had not behaved particularly and with loyalty, the Union would have collapsed."[159] With this mindset, it was quite natural on his part to think of a long-term plan to have a regular, permanent bureaucratic structure. He felt it was necessary to involve the provinces for the creation of an efficient and permanent bureaucracy which would meet the challenges of balkanisation as well as diversities. In the conference of the Provincial Premiers he succeeded in influencing them in favour of a uniform, merit-oriented pattern of appointment of civil servants to be made regularly by an independent body like Federal Public Service Commission with due provision for upgradation of some of the provincial employees into the Central cadre. He also gave the assurance of consulting the corresponding state in case of removal of any such employee posted therein. To enhance the efficiency of the bureaucracy, a training school was initiated for the first batch of IAS in the Metcalfe House in New Delhi. A committee was constituted under the supervision of John Mathai to find out the ways and means for reorganisation of the staff in the Secretariat. He not only appealed for a better pay scale for the bureaucrats but also warned against making frequent changes in it.[160].

Vallabhbhai believed that an efficient, disciplined and contented service was the *sine qua non* of sound administration under a democratic regime. So he took initiative to give them constitutional protection against legislative interference[161]. He was instrumental in the Constituent Assembly to introduce Article 283-A for it.[162] Article 311 was introduced to protect the bureaucrats from the whims of politicians and Article 314 was brought to protect the privileges of the civil servants. He believed that such provisions though given as per the Indian Independence Act would make the service more confident. Such foresight reflected the realistic approach of the leader. Besides the legislative interference, Vallabhbhai also argued against ministerial interference to ensure security in the services. He said: "The key to efficient administration is the sense of security in the service at the top and non-interference by Congressmen or other people connected either with the Congressmen or with the ministers in the administration. The ministers should not give orders to any subordinate officers and they must deal with them through their superiors."[163] During his tenure as a minister, he tried to adhere to it to the best possible extent. He admitted. "My secretary can write a note . . . . oppose to my views. I have given that freedom to all my secretaries. I have told them, if you do not give your honest opinion for the fear that it will displease your Minister, than please you should better go.[164] True to his conviction that a democratic Government was dependent upon the balance between the minister and the civil servant, Vallabhbhai insisted upon H.V.R. Iengar, his Home Secretary to give opinion on the state reorganisation, allowed V.P. Menon, the Secretary of States to publish the draft of the Instrument of Accession, permitted C.D. Deshmukh the Finance Secretary to make investigation on the defaulters of Income Tax and supported H.M. Patel, the Secretary for the Partition Council regarding the decision on division of assets with Pakistan.[165] He reacted against Nehru's suggestion of dismissing officers without evidence for abetting communal violence[166]. He also supported N. Bakshi, an I.A.S. officer in Bihar in making investigation in the Molasses scandal and Bettiah loot case in which some of the politicians of the state were apparently involved. When communal riot broke out in Ajmer, Nehru was supposed to visit the affected area. But in the last moment he cancelled his visit and deputed the Home Secretary H.V.R. Iengar. Vallabhbhai argued with Nehru over the sending of Ienger to Ajmer, while Shankar Prasad, the Chief Commissioner of Ajmer-Mewar had already reviewed the situation there. Defending the officer, he said: "Shankar Prasad is one of the ablest officers in U.P. whose efficiency and honesty and impartiality are beyond reproach . . . . Your sending Iengar to Ajmer was not right and its reaction on the public mind as well as on the mind of the officer concerned cannot be far from desirable."[167] Vallabhbhai reposed full faith in the officers and gave them full freedom to carry out their duties. H.V.R. Ienger himself admitted: "The Sardar expected those whom he trusted with responsibility to exercise the discretionary powers, rested in them to the full and he left them with no doubt that he would back them to the full, accepting responsibility himself if anything went wrong and giving full credit to them when things went well."[168]

Vallabhbhai was in favour of assuring protection to the Bureaucracy to enable it to function efficiently. But he urged sparing use of such privileges. As such the protections were restricted for the personnel of all-India service only to enable them to maintain stability.[169] He also expected from the bureaucrats certain commitments towards the society. He urged them: "It will be your bounden duty to treat the common men in India as your own or to put it correctly to feel yourself to be one of them and amongst them and you will have to learn not to despise or to disregard them. In other words, you will have to adapt yourselves to democratic way of administration."[170] It was this responsibility that made Vallabhbhai realise the necessity of a code of conduct for the Civil Servants. He could hardly forget the havoc created by the British officers in the Punjab at the time of independence. His fear about the presence of black sheep in the services made him resolve about the need of such a code. He advised them to be above party politics. He appealed: "I would advise you to maintain to the utmost the impartiality and incorruptibility of administration. A civil servant can not afford to and must not take part in politics. Nor must he involve himself in communal wrangles. To depart from the path of rectitude in either of these respects is to debase public service and to lower the dignity."[171] He introduced a bill in the Central Assembly, even prior to independence to regulate the public servants against corruptions which were on the rise because of the war conditions and inadequate legislative measures.[172] He also supported the measures taken by the Bombay Government to keep the public servants aloof from communal organisations.[173]

Vallabhbhai thought of reorganising the police force to bring the communal and fissiparous tendencies under control. At the time of independence, it was found that the problem of communalisation, lack of discipline and infrastructure and frequent interference had made the Police an ineffective body. Moreover, tension in the borders put a lot of strain on the law and order situation and compelled him to change his earlier conviction in the necessity of a low profile police officer.

Looking at the problems, Vallabhbhai worked for the integration of the police force of the Princely States with the Provinces. He urged the provinces to be self-sufficient in forces. The Central Reserve Police Force was created to replace the earlier Crown Representative Force to take care of the law and order situation without depending upon the army.[174] He worked for the proper training and modernisation of the forces which included increase in the number and provision of outfits, arms, communication and equipments.[175] He extended full support to the police force for resorting to firing to tackle the mob especially during strikes.[176] Again, he backed Randhwa, the Deputy Commissioner of Police in Delhi to stall his untimely transfer, particularly at a time when the city was seized with communal violence just after independence.[177] While reacting against the attack on the police force, deployed to maintain law and order, Vallabhbhai appealed to the people to extend cooperation to them to ensure the minimum use of force and survival of democracy. He said: ". . . . that a democratic Government cannot function on the basis of a police state. It can only function on the willing consent and cooperation of the people. In no other sphere is the cooperation of the public more needed than in the field work of the police, whether it is in connection with the prevention and detection of crime or while dealing with unruly mobs of recalcitrant assemblies of men . . . . I warn you that if we can not give the police the respect and position that is due to them as police of a free country, we should loose our freedom."[178] Besides this, he wanted to groom an effective intelligence network as a support mechanism to the police. So he insisted upon the removal of the European domination and communal biases in it and urged for its proper training.[179]

5.3.2.3 Reorganisation of the Party

Vallabhbhai had great hopes and expectations from the party. He believed that it had to play a responsible role in thwarting the British designs in the provinces. So he laid great emphasis on its reorganisation. As the Chairman of the Parliamentary Board in the mid-thirties he had issued directions to the Congress premiers to avoid the Governors and to carry out administration as promised at the time of the election. He had supported the Tripuri Congress Resolution (1939), which advocated for close coordination between the Congress Party and the Congress ministries in the states. Vallabhbhai as the Chairman of the Congress Parliamentary Sub-Committee did not hesitate to take action against the Ministers of Central Province and Bombay facing changes of corruption in order to discipline the party at the provincial level.[180] Being part of the Interim Government, he extended full support to the Provincial Governments like the Central Province of Assam against British interference. He appealed to the police personnel directly in the Central Province and Bihar to support the Provincial Governments and incurred the displeasure of Sir Philip Leasure, the Inspector General of Police.[181] As the Home Member, he dared to confront the Governor-General by supporting the Government of Assam on the issue of the eviction of unauthorised squatting.[182] He also came to the rescue of the Bihar Government during the communal riot by extending all necessary help.[183]

But after independence, Vallabhbhai could hardly rely upon the Central Party High Command to gear up the provincial administration. With the change in power equation, the Party had not only been converted into an election conducting machinery, but also became a victim of ideological dissension. The three crucial elections for the post of the Party President, conducted in between 1947 to 1950 and the rift-ridden party sessions in Meerut (1946) and Nasik (1950), were proof of its decline. Vallabhbhai realised that with such bickerings the Party could hardly take care of the provinces like Assam, Uttar Pradesh, Bihar and the Punjab which were affected by growing indiscipline and corruption. All these had tremendous bearing upon the law and order situation. Hence, he felt the necessity of direct intervention when necessary. He argued: "As far as possible to look after the country we have been doing our best to influence the provinces by moral pressures as well as by the intimate contact I have with all the provincial ministers and leaders as a result of a very long period of comradership."[184] He appealed to the Provincial Congress Governments to have cordial relationship with the Governors appointed by the Central Government.[185] He justified the central supervision to be "essentially in the nature of a safety valve."[186] He not only rebuked the Bihar Government for the Molasses scandal but also demanded a report from it. He warned: "It is amasing that such a thing should have happened in such an unseemly fashion. If the evil is as expensive and as high placed, your Government should have dealt with the matter drastically before it becomes public . . . . I should very much like you to send me an immediate report on the above matter."[187] Even during the process of state integration he supervised the formation of the Provincial Governments in Madhya Bharat, Vindhya Pradesh and Patiala and East Punjab States Union (PEPSU). He warned them of central intervention in case of their failure to ensure stability.[188]

Vallabhbhai was also in favour of giving independence to the provinces to solve their local problems, whenever it was possible. After independence, he advised the local Congress units in UP, Bihar and Bengal to ignore petty rivalries and to solve their own problems without depending upon external intervention. The Nehru-Patel difference also had its impact in the Provinces like U.P. where the local unit was split into two factions led by Rafi Ahmed Kidwai and Govind Vallabh Pant. Kidwai used to seek Nehru's help regularly even on petty issues. Vallabhbhai was worried over its impact on Provincial administration. He advised the Provincial leaders to avoid such practices. He argued: "we also seem to forget the elementary principle that day-to-day administration can not be conducted satisfactorily by constant interference from outside and that the responsibility for administration must ultimately rest with those who having the confidence of the majority are charged with that responsibility."[189] He urged the local Congress ministry to absorb long existing dissention within itself. While dissuading M.S. Hasan, a Minister of Central Province, he warned: "In any case it is up to you to restore the confidence... Otherwise it would be impossible to work with a sense of joint responsibility, which is essential for the working of a ministry."[190] He advised the Bengal Congress unit to have sufficient patience at a time of crisis to bear with the shortcomings of the new incumbent.[191] Vallabhbhai also wanted the provincial Congress units of Bihar and the Punjab to be organised in order to withstand the undue interference of Governors as expressed through their demands to examine individual files or to preside over the meetings of the provincial ministries.[192] Given his concern for the provinces, he expressed his lack of interest in bringing the Provincial Ministers like Rafi Ahmed Kidwai, H.K. Mahatab and K.M. Munshi to the Central Cabinet as he believed it might unsettle the political life at the local level.[193]

Reshaping of the Army

Vallabhbhai was highly conscious of the law and order situation in the country which was very often affected by the tension prevailing in the neighbouring countries and the unfriendly attitude of the big powers. He realised that in the long run it would affect the stability of the Nation–State. Although in the pre-independence period, he had advocated for the least use of armed forces, yet subsequently, he emphasised upon the rebuilding of the armed force because of the changes in the geo-political scenario.[194] Hence he argued: "The Congress is not against keeping National Army for the country's defence . . . . A few people in the Congress believe in the absolute Ahimsa of Gandhiji and if the Congress were to consist of only people believing in the absolute Ahimsa of Gandhi, it would reduce itself to a body consisting of very few individuals."[195]

The realisation of the importance of the army encouraged Vallabhbhai to think of its reorganisation. Given the sensitive nature of its responsibility, he first emphasised upon its indianisation to make it a 'national institution' in the true sense of the term.[196] During the colonial period, the Indian Army was mostly dominated by the members from the Muslim community.[197] Hence, at the time of the partition, as an important member of the Partition Council, he wanted a proper distribution of the armed personnel between India and Pakistan. The personnel were given the option to choose the country they wanted to serve. Later he insisted on giving it a secular look. He argued: "there should be no difference between the Hindus, Sikhs and Muslims amongst the forces. It should be so in the whole of India, but more so in the armed forces."[198] Vallabhbhai advocated for the disbanding of the outlived units like the Maharastra Field Regiment.[199] He also supported the proper merger of the armed forces of the states into the Indian Army to bring uniformity in the services.[200] By Army, he referred to all the three branches like the Army, Air force and Navy. He came to know the efficiency and utility of the first two during the Kashmir and Hyderabad Military operations. Also the need to protect the long coastline of India made him realise the importance of the Navy.[201] While inaugurating the Armed Force Academy in Dehradun, he highlighted the significance of an integrated armed force.[202] He also encouraged the training programmes to be given by experienced British personnel even after independence.[203] He supported the creation of industries to cater to the needs of such a big armed force in the country.[204] He insisted that to counter the possible attack from countries like China, the army should be trained to make constant evaluation of itself, and be well-equipped with an efficient intelligence network and sufficient supply of arms and ammunitions.[205] Lastly, Vallabhbhai wanted to infuse qualities like discipline, unity, camaraderie etc. in the armed forces to make it committed for the cause of the Nation. He urged the armed personnel: ". . . . You must grow a healthy secular outlook which is the foundation of true democracy and that unshakable loyalty to the principles on which that democracy must rest."[206] Further, to ensure the independence of the services he warned against using it for maintenance of the day-to-day law and order which would affect its integrity and independence in the long run.[207]

Rejuvenation of Socio-economic Groups

Vallabhbhai depended largely on the state to implement various agendas of nation-building. A man with a pragmatic orientation, he understood the relevance of different socio-economic groups and the important role they would play in stabilising the Nation–State. He declared: "I admire institutions which believe in self-help because it is indirectly performing the work of services to the Nations."[208] He had utilised the integrative value of the caste groups during the freedom struggle. Later on, he not only urged for the grass roots devolution of power, but also expected the local bodies to be self-reliant as far as possible.[209] He encouraged the socio-economic organisations to contribute to the nation building activities by assisting the authority in the implementation of various developmental projects, raising the standard of health and education, maintenance of law and order and undertaking of relief measures. His intention was to develop these organisations as support mechanism and relieve the state from certain responsibilities in order to make it more efficient during the transition period.

On Economic Planning

Vallabhbhai's policy of guarded nationalisation substantiated his keenness to involve groups other than the state in the economic planning.[210] He pursued it further in the absence of proper infrastructure and Government machinery. So he gave more importance to creation rather than taking over of the industries.[211] The 1948 Industrial Policy Resolution contained some of his ideas on economic planning. The Resolution reflected his lack of faith in the centralised planning structure and his inclination for a balanced growth of both the public and private sectors. He argued: "A government, which engages itself in trading activities will come to a grief. The essential function of the Government is to ensure increased production and fair distribution of available resources... In both industries and trade, there was a limit in which the Government could go as far as commitments were concerned. Therefore, it was essentially the function of the private enterprise to step in."[212] In fact, he appreciated the Scindia Group of industries for making significant contribution in the field of shipping.[213] Besides the private sector, Vallabhbhai also welcomed individual initiative, rendered through the cooperative societies. Even prior to independence, he had supported the growth of the village industries associations and institutions like the Anand Dairy Farm. He wanted to develop cooperative spirit among people through the system of education.[214] He was in favour of promoting *Khadi* as a mark of self-sufficiency.[215] He appreciated the efforts of the Vedchhi Ashrama and the Charkha Sangha for production of *Khadi* and contributing to some extent to tide over the cloth crisis which the country was facing immediately after independence.[216] Thus, his vision not only created opportunities for self-help but also provided enough scope for increase in productivity and thereby helped the Government tide over the administrative challenges which emerged as a result of the severe food crisis and the problem of revenue deficit.

On Maintenance of Law and Order

The mammoth task of maintaining law and order in the country encouraged Vallabhbhai to look beyond the Government. He realised the significance of various voluntary groups for the purpose. He asked the Provinces to create the Prantiya Raksha Dal which not only helped to restore discipline but also prevented the unemployed youth from going astray.[217] He appreciated the collaboration between the Press Trust of India, the non-official news agency and the Reuters and hoped that it would disseminate correct information and help the authority in maintaining law and order.[218]

On Health

Vallabhbhai appeared to be keen on the development of infrastructures in the health sector with private initiative. Even prior to independence, he encouraged the growth of private institutions like Arogya Bhawan and Sheth Vadilal Sarabhai

General Hospital. Later on, he endorsed the appeal of the Health Minister of India for private charity.[219] Many times he expressed gratitude to the industrialists for developing medical centres to assist the authority in spreading health facilities to the rural areas. He argued: "To maintain peace internally the country should have institutions to render service to the community, but these institutions should be created only by public endeavour. When the country was under foreign rule, we had developed the habit of looking up to the Government to create these things, but now that we had become independent, we should cease to think on such lines. In England and other foreign countries the people helped themselves in these matters."[220] Thus, the engagement of the private sector in developing health facilities provided a great relief to the Government gruelling under innumerable challenges immediately after the partition of the country.

On Education

Vallabhbhai encouraged the involvement of private groups in the field of education as long as the basic purpose of 'national reconstruction' was not diluted. In the pre-independence period he promoted organisations like the Kelavani Mandal and Gujarat Vidyapitha to infuse national ethos. In the subsequent period he motivated the Charotar Education Society and the Vedchhi Ashram for the same purpose. He was in favour of the social organisations playing an important role at least in the growth of infrastructures, needed by these educational institutions.[221] His long cherished vision was to develop an effective system of education that would infuse a sense of commitment among the youth and motivate them to counter the divisive forces.

On Rehabilitation of Distressed People

Vallabhbhai supported the social organisations who were working for upliftment of the society. He appreciated the role of the Jyoti Sangha and Kanya Ashrama in spreading education among girls and helping the backward communities.[222] He also commended the role of the Kasturba Trust in opening avenues for the widows and spreading education among women in rural areas.[223] He did not hesitate to involve voluntary organisations in providing relief to the people affected by natural calamities to enable the Government to look after the safety and security of the country. He appealed to the voluntary organisations to look after the relief work of the draught affected people of Saurastra. Highlighting their importance he said: "As we have our own Government, now if the officers are good and efficient they can render good service to the people. But, the public workers can do a lot in comparison to the limited capacity of the Government officials. So, our workers should make the maximum use of all Government assistance."[224]

5.4 The Emerging Pattern

Vallabhbhai played a key role in various nation building activities. His conviction in the capability of the state motivated him to show keen interest in the evolution of a representative constitutional framework not only to ensure a sense of unity but also to contain the authority within a definite framework of law. He headed various Sub-committees in the Constituent Assembly and was instrumental for the incorporation of provisions like the Fundamental Rights, rights for the Minorities and an Independent Judiciary in the Constitution. Obviously, his efforts revealed his democratic inclination.

Vallabhbhai also accorded tremendous importance to the problem of integration of the Nation–State. He was one of the first leaders who could anticipate the British design of balkanising the country. Hence, he opted for the Ministry of Home and States to convince the rulers of the Princely States to join with India. He could win over the Princes by making them realise their waning influence, offering them lucrative 'Privy Purse', and by using the good offices of many influential people. Force as a technique was used sparingly as the last resort only in case of Kashmir, Junagarh and Hyderabad. The process of centralisation helped him to ensure unity especially in the phase of transition. Thus, he played a key role in the emotional integration of the country and facilitated the evolution of a united and strong Indian Nation–State.

Vallabhbhai created an efficient administrative machinery to ensure the stability of the newly created Nation–State. A true nationalist, he was worried about Cabinet dissension, the indifferent bureaucracy, the corrupt-ridden and inexperienced provincial political set-up and the hostility of some of the neighbours. The consequent problems of law and order produced a threat to refugee rehabilitation and affected the economic development of the country. In this context, Vallabhbhai's endeavour to infuse a spirit of collective responsibility in the Cabinet, develop an effective and well-regulated bureaucratic and police machinery with proper accountability, revive the sense of confidence of the Party workers in the Provinces, indianise and discipline the Army, reflected his democratic mindset. He was in favour of providing sufficient space to various socio-economic groups to share the nation building burden and thereby make the Government more effective. All these bold initiatives suggested and taken by Vallabhbhai unveiled the foresight of a true nation builder.

Notes and References

1. *The Times of India*, 7 April, 1947.

2 David Hardiman, *Peasant Nationalists of Gujarat: 1917-34* (New Delhi: Oxford, 1981, p. 44). V.B. Kulkarni, *The Indian Triumvirate: A Political Biography of Gandhi-Patel-Nehru* (Bombay: Bharatiya Vidya Bhavan, 1969, p. 263).

3. G.M. Nandurkar (ed.), *Sardarshri na Patro,*Vol. IV (Ahmedabad: 1976).

4. *Bombay Chronicle*, 29 December, 1939.

5. *Ibid.*, 29 July, 1942.

6. P.N. Chopra (ed.), *The Collected Works of Sardar Vallabhbhai Patel*, Vol. X (New Delhi: Konark Publishers Pvt. Ltd., 1997, p. 229).

7. B. Shiva Rao,"Sardar Patel and the Constitution", in Verinder Grover (ed.) *Political Thinkers of Modern India*, Vol. 18 (New Delhi: Deep and Deep Publications, 1992, p. 400).

8. P.N. Chopra, *The Sardar of India* (New Delhi: Allied Publishers, 1995, p. 277).
9. *Constituent Assembly Debates*, 29 April, 1947.
10. *Ibid.*, 30 April, 1947.
11. *Ibid*, 29 April, 1947.
12. *Ibid.*
13. G.M. Nandurkar (ed.) *This was Sardar: The Commemorative Volume* (Ahmedabad: 1974, p. 143).
14. *Constituent Assembly Debates*, 29 April, 1947.
15. *Ibid.*, 2 May, 1947.
16. *Ibid.*
17. *Ibid., 30* August, 1947.
18. *Ibid.*, 26 May, 1949.
19. *Ibid.*, 1 May, 1947.
20. *Bombay Chronicle*, 25 February, 1931.
21. *Constituent Assembly Debates*, 27 August, 1947.
22. *Ibid.*, 25 May, 1947.
23. *Ibid.*, 27 April, 2947.
24. *Ibid.*, 1 May, 1947.
25. *Ibid.*, 27 August, 1947.
26. *Ibid.*,
27. *Ibid.*, 25 May, 1949.
28. *Ibid.*, 26 May, 1949.
29. *Gujarat Samachar*, 2 October, 1934. *Ibid.*, 9 January, 1935.
30. *Constituent Assembly Debates*, 12 October, 1949.
31. *Ibid.*, 15 July, 1947.
32. *Ibid.*, 12 October, 1949.
33. V. Shankar (ed.), Sardar Patel's Select Correspondence, Vol. 2 (Ahmedabad: Navajivan, 1976, p. 428).
34. *Constituent Assembly Debates*, 15 July, 1947.
35. Vallabhbhai Patel to O.P. Ramaswamy Reddy, 12 December, 1947 in

V. Shankar (ed.), *Sardar Patel: Select Correspondence* (1945-50), Vol. 2 (Ahmedabad: Navajivan, 1976, p. 435).

36. Rafiq Zakaria, *Sardar Patel and Indian Muslims* (Bombay: Bharatiya Vidya Bhavan, 1996, p. 95).
37. G.M. Nandurkar (ed.), *Sardar's Letters Mostly Unknown*, Post-Centenary Vol. I (Ahmedabad: Navajivan, 1980, p. 90).
38. Sir William Lee Warner, *The Native States of India* (London: Macmillan, 1960, p. 31).
39. Navajivan, 7 April, 1929.
40. In the late thirties many Princely States in India witnessed the Prajamandal Movements which were launched by the local leaders against the atrocious rulers and feudal lords.
41. Gujarat Samachar, 2 October, 1934.
42. G.M. Nandurkar (ed.), *Sardar's Letters Mostly Unknown*, Vol. II (Ahmedabad: Navajivan, 1977).
43. Maulana Abul Kalam Azad, *India Wins Freedom* (New Delhi: Orient Longman, 1959, p. 178).
44. Dr. Zakir Hussain, *The Statesman*, 1 November, 1968.
45. Durgadas (ed.), *Sardar Patel's Correspondence*, Vol. V (Ahmedabad: Navajivan, 1971, pp. 242-3).
46. B. Krishna, *Sardar Patel: India's Iron Man* (New Delhi: Indus, 1945, p. 321).
47. Government of India, File of Political Department, No.12, Political (Secret), 1924-6, No.1-49, pp. 7-9.
48. G.M. Nandurkar (ed.), *Sardar Patel: in Tune with the Millions*, Vol. I (Ahmedabad: 1970, p. 57).
49. P.N. Chopra, (ed.), *The Collected Works of Sardar Vallabhbhai Patel*, Vol. XII, *op. cit.*, p. 121.
50. B. Krishna, *Sardar Patel: India's Iron Man, op. cit.*, pp. 322-3.
51. P.N. Chopra, (ed.), *The Collected Works of Sardar Vallabhbhai Patel*, Vol. XII, *op. cit.*, p. 43.
52. John Wood, *The Political Integration of British and Princely Gujarat: The Historical Political Variable in Indian States Politics*, (New York: Columbia, 1971, p. 243).

53. D.R. Manekar, *Accession to Extinction* (New Delhi: Vikash Publishers, 1974, p. 115).
54. Durgadas, (ed.), *Sardar Patel's Correspondence*, Vol. V, *op. cit.*, pp. 515-6.
55. B. Krishna, *Sardar Vallabhbhai Patel: India's Iron Man, op. cit.*, p. 339.
56. *Ibid.*, p. 352.
57. Vallabhbhai Patel to Mountbatten, 10 August, 1947, *Patel Papers*, Navajivan, Ahmedabad.
58. B. Krishna, *Sardar Vallabhbhai Patel: India's Iron Man, op. cit.*, p. 352.
59. Durgadas (ed.), *Sardar Patel's Correspondence*. Vol. VII, *op. cit.*, pp. 426-7.
60. V. Shankar, *My Reminiscence of Sardar Patel*, Vol. I (New Delhi: Macmillan, 1974, p. 127.)
61. The Round Table Quarterly, Review of the British House of Commonwealth Affairs, December 1948, pp. 9-14, White Paper on Jammu and Kashmir, Government of India, March, 1948, p. 9. Meher Chand Mahajan, *Bhavan's Journal*, 5 December, 1965, p. 29.
62. White Paper on Hyderabad, Government of India Publication, New Delhi, 1948, p. 48.
63. Durgadas, (ed.), *Sardar Patel's Correspondence*, Vol. I, *op. cit.*, p. 263.
64. S.P.P. Throat, in B. Krishna, *Sardar Vallabhbhai Patel: India's Iron Man, op. cit.*, p. 397.
65. H.V. Kamath, "Sardar Vallabhbhai Patel: Some Memoirs", *Bhavan's Journal*, 16 January 1982, p. 63.
66. Rabindranath Kumar, *Role of Sardar Patel in the Integration of States* (Muzaffarpur: Prabha Publications, 1987, p. 142).
67. G.M. Nandurkar (ed.), *Sardar Patel: In Tune with the Millions*, Vol. I (Ahmedabad: Navajivan, 1976).
68. *The Hindustan Times*, 20 April 1939.
69. D.V. Tahamankar, *Sardar Patel* (London: George Allen and Unwin Ltd., 1970, pp. 218-35). C.H. Phillip, Mary Dareen and Waing Wright (ed.), *The Partition of India: Policies and Perspectives (1935-47)* (London: George Allen and Unwin Ltd., 1970, p. 95).
70. *Constituent Assembly Debates*, 12 October, 1949.

71. Rani Dhavan Shankardass, *Sardar Patel: Power and Organisation in Indian Politics* (New Delhi: Orient Longman, 1988, p. 285).
72. D.R. Manekar, *Accession to Extinction op. cit.*, pp. 118-20.
73. Durgadas, (ed.), Sardar Patel's Correspondence, Vol. VII, *op. cit.*, p. 526.
74. D.R. Manekar, *Accession to Extinction op. cit.*, pp. 131-2.
75. B. Krishna, *Sardar Vallabhbhai Patel: India's Iron Man, op. cit.*, p. 423.
76. *Ibid.*, pp. 439-40.
77. *The Hindustan Times*, 26 January, 1949.
78. *The Constituent Assembly Debates*, 12 October, 1949.
79. Sucheta Mahajan, *Independence and Partition*, (New Delhi: Sage Publication, 2000, pp. 301-2).
80. Durgadas, (ed.), Sardar Patel's Correspondence, Vol. III, *op. cit.*, pp. 301-2.
81. Adul Kalam Azad, *India Wins Freedom, op. cit.*, p. 165.
82. *Ibid.*, p. 176.
83. S. Gopal, *Jawaharlal Nehru: Selected Works*, 2nd Series, Vol. I (New Delhi: 1984, p. 187).
84. V. Shankar, *My Reminiscence of Sardar Patel*, Vol. I, *op. cit.*, p. 23.
85. Adul Kalam Azad, *India Wins Freedom, op. cit.*, p. 190.
86. G.M. Nandurkar (ed.), *Sardar Patel: in Tune with the Millions*, Vol. I (Ahmedabad: 1975, p. 4).
87. V. Shankar, *My Reminiscence of sardar Patel*, Vol. I, *op. cit.*, pp. 16-7.
88. V. Shankar, *Ibid.*, p. 93.

    N.V. Gadgil, *Government from Inside, op. cit.*, p. 161.
89. M.O. Mathai, *Reminscence of the Nehru Age*, (New Delhi: Vikash Pvt. Ltd., 1978, p. 242). N.V. Gadgil, *Government from Inside, op. cit.*, p. 145.
90. V. Shankar, *My Reminiscence of Sardar Patel*, Vol. II, *op. cit.*, pp. 91-7.
91. V. Shankar, (ed.), *Sardar Patel: Select Correspondence*, Vol. 2 (Ahmedabad: 1976, p. 142).
92. N.D. Parikh, Vol. 2 (Ahmedabad: 1956, p. 220).

93. Maniben Patel, "Focus on Sardar Patel", in B.K. Ahluwalia (ed.), *Facets of Sardar Patel* (New Delhi: Kalyani Publishers, p. 74).

94. Vallabhbhai Patel to Jawaharlal Nehru, 29 September 1948, Patel Papers, Navajivan, Ahmedabad. V. Shankar, *My Reminiscence of Sardar Patel*, Vol. II, *op. cit.*, p. 147.

95. P.N. Chopra and Prabha Chopra, (ed.), *Inside Story of Sardar Patel: The Diary of Maniben Patel: 1936-50* (New Delhi: Vision Books, 2001, p. 19).

96. Durgadas, (ed.), *Sardar Patel's Correspondence*, Vol. IV, *op. cit.*, p. 66.

97. V. Shankar, *My Reminiscence of Sardar Patel*, Vol. II, *op. cit.*, p. 145.

98. Rajmohan Gandhi, *Patel: A Life* (Ahmedabad: Navajivan, 1991, p. 431). Durgadas, (ed.), *Sardar Patel's Correspondence*, Vol. IV, *op. cit.*, p. 413, Rafiq Zakaria, *Sardar Patel and Indian Muslims*, *op. cit.*, pp. 55-6.

99. S. Gopal, *Jawaharlal Nehru: Selected Works*, Vol.14, p. 174. Vallabhbhai Patel to Venkatarama Sastry, 16 July, 1949, *Patel Papers*, Navajivan, Ahmedabad.

100. N.V. Gadgil, Government from Inside, *op. cit.*, p. 147. V. Shankar, *My Reminiscence of Sardar Patel*, Vol. I, *op. cit.*, p. 136.

101. G.M. Nandurkar (ed.), *Sardar Patel: in Tune with the Millions*, Vol. (II), *op. cit.*, p. 202, V. Shankar, *My Reminiscence of Sardar Patel*, Vol. I, *op. cit.*, p. 163.

102. Vallabhbhai Patel's address at the Rajpipla Praja Mandal Conference, 29 December 1939, in P.N. Chopra (ed.), *The Collected Works of Sardar Vallabhbhai Patel*, Vol. VIII, *op. cit.*, p. 202. Rani Dhavan Shankardass, *Vallabhbhai Patel: Power and Organisation in Indian Politics*, *op. cit.*, p. 204.

103. G.M. Nandurkar (ed.), *Sardar Patel: in Tune with the Millions*, Vol. II, *op. cit.*, p. 221.,

. V. Shankar, *My Reminiscence of Sardar Patel*, Vol. II, *op. cit.*, p. 106.

104. V. Shankar, (ed.), *Sardar Patel: Select Correspondence*, Vol. 2, *op. cit.*, p. 193.

105. Sucheta Mahajan, *Independence and Partition*, *op. cit.*, p. 118.

106. U.P. Home Political, 18 April, 1941.

107. B. Krishna, *Sardar Patel: India's Iron Man*, *op. cit.*, p. 476.

108. S. Gopal, Jawaharlal Nehru: Selected Works, Vol. I, *op. cit.*, p. 541.
109. Durgadas, (ed.), *Sardar Patel's Correspondence,* Vol. IX, *op. cit.*, p. 17.
110. N.V. Gadgil, Government From Inside, *op. cit.*, p. 23.
111. V. Shankar, *My Reminiscence of Sardar Patel,* Vol. I, *op. cit.*, p. 23.
112. Abdul Majid Khan, *A Leader by Merit* (Lahore: 1946, p. 228).
113. *The Hindustan Times*, 21 February, 1938.
114. *The Times of India*, 16 April, 1938.
115. Home Department (Political), File No.18 April, 1938.
116. Vallabhbhai Patel to Rajendra Prasad, 2 October 1937, Rajendra Prasad Papers, National Archives of India, New Delhi. Vallabhbhai Patel to B.G. Kher, 11 July 1938, B.G. Kher Papers, NMML, New Delhi.
117. Vallabhbhai Patel to Rajendra Prasad, 9 March 1938, *Rajendra Prasad Papers,* National Archives of India, New Delhi.
118. Vallabhbhai Patel to Jawaharlal Nehru, 19 November, 1939, AICC Papers, New Delhi.
119. B. Shiva Rao, *Freedom Movement* (New Delhi: Orient Longman, 1972, p. 128).
120. Durgadas, (ed.), Sardar Patel's Correspondence, Vol. 3 *op. cit.*, p. 182.
121. *Ibid.*, p. 174.
122. V. Shankar, (ed.), *Sardar Patel: Select Correspondence*, Vol. 2, *op. cit.*, p. 407.
123. *The Hindustan Times*, 20 September, 1950.
124. *Ibid.*, 3 January 1948.
125. G.M. Nandurkar (ed.), *Sardar's Letters Mostly Unknown*, Vol. I, *op. cit.*, p. 165.
126. *The Hindustan Times*, 25 February, 1949.
127. S. Gopal, *Jawaharlal Nehru: Selected Works*, Vo.13, *op. cit.*, p. 331.
128. G.M. Nandurkar (ed.), *Sardar's Letters Mostly Unknown*, Vol. (I), *op. cit.*, p. 141.
129. V. Shankar, *My Reminiscences of Sardar Patel,* Vol. 2, *op. cit.*, p. 107.
130. T.N. Chaturvedi, *Sardar's Contribution to Public Administration*, Verinder Grover, (ed.), Vol. 10, *op. cit.*, p. 207.

131. Philip Mason in B. Krishna *Sardar Vallabhbhai Patel: India's Iron Man, op. cit.*, p. 492.
132. Durgadas, (ed.), *Sardar Patel's Correspondence*, Vol. IV, *op. cit.*, p. 527.
133. V. Shankar, (ed.), *Sardar Patel: Select Correspondence,* Vol. 2, *op. cit.*, p. 161.
134. Vallabhbhai Patel to Dayabhai, 6 December, 1930, *Patel Papers*, Navajivan, Ahmedabad.
135. Rajmohan Gandhi, *Patel: A Life*, *op. cit.*, p. 302.
136. V. Shankar, *My Reminiscence of Sardar Patel*, Vol. I, *op. cit.*, p. 26.
137. N.V. Gadil, *Government From Inside, op. cit.*, p. 49.
138. Vallabhbhai Patel to Jawaharlal Nehru, 5 February, 1948, *Patel Papers*, Navajivan, Ahmedabad.
139. *The Hindustan Times*, 3 October, 1950.
140. Vallabhbhai Patel to Jawaharlal Nehru, 19 October, 1948, *Patel Papers*, Navajivan, Ahmedabad.
141. V. Shankar, *My Reminiscence of Sardar Patel*, Vol. 2, *op. cit.*, pp. 136-37.
142. B. Krishna, *Sardar Vallabhbhai Patel: India's Iron Man, op. cit.*, p. 505.
143. N.V. Gadgil, *Government from Inside, op. cit.*, p. 170.
144. Vallabhbhai Patel to Jawaharlal Nehru, 12 June, 1948, *Patel Papers*, Navajivan, Ahmedabad.
145. Vallabhbhai Patel to Jawaharlal Nehru, 29 December, 1947, Patel Papers, Navajivan, Ahmedabad. Vallabhbhai Patel to Jawaharlal Nehru, 4 June 1948 in G.M. Nandurkar (ed.) *Sardar's Letters Mostly Unknown*, Vol. I (Ahmedabad: 1980.)
146. N.V. Gadgil, *Government from Inside*, *op. cit.*, p. 87.
147. *Ibid.*, p. 91.
148. V. Shankar, *My Reminiscence of Sardar Patel*, Vol. II, *op. cit.*, p. 85.
149. N.V. Gadgil, *Government from Inside*, *op. cit.*, p.
150. *Ibid.*, p. 208.
151. L.N. Sarin, *Sardar Patel* (New Delhi: S. Chand & Co., 1972, p. 14).
152. Verinder Grover, (ed.), *Political Thinkers of Modern India,* Vol. 18, *op. cit.*, p. 203.

153. Navajivan, 5 June, 1921.

154. Vallabhbhai Patel to B.G. Kher, B.G. Kher Papers, 14 July, 1938, New Delhi, NMML, Bombay Chronicle 29 November, 1946.

155. Bombay Chronicle 21 April, 1947.

156. P.N. Chopra (ed.), *The Collected Works of Sardar Vallabhbhai Patel,* Vol. XII, *op. cit.*, p. 117.

157. Leonard Mosley, in B. Krishna, *Sardar Vallabhbhai Patel: India's Iron Man, op. cit.*, p. 476.

158. P.N. Chopra (ed.), *The Collected Works of Sardar Vallabhbhai Patel,* Vol. XII, *op. cit.*, p. 113.

159. Constituent Assembly Debates, 16 May, 1949.

160. Vallabhbhai Patel, 16 May 1949, *Patel Papers*, Ahmedabad.

161. B. Krishna, *Sardar Vallabhbhai Patel: India's Iron Man, op. cit.*, p. 276.

162. Constituent Assembly Debates, 10 October, 1949.

163. Durgadas, (ed.), Sardar Patel's Correspondence, Vol. V, *op. cit.*, p. 109.

164. G.M. Nandurkar (ed.), *Sardar in Tune with the Millions*, Vol. I, *op. cit.*, p. 2.

165. V.P. Menon, *The Story of the Integration of States, op. cit.*, p. 41.

    H.V. R. Ienger, "The Image of the Police", *The Indian Express*, 8 September, 1966.

    V. Shankar, *My Reminiscence of Sardar Patel,* Vol. I, *op. cit.*, p. 185.

    H.M. Patel, "Sardar and the First Year of Independence" in *Sardar Patel Memorial Lecture Series* (Vallabh Vidya Nagar: 1982, p. 25).

166. Durgadas, (ed.), Sardar Patel's Correspondence, Vol. IV, *op. cit.*, p. 303.

167. V. Shankar, (ed.), *Sardar Patel: Select Correspondence* Vol. 2, *op. cit.*, p. 188.

168. H.V.R. Iengar, "Officials and Ministers", *The Indian Express*, 8 July, 1964.

169. V. Shankar, (ed.), *Sardar Patel: Select Correspondence* Vol. 2, *op. cit.*, p. 162.

170. *Bombay Chronicle*, 21 April, 1947.

171. *Ibid.*

172. *Bombay Chronicle*, 19 November, 1946.

173. *The Hindustan Times*, 18 January, 1948.

174. *Ibid.*, 18 March 1949. *Ibid.*, 23 December, 1949.

175. *Ibid.*, 13 January, 1950.

176. *Ibid.*, 22 March, 1950.

177. Rajmohan Gandhi, *Patel: A Life*, *op. cit.*, p. 432.

178. *The Hindustan Times*, 13 January, 1950.

179. *Ibid.*, 18 March 1949 and 13 January, 1950.

180. Vallabhbhai Patel to N.B. Khare, 30 May 1938, AICC Papers, NMML, New Delhi. Vallabhbhai Patel to Subhas Bose, 1 June 1938, AICC Papers, NMML, New Delhi.

181. V. Shankar, (ed.), *Sardar Patel: Select Correspondence*, Vol. 2, *op. cit.*, p. 341. Vallabhbhai to Wavell, 14 March 1947, Patel Papers, Navajivan, Ahmedabad.

182. V. Shankar, (ed.), *Sardar Patel: Select Correspondence*, Vol. I, *op. cit.*, p. 390.

183. *Ibid.*, p. 385.

184. *The Hindustan Times*, 22 March, 1950.

185. Vallabhbhai Patel to Krishna Sinha, 25 September 1947 in V. Shankar, (ed.), Select Correspondence, Vol. 2, p. 423.

Vallabhbhai to Jai Ram Das Daulat Ram, 25 November, 1947, *Ibid.*, p. 428.

186. *Ibid.*, 13 October, 1949.

187. Vallabhbhai Patel to Krishna Sinha, 2 November, 1946, *Patel Papers*, Navajivan, Ahmedabad.

188. *The Hindustan Times*, 2 October, 1950.

189. *Ibid.*, 20 September, 1950.

190. V. Shankar, (ed.), *Sardar Patel: Select Correspondence*, Vol. 2, *op. cit.*, p. 392.

191. P.N. Chopra (ed.), *The Collected Works of Sardar Vallabhbhai Patel*, Vol. XV, *op. cit.*, p. 11.

192. V. Shankar, (ed.), *Sardar Patel: Select Correspondence*, Vol. 2, *op. cit.*, p. 393.

193. N.V. Gadgil, Government from Inside, *op. cit.*, p. 127.
194. *Bombay Chronicle*, 11 October, 1937.
195. P.N. Chopra (ed.), *The Collected Works of Sardar Vallabhbhai Patel*, Vol. X, *op. cit.*, p. 235.
196. *The Hindustan Times*, 5 June, 1949.
197. Rani Dhavan Shankardas, *Vallabhbhai Patel: Power and Organisation in Indian Politics, op. cit.*, p. 241.
198. *The Hindustan Times*, 2 October, 1948.
199. P.N. Chopra (ed.), *The Collected Works of Sardar Vallabhbhai Patel*, Vol. XIII, *op. cit.*, p. 104.
200. *Ibid.*, Vol. XIV, p. 101.
201. *The Hindustan Times*, 13 May, 1950.
202. *Ibid.*, 5 June, 1949.
203. *Ibid.*, 13 May, 1950.
204. P.N. Chopra (ed.), *The Collected Works of Sardar Vallabhbhai Patel*, Vol. XIII, *op. cit.*, p. 16.
205. *Ibid.*, Vol. XV, *op. cit.*, p. 278.
206. *The Hindustan Times*, 5 June, 1949.
207. *Ibid.*, 13 December, 1948.
208. *Gujarat Samachar*, 3 October, 1934.
209. *The Hindustan Times*, 26 February, 1949.
210. *Bombay Chronicle*, 11 September, 1937.
211. *The Hindustan Times*, 28 February, 1949.
212. *Ibid.*, 6 January, 1950.
213. *Ibid.*, 21 November, 1948.
214. P.N. Chopra (ed.), *The Collected Works of Sardar Vallabhbhai Patel*, Vol. XIII, *op. cit.*, p. 304.
215. *Gujarat Samachar*, 3 October, 1934.
216. *The Hindustan Times*, 18 January, 1949.
217. *Ibid.*, 18 March, 1949.
218. *The Hindustan Times*, 24 September, 1948.
219. *Ibid.*, 7 April, 1949.

220. *Ibid.*, 23 May, 1950.

221. *Bombay Chronicle*, 2 August 1937. P.N. Chopra (ed.) *The Collected Works of Sardar Vallabhbhai Patel,* Vol. XV, *op. cit.*, p. 96.

222. *Gujarat Samachar*, 3 October 1934. P.N. Chopra, (ed.), *The Collected Works of Sardar Vallabhbhai Patel,* Vol. XV, *op. cit.*, p. 136.

223. *Ibid.*, Vol. X, *op. cit.*, p. 44.

224. G.M. Nandurkar (ed.), *Sardar's Letters Mostly Unknown*, Vol. II, *op. cit.*, p. 108.

6

Conclusion

I

Political Thought provides for alternative models of state-individual relationship for realisation of the Best Political Life. It reflects upon the nature, structure and function of the State and focuses upon the essential political values like Rights, Liberty, Equality, Justice and Political Obligation. Irrespective of variations and differences among thinkers in the interpretation of such perennial political issues, its relevance lies in providing alternative conceptual schemes and models on State and state-individual relationship from which mankind may choose, emulate and approximate the preferred model for realising the goal of "the Best Political Existence".

In these intellectual endeavours of thinkers and scholars the World over, from antiquity till date, Indian intellectuals have also contributed immensely. Indian Political Thought, focusing on 'Integral Humanism' has provided a beacon-light to mankind, and over the years, it has carved out a place of special significance and eminence by its own distinctiveness. Political thinkers of modern India have also reflected upon State, and State-Individual relationship in varieties of ways and forms, basing on the concept of 'Integral Humanism' that constitutes the cornerstone of Indian Political Thought. Among the Indian intellectuals and statesmen who have contributed significantly towards the growth of the Modern Indian Political Thought, Vallabhbhai Patel stands out forgiving valuable suggestions for the realisation of the Best Political Existence for the people of India in contemporary time. His eminence derives from the fact that he was a great freedom fighter and an astute architect of modern India. In the long span of his political career as a political activist and for a brief period as the "Iron Pillar" of the Government of India, he succinctly played roles as a party organiser, negotiator, Constitution-maker, consolidator and integrator of the Indian Nation–State. In the process, he endeavoured to realise for the people of India his vision of the Best Political Life. Hence, his political ideas and values have been studied and analysed and the emerging pattern has been delineated.

II

The enquiry into the pattern of political values of Vallabhbhai has been undertaken in the context of the concepts of Rights and Liberty on the one hand, and Equality and Justice on the other.

It has been found that Vallabhbhai, throughout his life championed the cause of personal rights of the individual. He fought against the British authority for the protection of Individual Rights and Liberty. He continued his efforts after independence as part of the Government. He was quite emphatic on the Right against Exploitation, Freedom of Speech and Expression, Right to Life, Right to Property, Right to Religion and various other political rights. He protested against the high-handedness of the officials, exploitative British revenue policies, and maladministration in the Princely States to defend the Right against Exploitation. In pursuance of his faith in the Freedom of Speech and Expression as a pre-requisite for the growth of individual's personality, he criticised the British authority for the unwanted mutilation of the policy of education, indifference towards the political prisoners, abuse of freedom of movement, and undesired restrictions on the Press. Vallabhbhai's passion for a moderate style of living, obsession for good health and aversion towards fasting, proved his genuine concern for the Right to

Life. Given his agrarian background, he seemed to have realised the significance of private property and reacted against the British policy of arbitrary confiscation. He also advised the Government of India against indiscreet land reform and hasty nationalisation. His keenness to defend the Right to Religion was revealed from his effort to reform the undesirable traditional rituals of the Hindu religion, raise public fund for renovation of religious structures, discard the idea of making India a Hindu State, ban political organisations with religious leanings, and extend sympathy to people of all faith. His exhortation to people to participate in elections, grooming of the Congress Party to seize all opportunities to hold public office and his resistance to the authority in case of arbitrariness and despotism, proved his concern for political rights. To protect all these rights effectively, he suggested revitalisation of grass roots bodies with due financial autonomy, mobilisation of people with the help of caste groups and political parties, and incorporation of essential provisions like Fundamental Rights and Independent Judiciary in the Constitution of India. All these indicate that he was a champion of Individual Rights.

At the same time, Vallabhbhai's pragmatic outlook made him realise the objectives of the freedom struggle and the needs of nation-building activities which demanded regulation of rights for the unity, integration, peace and stability of the state. He believed that rights without restraint would be mere licence. He realised that the fallible of human nature could be set right by the due sanctions of the authority. Hence, irrespective of his inclination for the Right against Exploitation, he urged the people during freedom struggle to bear at times with the exploitative policies of the British authority and the Princes to pave the way for a conducive atmosphere, needed for negotiation. He appealed to support the policy of reservation for certain weaker sections of the society to enhance the quality of freedom in the long run. He also urged for constitutional protection for the civil servants to overcome the administrative challenges during the transitional period. He wanted to restrict the Freedom of Speech and Expression to guarantee public decency, particularly in an atmosphere surcharged with communal tension. He advocated for a Government supervised education policy and well-regulated Press to ensure the Freedom of Speech and Expression effectively. He compromised with the Right to Life as he supported capital punishment and police firing, and ensured law and order immediately after the partition. In spite of his support for the Right to Property, he stood by the Government of India's effort for gradual land reform, nationalisation of certain key industries, control over the supply of certain essential items and imposition of proportional tax like the Income Tax to enable the Government to fulfill its obligations towards the people. His secular approach seemed to have been affected by the apparently hawkish attitude of the Muslim League which influenced him to support stringent legislative measures like the Permit System and Property Evacuee Bill to bring an early end to refugee rehabilitation. Last but not the least, the partition complications compelled him to restrict political rights including the right to resist the state authority. He took drastic steps to initiate Bills on Preventive Detention and Prevention of Strikes in Essential Services to solve the impending problems like food crisis and refugee rehabilitation.

While asserting individual's rights and liberty in a judicious way, Vallabhbhai also expressed concern for the unprivileged sections of people such as women, backward communities and labour class. He was highly critical of the prevailing social practices which degraded the status of these sections of people. He criticised child marriage, dowry practice, purdah system and the torture of widow as abominable traditions that caused indignity and misery to women. He expressed his dismay at the practice of untouchability and the consequent rampant conversion and caste violence. He showed concern over the inhuman existence of the backward communities which very often forced them to become bonded-labourers Vallabhbhai also highlighted the plight of the working class, manifested in its lack of organisation, ignorance and aloofness to national interest. He urged them to resort to arbitration rather than strike to ameliorate their fate in a genuine way. He tried to improve the condition of people of all these categories by emphasising upon spread of education, women empowerment, labour reorganisation and selective reservation in jobs and representative bodies for some of them. He motivated both the Government and non-Government sectors to come forward to implement the measures required for the overall development of these sections. Vallabhbhai's articulation of resistance determines the nature of political obligation he was advocating for. As a person with liberal mindset, he visualised the state as a means. He supported guarded confrontationist measures such as strike to ensure that rights of the people are protected by the state.

Thus, the pattern of political values of Vallabhbhai is found to be characterised by a synthesis of his ideas and perspectives on individual's rights, liberty, equality and social justice. He seems to be a fiery champion of individual rights and liberty with a conviction that these political values are the essential pre-requisites for the development of the individual as well as the progress of culture and civilisation. At the same time, he presents himself as a stern asserter of state-authority, on utilitarian consideration to ensure just social order, national security and unity. He seems to combine the values of individual rights with necessity for state-authority and emphasises that rights and liberty should be exercised within the confines of law and provisions of the Constitution. His assertion of rights and liberty presenting them as necessary for individual good is not antithetical to the values of social justice. He is found to be very much worried over injustice meted out to the downtrodden and the weaker sections of the society. No doubt, his zeal is found to have been affected from time to time by the compulsions of freedom struggle and nation-building activities. However, the pragmatic mindset of a *Patidar* in him has probably induced him to be conservative and cautious of any hasty socio-economic changes. Thus, the pattern of political values of Vallabhbhai presents a fine synthesis of liberalism, conservatism and welfarism.

III

Besides ascertaining the pattern of political values of Vallabhbhai, an endeavour has been undertaken to enquire into and portray his vision of Nation–State, involving the nature of State as well as the state-individual relationship. The enquiry has revealed that his vision of state is in tune with the pattern of his political values. In his concept, the state is founded on and its people are held together by a high sense of nationalism and patriotism. He intends to ensure individual liberty in conformity with the provisions of the Constitution and simultaneously to establish a just society through appropriate state action and social reforms. In this context, it may be noted that Vallabhbhai's conviction in the existence of a strong state was rooted in the boldness of the character of his father, independent mindset of his *Patidar* community, exposure to nationalistic ethos in school and the dynamic spirit of his legal profession. Moreover, the influence of national leaders such as Ranade, Tilak, and Gandhi most probably helped him nurture his passion for a nationalistic, democratic and just state.

The necessity of creating a Nation–State motivated Vallabhbhai to design a comprehensive strategy in view of the changing national and international scenario. Firstly, he emphasised upon the rearrangement of the existing social relationship. In this context, on the one hand, he pressed for the emancipation of backward communities through the Gandhian constructive programme, while on the other he utilised skillfully the higher castes for social integration and political mobilisation. Hence, he propagated the *Khadi*-culture, spread the message against untouchability and simultaneously guarded the interest of the upper caste people by following suitable policies. It reflected his pragmatic approach which helped him to get the desired result with the least possible change. Vallabhbhai also harped upon the emancipation of women and Hindu-Muslim unity to reduce the existing social and ethnic cleavages. His intention was to strengthen the plural basis of Nation–State. During the initial stage of the freedom struggle, he preferred to use and encourage the Gandhian non-violent techniques to cope with dissensions prevailing particularly in the traditional society of India. However, subsequently, with the change of time he switched over to electoral participation as a technique of effective political mobilisation to encash the newly introduced constitutional opportunities. For this purpose, the Congress Party, under his leadership and guidance, played a significant role. The long-drawn struggle finally paid off, though it was at the cost of partition. Vallabhbhai accepted it as the best possible outcome in the given situation and tried to carry the party with him at the tragic moment. Thus, he is found to have envisioned for the people of India, a state which is democratic in structure, nationalistic in foundation, and welfarist in spirit and function.

IV

Vallabhbhai has sought to realise his vision of nation-state through suitable nation-building activities soon after independence. His tremendous significance as a nation-builder is revealed in the roles he played in the context of framing the Constitution of India, consolidation of the nascent Nation–State by integrating the Princely States with it and reorienting the Bureaucracy for administrative efficiency and effectiveness.

Vallabhbhai emphasised upon evolving a constitutional framework for independent India not only to reflect the self-pride of people of a free country but also to define the jurisdiction of the authority through rule of law. He readily accepted the Cabinet Mission Plan to give the maximum possible representation to the Constituent Assembly in the prevailing phase of transition. As the Chairman of the Fundamental Rights Sub-committee, Minorities Sub-committee and the Provincial Constitution Sub-committee, he played a decisive role in defining the Individual-State relationship. His initiative to incorporate in the Constitution provisions for a set of Fundamental Rights, independent judiciary and special protective measures for the minorities proved his sincerity as the champion of individual's rights and dignity whereas his effort to provide in the Constitution a set of instructions called the 'Directive Principles of State Policy' and measures like protective discrimination or the policy of reservation for certain unprivileged sections, reflected his inclination to make the state an instrument of social change. Moreover, the constitutional provisions that make the Union Government more powerful than the provincial governments in the federal set-up are the outcome of his astute thinking for a strong state and integrated India capable of coping with external and internal challenges. It reflected his pragmatic mindset keen to balance the freedom of individual with the authority of state. Also, as the much acclaimed 'Iron Man' of India, Vallabhbhai played a crucial role in consolidating the Indian territory soon after independence. He integrated the Princely States slowly and skillfully through the process of annexation, reconstitution and centralisation. He relied mostly upon techniques such as conciliation, good offices of well connected people, diplomacy and bargaining. In the process, he thought it was wise to grant 'Privy Purse' to the Princes to secure their merger with the Indian Union. He used force sparingly and only in case of Junagarh, Hyderabad, and Jammu and Kashmir wherein he was compelled to take harsh measures given their sensitive geographical location, demographic composition and high ambition of the rulers. The minimal use of force created a consensual basis for the Nation–State.

Vallabhbhai's role as the Deputy Prime Minister was in tune with his zeal to strengthen the Nation–State. At the level of the Government, he took measures to reduce dissensions within the Cabinet and helped in reasserting the principle of collective responsibility. Further, as the Minister of Home Affairs he was instrumental in remodelling the Bureaucracy and Army to adapt them to the new situation and to be more integrated, efficient and effective. All these measures introduced to a large extent as 'contextual necessity', contributed immensely to the strengthening of the nascent Nation–State by way of obtaining support and allegiance of the people to the Government of India. Vallabhbhai also encouraged various socio-economic groups to come forward to assist the state not only in administration and maintenance of law and order but also in other developmental works relating to health, education, economic planning, and supply of relief measures to the distressed people. His policies of guarded nationalisation with a definite space for private sectors and reliance upon private charity to raise infrastructures on health and education reflected his sincerity of approach.

Thus, Vallabhbhai's role as a nation builder reflects and manifests his political value-pattern which is a synthesis of the values of liberalism democracy, conservatism, nationalism, and welfarism in various degrees.

V

On the whole, the pattern of political ideas of Vallabhbhai has been discerned on the basis of enquiry and analysis of some important statements and opinions made by him on various socio-political issues and scrutiny of the roles he played at different stages of his life. His pattern of political ideas is found to be a synthesis of various political inclinations. He is found to be conservative for he holds the Right to Property as inalienable. He also favours the socio-cultural traditions and the conventional pattern of social organisation. However, his conservatism is largely a product of his deep-rooted sense of pragmatism and of expediency. He seems to be liberal by temperament for he accords tremendous importance to individual rights and liberty, considers them as essential for the growth and development of individual's personality and dignity and favours constitutional guarantee for their protection and effective exercise. However, his inclination to regulate the rights through the required measures by a legitimate state intervention is in tune with the liberal mindset, keen to enhance the quality of freedom. He is found to be a democrat in belief for he promotes individual initiatives, emphasises on popular, equal and active participation of the people in the political process. He also encourages political mobilisation of various social groups, favours the least possible use of force, necessary only to ensure the unity of the state and voices for a responsive and responsible Government attuned to public opinion. He is emerges as a welfarist as he favours state-sponsored welfare measures for the gradual development of the downtrodden and the weaker sections of the society. Above all, appears to be a staunch nationalist and patriot in spirit as he is mostly concerned for building a strong, united and integrated India capable of maintaining its dignity both within and outside. In fact, his nationalism seems to be a vital motivating factor behind many of his ideas and actions.

All these socio-political inclinations and values are found to have been harmoniously synthesised and reflected in the various roles played by Vallabhbhai as a socio-political activist and a national leader during the freedom struggle and also during the post-independence period. He seems to be simultaneously a sane conservative, a fiery liberal-individualist, an ardent democrat, an advocate of welfarism, a staunch nationalist and a committed patriot. The liberal-democratic ideology with due emphasis upon conservatism, pragmatism, welfarism and nationalism seems to characterise the mindset of Vallabhbhai which is perfectly in tune with 'Integral Humanism', the quintessence of Indian Political Thought.

Bibliography

1. Private Papers

Atlee Papers, (Microfilm), National Archives of India, New Delhi.

B.G. Kher Papers, Nehru Memorial Museum and Library, New Delhi.

Bulabhai Desai Papers, Nehru Memorial Museum and Library, New Delhi.

G.B. Pant Papers, National Archives of India, New Delhi.

J.B. Kripalani Papers. Nehru Memorial Museum and Library, New Delhi.

Jamnalal Bajaj Papers, Nehru Memorial Museum and Library, New Delhi.

Jawaharlal Nehru Papers, Nehru Memorial Museum and Library, New Delhi.

K.M. Munshi Papers, Bharatiya Vidya Bhavan, Bombay.

Lord Irwin Papers, Nehru Memorial Museum and Library, New Delhi.

M.K. Gandhi Papers, Gandhi Smarak Nidhi, Rajghat, New Delhi.

Mountbatten Papers (Microfilm), Nehru Memorial Museum and Library, New Delhi.

N.B. Khare Papers, National Archives of India, New Delhi.

Purushottamdas, Thakurdas Papers, Nehru Memorial Museum and Library, New Delhi.

Rajendra Prasad Papers, National Archives of India, New Delhi.

Vallabhbhai Patel Papers, Navajivan, Ahmedabad.

2. Papers of Organisations

(In Nehru Memorial Museum and Library, New Delhi).

All India Congress Committee Papers.

Bombay Provincial Congress Committee Papers.

3. Unpublished Government Records

(In the National Archives of India, New Delhi).

Government of India, Home Department (Political), *Fortnightly Reports on Political Situation in India*, for the years 1921, 1928, 1929, 1930 and 1931, File No.1/28, 17/29, 18/1-12 and 33.

Government of India, Home Department (Political) 1922, *Secret Abstract on Bordoli Civil Disobedience Movement*, 1921-22, File No. 489.

Government of India, Home Department (Political) 1928, *Agitation in the Bordoli Taluka, Bombay Presidency, Against the Payment of Land* Revenue, 1928, File No. 75.

Government of India, Home Department (Political) 1930, *Salt Satyagraha Campaign in the Bombay Presidency*, under the Leadership of Mr. M.K. Gandhi, File No. 247-11/30.

Government of India, Home Department (Political) 1930, *Formation of New Land League under the Presidentship of Vallabhbhai Patel*, File No. 421.

Government of India, Home Department (Political) 1931, Intimation from the Bombay Government that Mr. Vallabhbhai Patel has no Right to the Title of Sardar, File No. 243.

Government of India Records, Home, Political Department, 1943-47.

(In the Maharashtra State Record Office, Bombay, India)

Government of Bombay, Revenue Department (B Branch), 1928, *Revision Settlement of Bordoli Taluka*, 1928, File No. 7259/24, Part-VIII.

Government of Bombay, Revenue Department (B-Branch), 1928, *Letters from the Secretary*, Government of Bombay, Revenue Department, to the Secretary, Government of India, Home Department, File No.7259, B/24, Part-XVII.

(In the Maharashtra State Gazetteer Office, Bombay, India)

Government of Bombay, Home Department (Special Branch), 1928, *Extracts on Bordoli Satyagraha*, 1928, File No. 584-E, Part II.

Government of Bombay, Home Department (Special Branch), 1928, *Secret Police Abstract, on Bordoli Satyagraha*, File No. B-17.

(In the Maharastra Sachivalaya, Home Ministry, Bombay, India)

Government of Bombay, Home Department (Special Branch), 1928, *Paper cuttings on Bordoli Satyagraha*, 1928, File No. 584-E, Part II.

Government of Bombay, Home Department (Special Branch), 1928, *Proposals to Prosecute Vallabhbhai Patel and Policy of Government Regarding Prosecution of Patel and Leaders*, File No. 584-E, Part VII.

Government of Bombay, Home Department (Special Branch) 1929, *Bordoli in British Press*, File No. 584-E, Part X.

4. Official Publications

Gazetteer of the Bombay Presidency, Bombay Presidency, Gujarat, Surat and Broach (Bombay, 1877), Vol. 1 and 2.

Gazetteer of India, 1921, Bombay Presidency, (Bombay, 1922).

Sedgwick, L.J., *Census of India*, 1921, Bombay Presidency (Bombay, 1922).

Jayakar, M.S. and Anderson, F.G.H., *The Second Revision Settlement of the Bordoli Taluka and Valod Mahal of the Surat District*, (Bombay, 1927).

Broomfield R.S. and Maxwell, R.M., *Reports of the Special Enquiry into the 'Second' Revision Settlements of the Bordoli and Chorasi Talukas*: (Bombay, 1929).

Proposal for Indian Constitutional Reform, (White Paper, March 1933).

Report of the Joint Committee on Indian Constitutional Reform (London, 1934).

Government of India Act, 1935.

Indian Annual Register, Jan.-June, 1928, Vol. I.

Indian Annual Register, July-Dec., 1928, Vol. II.

Indian Annual Register, Jan.-June, 1937, Vol. I.

Indian Annual Register, July-Dec., 1937, Vol. II.

Indian Annual Register, Jan-June, 1938, Vol. I.

Indian Annual Register, July-Dec., 1938, Vol. II.

Indian Annual Register, Jan-June, 1939, Vol. I.

Indian Annual Register, July-Dec., 1939, Vol. II.

Legislative Assembly Debates, Jan.-Dec., 1939.

White Paper on Indian States (Publication Division, Government of India: New Delhi, 1948).

White Paper on Hyderabad (Publication Division, Government of India: Delhi, 1948).

White Paper on Jammu and Kashmir (Publication Division, Government of India: Delhi, 1950).

Proceedings of the Conferences of the Ruling Princes and Chiefs: 1921-1947 (Narendra Mahal, Government of India Publication: Delhi, 1950).

Gazetteer of India, Gujarat State, Surat District (Ahmedabad, 1962).

Constituent Assembly Debates, (Reprinted: Lok Sabha Secretariat, New Delhi, 1966).

The Bombay Land Revenue Code, 1879 (Ahmedabad, 1967).

5. Collection of Documents, Letters and Speeches

Chopra, P.N. and Chopra Prabha (ed.), *Inside Story of Sardar Patel: The Diary of Maniben Patel: 1936-50* (New Delhi: Vision Books, 2001).

Chopra, P.N. (ed.), *The Collected Works of Sardar Vallabhbhai Patel*, 15 Vols. (New Delhi: Konark Pvt. Ltd., 1990-99).

Chopra, P.N., (ed.), *Thematic Volumes on Vallabhbhai Patel: Kashmir and Hyderabad* (New Delhi: Konark Pvt. Ltd., 2000).

Durgadas (ed.)., *Sardar Patel's Correspondence: 1945-50*, 10 Vols. (Ahmedabad:, Navajivan, 1971).

Gandhi, M.K., *Collected Works* (New Delhi: 1979-84).

Gandhi, M.K., *Letters to Sardar Patel* (Ahmedabad: *Navajivan*, 1957).

Gopal, S. (ed.), *Jawaharlal Nehru: Selected Works*, 15 Vols. (New Delhi: 1981).

Jamil-ud-din (ed.), *Jinnah: Speeches and Writings*, 2 Vols. (Lahore: 1964).

Linlithgow, *Marquess of Speeches and Statements, 1936-43* (New Delhi: 1945).

Nandurkar, G.M., (ed.), *Sardar Patel Centenary* 5 Vols. (Ahmedabad: 1974-78).

Nandurkar, G.M., (ed.), *Sardar's Letters: Post-Centenary Series* 3 Vols. (Ahmedabad: 1980-83).

Nandurkar, G.M., (ed.), *Sardarshri Ke Patra* 2 Vols. (Ahmedabad: 1981).

Nandurkar, G.M., (ed.), *Sardarshri Na Patro* 3 Vols. (Ahmedabad: 1975-78).

Parikh, Narahari and Shah, Uttamchand Dwarikadas, *Sardar Patel ke Bhashan* (Ahmedabad: Navajivan, 1950).

Parikh, Narahari, *Speeches by Lord Mountbatten, 1947-48* (New Delhi: 1948).

Prasad, Rajendra, *Correspondence and Select Documents*, Vol. 1-9 (Bombay: 1987).

Publication Division, *For a United India: Speeches of Sardar Vallabhbhai Patel*, 1947-50 (New Delhi: 1967).

Publication Division, *Sardar Patel: On Indian Problems* (New Delhi: 1949).

Shankar, V., (ed.), *Sardar Patel: Select Correspondence, 1945-50*, 2 Vols., (Ahmedabad: *Navajivan*, 1977).

6. News Papers and Magazines

Anandbazar Patrika

Bombay Chronicle

Bombay Sentinel

Bordoli *Satyagraha* Patrika

Gujarat Samachar

Harijan

Hitavada

Indian Annual Register

Mainstream

Navajivan

Prajabandhu

Shankar's Weekly

The Dawn

The Hindu

The Hindustan Times

The Illustrated Weekly of India

The Indian Express

The Statesman

The Times of India

Tribune

Young India

7. Books

Ahluwalia, B.K. and Ahluwalia, Sashi, *Sardar Patel: A Rebel and Ruler* (New Delhi: Akbe Group, 1981).

Ahluwalia, B.K., *Sardar Patel: A Life* (New Delhi: Sagar Publications, 1974).

Ahluwalia, B.K., *Facets of Sardar Patel* (Ludhiana: Kalyani, 1974).

Ahmed, Imtiaz, Ghosh, Partha and Reifeld, Helmut (eds.), *Pluralism and Equality : Values in Indian Society and Politics* (New Delhi: Sage Publications, 2000).

Altekar, A.S., *State and Government in Ancient India* (New Delhi: 1958).

Ambedkar, B.R., *Pakistan or the Partition of India* (Bombay: 1946).

Anthony, Frank, *Britain's Betrayal in India* (New Delhi: Allied Publishers, 1969).

Appadorai, A., *Indian Political Thinking in the Twentieth Century: An Introductory Survey* (Calcutta: Oxford University Press, 1987).

Ashraf, Ali, *Politics of Development and Decay: A Study of Politics and City Government in Ahmedabad and Kanpur* (May 1975, Mimeograph, submitted to ICSSR).

Azad Abul Kalam, *India Wins Freedom* (Calcutta: Orient Longman, 1959).

Bakshi, S.R., *The Bordoli Satyagraha* (New Delhi: Akashdeep Publishing House, 1988).

Bakshi, S.R., *Sardar Patel: His Political Ideology* (New Delhi: Anmol, 1990).

Barker, Earnest, *Principles of Social and Political Theory* (Calcutta: Oxford University Press, 1951).

Barry, Norman, *An Introduction to Modern Political Theory* (London: Macmillan, 1981).

Basham, A.L., *The Wonder that was India* (New Delhi: Rupa & Co., 1954).

Berman, Jan, *Peasants Migrants and Paupers: Rural Labour Circulation and Capitalist Production in West India* (New Delhi: 1985).

Black, Max, *Critical Thinking* (New York: Prentice-Hall, 1952).

Bluhm William, T., *Theories of Political System* (Englewood Cliff, N.J.: Prentice-Hall, 1965).

Brecher, Michael, *Nehru* (London: Oxford University Press, 1959).

Brecht, Arnold, *Political Theory: The Foundation of Twentieth Century Political Thought* (Bombay: *The Times of India Press*, 1970). Originally Published by the Princeton University Press, USA, 1959.

Brown, Judith, *Gandhi's Rise to Power* (London: Cambridge University Press, 1972).

Campell-Johnson, Alan, *Mission with Mountbatten* (Bombay: Jaico Publishers, 1951).

Chandra, Bipan, *Nationalism and Colonialism in Modern India* (New Delhi, Orient Longman, 1979).

Chopra, P.N. (ed.), *Quit India: The Wittenden Report* (Faridabad: 1976).

Chopra, P.N., *The Sardar of India: Biography of Vallabhbhai Patel* (New Delhi: Allied Publishers Ltd., 1995).

Chudgar, P.L., *Indian Princes Under British Protection: A Study of their Personal Race, their Constitutional Position and Their Future* (London: 1929).

Cohen, Moris R. and Nagel, Earnest *An Introduction to Logic and Scientific Method* (New York: Harcourt Brace, 1934).

Collins, Larry and Lapierre, Duminique, *Freedom at Midnight* (New Delhi: Vikash Publishing House, 1976).

Corfield, Sir Cornard, *The Princely India I Know: From Reading to Mountbatten* (Madras: 1975).

Coupland, R., *The Indian Politics, 1936-42* (Oxford: 1942).

Das, Manmathnath, *Partition and Independence of India* (New Delhi: Vision, 1982).

Desai, A.R., *Social Background of Indian Nationalism* (Bombay: Popular Prakashan, 1948).

Desai, Ishwarlal, I., *Bordoloi Satyagraha* (Surat: 1970).

Desai, Mahadev, *The Story of Bordoli* (Ahmedabad: Navajivan, 1929).

Desai, Morarji, *The Story of My Life* (New Delhi: Macmillan, 1974).

Dhangare, D.N., *Peasant Movements in India: 1920-50* (New Delhi: Oxford, 1991).

Dunning, William Archibald, *A History of Political Theories: Ancient and Medieval* (Allahabad: Central Book Depot, 1970).

Durgadas, *Sardar Patel: The Politician and The Statesman* (Vidyanagar: 1972).

Durgadas, *Sardar Patel: India from Curzon to Nehru and After* (London: 1969).

Duta, R. Palme, *India Today* (Bombay: 1947).

Dutt, Krishan, *Sardar Patel and the Bordoli Movement* (Meerut: Anu Books, 1968).

Dwarkadas, Kanji, *Ten Years to Freedom* (Bombay: Popular Prakashan, 1968).

Dyke, Vermon Van, *Political Science: A Philosophical Analysis* (Stanford, California: Stanford University Press, 1960).

Erikson, Erik, *Gandhi's Truth* (London: Faber and Faber, 1970).

Gadgil, N.V., *Government from Inside* (Meerut: Meenakshi, 1968).

Gandhi, M.K., *The Indian State's Problems* (Ahmedabad: Navajivan, 1941).

Gandhi, Rajmohan, *Patel: A Life* (Ahmedabad: Sardar Vallabhbhai Patel Memorial Society and Navajivan, 1991).

Gillon, Keeneth, *Ahmedabad: A Study in Urban History* (University of California Press: 1968).

Govinddass, Sheth, *Sardar Patel* (New Delhi: 1968).

Grover, Verinder (ed.), *Political Thinkers of Modern India; Vallabhbhai Patel,* Vol. 18 (New Delhi: Deep and Deep Publications).

Hacker, Andrew, *Political Theory: Philosophy, Ideology, Science* (New York: Macmillan, 1961).

Hardiman, David, *Peasant Nationalists of Gujarat: Kheda District, 1917-34* (New Delhi: Oxford University, 1981).

Heimann, Betty, *Facets of Indian Thought* (London: George Allen and Unwin, 1964).

Held, David, *Political Theory and the Modern State: Essays on State, Power and Democracy* (London: Polity Press and Basil Blackwell Ltd., 1984).

Held, David, (ed.), *Political Theory Today* (London: Polity Press, 1990).

Heredia, Susane, *A Patriot for Me* (Bombay: Orient Longman, 1972).

Heywood, Andrew, *Political Theory* (London: Macmillan, 1994).

Hodson, H.W., *The Great Divide* (London: Hutchinson, 1969).

Jain, Rajula, *Vallabhbhai Patel and the Indian National Congress: A Study (1934-1939)* (New Delhi: Gyan Sagar Publication, 1997).

Jalal, Aesha, *The Sole Spokesman: Jinnah, The Muslim League and the Demand for Pakistan* (Cambridge: 1985).

Jaysbee, S., *The Iron Man of India* (New Delhi: R.P. Bookwala and Co.).

Jenkin, Thomas P., *The Study of Political Theory* (Garden City: Double Day, 1955).

Jones, Rodney, *Urban Politics in India* (New Delhi: Vikash Publishing House, 1975).

Kaushik, P.D., *The Congress Ideology and Programme 1920-47: Ideological Foundation of Indian Nationalism during the Gandhian Era* (Delhi: 1964).

Kaviraj, Sudipta (ed.), *Politics in India* (New Delhi: Oxford University Press, 1997).

Khan, Abdul Majid, *Leader by Merit* (Lahore: Indian Printing Works, 1946).

Khilnani Sunil, *The Idea of India* (London: Penguin, 1997).

Kochanek, S.A., *The Congress Party of India* (Princeton Press, 1968).

Kothari, Rajni, *Politics in India* (New Delhi: Orient Longman, 1970).

Kripalani, J.B., *Fateful Years.* (Bombay: 1948).

Krishna, B., *Sardar Vallabhbhai Patel: India's Iron Man* (New Delhi: Indus, 1995).

Kshirasagar, Shivram, *The Indomitable Sardar and the Triumph of Borsad* (Vallabh Vidya Nagar: 1973).

Kulkarni, V.B., *The Indian Triumvirate: A Political Biography of Gandhi-Patel-Nehru* (Bombay: Bharatiya Vidya Bhavan, 1964).

Kumar Rabindra, *Sardar Vallabhbhai Patel: A Recollection* (New Delhi: Atlantic Publishers and Distributors, 1990).

Kumar, Rabindra Nath, *Role of Sardar Patel in the Integration of India* (Muzaffarpur: Prabha Publications, 1987).

Lee-Warner, William, *The Native States of India* (London: 1910).

Lohia, Rammanohar, *Guilty Men of India's Partition* (Allahabad: Kitabstan, 1960).

Low, D.A. (ed.), *Congress and the Raj* (London: 1977).

Lumby, E.W.R., *The Transfer of Power in India, 1945-47* (London: 1954).

Lyon, Michael, *Sardar Patel and Indian Independence* (New Delhi: Konark Pvt. Ltd., 1996).

Mahajan, Sucheta, *Independence and Partition* (New Delhi: Sage Publications, 2000).

Maheswari, S.R., *Administrative Thinkers* (New Delhi: Macmillan, 1998).

Mankekor, D.R., *Accession to Extinction* (Delhi: Vikash Publishers, 1974).

Mathai, M.O., *Reminiscence of the Nehru Age* (New Delhi: Vikash Publishing House, 1978).

Meehan, E.J., *Contemporary Political Thought: A Critical Study* (Homewood, Illinois: The Dorsey Press, 1967).

Mehta, Asoka, *Economic Consequences of Sardar Patel* (Hyderabad: Chetna, 1949).

Mehta, Asoka, *We Accuse the INTUC* (Hind Mazdoor Sabha, 1949).

Mehta, Shirin, *The Peasantry and Nationalism: A Study of the Bordoli Satyagraha* (New Delhi: Manohar, 1984).

Mehta, V.R., *Ideology, Modernisation and Politics in India* (New Delhi: Manohar, 1983).

Menon, V.P., *The Story of the Integration of the Indian States* (Calcutta: Orient Longman, 1956).

Menon, V.P., *The Transfer of Power to India* (Calcutta: Orient Longman, 1957).

Merriam, Allen, Hayes, *Gandhi Vs. Jinnah: The Debate over the Partition of India* (Calcutta: 1980).

Mishra, D.P., *Living An Era*, 2 Vols. (New Delhi: Vikash Publishing House, 1978).

Mookerjee, Shyama Prasad, *Leaves from a Diary* (Calcutta: 1993).

Moon, Penderel (ed.), *Wavell: The Viceroy's Journal* (London: Oxford University Press, 1973).

Moon, Penderel, *Divide and Quit* (Brekley: University of California, 1962).

Moore, R.J., *Escape from Empire: Government and The Indian Problem* (London: Oxford, 1983).

Moore, R.J., *Endogames of Empire* (New Delhi: Oxford, 1988).

Mosley, Leonard, *The Last Days of British Raj* (London: 1962).

Munshi, K.M., *The End of an Era* (Bombay: Bhavan, 1967).

Munshi, K.M., *Pilgrimage to Freedom* (Bombay: Bhavan, 1967).

Murthi, R.K., *The Man and His Contemporaries* (New Delhi: Sterling Publishers Pvt. Ltd., 1976).

Palkhivala, N.A., *Enduring Relevance of Sardar Patel* (New Delhi: Publication Division, 1993).

Pande, B.N. (ed.), *The Indian National Movement: 1885-1947*, Select Documents (London: 1979).

Panikkar, K.M., *The Idea of Sovereignty of State in Indian Political Thought* (Bombay: Bharatiya Vidya Bhavan, 1963).

Panjabi, K.L., *The Indomitable Sardar* (Bombay: Bharatiya Vidya Bhavan, 1962).

Pantham, Thomas and Deutsch, Keeneth, L. (ed.), *Political Thought in Modern India* (New Delhi: Sage Publications, 1986).

Pantham, Thomas, *Political Theories and Social Reconstructions: A Critical Survey of the Literature on India* (New Delhi: Sage Publications, 1995).

Parekh, Bhikhu and Pantham, Thomas, *Political Discourse: Explanations in Indian and Western Political Thought* (New Delhi: Sage Publications: 1987).

Parikh, Narahari, *Sardar Vallabhbhai Patel*, 2 Vols. (Ahmedabad: Navajivan, 1953-56).

Park, Richard. L. and Tinker, Irene (ed.), *Leadership and Political Institutions of India* (New Jersey: 1959).

Patel, G.I., *Vithalbhai Patel: Life and Times*. 2 Vols. (Bombay: 1950).

Patel, Maniben, *Borsad Satyagraha* (Ahmedabad: 1972).

Patel, P.U., *India's Man of Destiny* (Bombay: 1964).

Patel, Raojibhai, *Hind Ke Sardar* (Ahmedabad: Navajivan, 1972).

Patel, S.H., *The Congress Party and the Princely States* (Bombay: 1981).

Pathak, Devavrat Nanubhai and Sheth, Pravin, *Sardar Vallabhbhai Patel: From Civic to National Leadership* (Ahmedabad: Navajivan, 1980).

Phadnis, Urmila, *Towards the Integration of Indian States: 1919-1949* (London, 1968).

Philips, C.H. and Wainwright, M.D. (ed.), *The Partition of India: Policies and Perspectives, 1935-47* (London: 1970).

Plant, Raymond, *Modern Political Theory* (London: Blackwell Publishers, 1991).

Pocock, David, *Kanbi and Patidar: A Study of the Patidar Community of Gujarat* (London, Oxford, 1972).

Prasad, Beni, *States in Ancient India* (Allahabad: 1929).

Prasad, Rajendra, *Autobiography* (Bombay: 1957)

Prasad, S.N. and Pal, Dharm, *Operation in Jammu and Kashmir* (New Delhi: Ministry of Defence, 1987).

Prasad, S.N., *Operation Polo: The Police Action Against Hyderabad, 1948* (New Delhi: Ministry of Defence, 1972).

Publication Division, *Sardar Patel* (New Delhi: 1975).

Pyarelal, *Mahatma Gandhi: The Last Phase*, 2 Vols. (Ahmedabad: Navajivan).

Rajagopalachari, C., *Reconciliation* (Bombay: Hind Kitab, 1946).

Rajagopalachari, C., *The Way Out* (Bombay: 1943).

Ramusack, Barbara, *The Princes of India in the Twilight of Empire: Dissolution of A Patron-Client System: 1914-39* (Columbus: Ohio, 1978).

Rao, B.S., *The Framing of India's Constitution: A Study* (Nasik: Government of India Press, 1968.)

Raphel, D.D., *Problems of Political Philosophy* (London: Pall-Mall Press, 1970).

Rau, B.N., *India's Constitution in the Making* (Madras: Orient Longman, 1960).

Ravindranath, P.K. (ed.), *Sardar Patel: A New Perspective* (Bombay: Sardar Patel Birth Centenary Celebrations Committee, 1978).

Reichenback, Hans, *The Rise of Scientific Philosophy* (Berkeley: University of California Press, 1951).

Rosen, Michael and Wolff, Jonathan (ed.), *Political Thought* (London: Oxford University Press, 1999).

Rudolph, Lloyd, I. and Rudolph, Susanne, Hoeber, *The Modernity of Tradition: Political Development in India* (New Delhi: Orient Longman, 1987). Originally published by the Chicago University Press, Chicago, 1967.

Russell, Bertand, *History of Western Political Philosophy* (London: George Allen and Unwin Ltd., 1961).

Sabine, George, H., *A History of Political Theory* (Calcutta: Oxford and IBH Publishing Co., 1973).

Saggi, P.D. (ed.), *A Nation's Homage: Life and work of Sardar Vallabhbhai Patel* (Bombay: Overseas Publishing House, 1951).

Sarin, L.N., *Sardar Patel* (New Delhi: S. Chand and Co. Pvt. Ltd., 1972).

Shah, Ghanshyam, *Protest Movements in Two States: A Study of the Gujarat and Bihar Movements* (Delhi, 1977).

Shah, Gunwant, *The Peerless Sardar* (Ahmedabad: Navajivan, 1984).

Shankar, V., *My Reminiscences of Sardar Patel*, 2 Vols. (New Delhi: Macmillan, 1974-75).

Shankardass, Rani Dhavan, *Vallabhbhai Patel: Power and Organisation in Indian Politics* (New Delhi: Orient Longman, 1988).

Shankardass, Rani Dhavan, *The First Congress Raj: Provincial Autonomy in Bombay* (Delhi: 1982).

Shekhdiwala, J. (ed.), *Sardar: An Anthology of Articles on Sardar Patel* (Vallabh Vidya Nagar: S.P. University, 1976).

Sheth, Hiralal, *The Iron Dictator: A Biographical Study of Gandhiji's Greatest General: Sardar Vallabhbhai Patel* (Lahore: Hero Publication, 1945).

Sibley Mulford, O., *Political Ideas and Ideologies: A History of Political Thought* (Delhi: Surjeet Publications, Indian Reprint, 1981), Originally published by Harper and Row, USA.

Singh, Anita Inder, *The Origin of the Partition of India: 1936-47* (New Delhi: 1987).

Singh, G.P. (ed.), *Sardar Patel: The Working of His Mind* (New Delhi: Rajhans Publications, 1948).

Singh, L.P., *Sardar Patel and the Indian Administration* (New Delhi: Uppal Publication, 1978).

Singh, Mubarak, *Sardar Vallabhbhai Patel: The Man of Few Words and Many Triumphs* (Lahore: 1945).

Singh, Yogendra, *Modernisation of Indian Tradition* (Jaipur: Rawat Publications, 1972).

Sitaramayya, Pattabhi, *The History of the Indian National Congress: 1935-47* (New Delhi: S. Chand & Co. 1969).

Strokes, Eric (ed.), *The Peasant and the Raj: Studies in Agrarian Society, Colonial India and Peasant Rebellion* (Cambridge: 1978).

Tahamankar, D.V., *Sardar Patel* (London: George Allen and Unwin, 1970).

Tendulkar, Vijaya, *The Last Days of Sardar Patel* (Bombay: Popular Prakashan, 1993).

Thomson, David (ed.), *Political Ideas* (London: Pelican Books, 1965).

Tiwari, A.R.G., *Ordeal of the Leader* (Vallab Vidya Nagar: S.P. University, 1984).

Tiwari, Arya Ramachandra, *Making of the Leader: Sardar Vallabhbhai Patel* (Vallabhbhai Vidyanagar: Sardar Patel University, 1967).

Tomlinson, B.R., Imperialism, Nationalism and Indian Politics: The Indian National Congress: 1932-42 (London: Cambridge, 1973).

Tomlinson, B.R., *The Indian National Congress and the Raj; 1929-42: The Penultimate Phase* (London: Macmillan, 1976).

Varma, Mukurbehari, *Loh Purush, Sardar Patel* (Delhi: 1970).

Varma, V.P., *Ancient and Medieval Indian Political Thought* (Agra: Laxmi Narayan Publication, 1989).

Varma, Vishwanath Prasad, *Studies in Hindu Political Thought and its Metaphysical Foundations* (New Delhi: 1974).

Wayper, C.L., *Political Thought* (New Delhi: B.I. Publications, Indian Edition, 1984).

Wolf, Eric, *Peasant Wars of the Twentieth Century* (London: 1971).

Wood, John, *The Political Integration of British and Princely Gujarat: The Historical and Political Variable in Indian State Politics* (New York: Columbia University, 1970).

Yagnik, Indulal, *Atmakatha,* Vols. I, II and III (Ahmedabad: 1967, 70 and 76).

Zakaria, Rafiq, *Sardar Patel and Indian Muslims* (Mumbai: Bharatiya Vidya Bhavan, 1996).

Zakaria, Rafiq, *The Man Who Divided India* (Mumbai: Popular Prakashan, 2001).

8. Articles

Aiyar, S.P., "Some Aspects of the Study of Modern Indian Political Thought", *The Indian Journal of Political Science*, Vol. XXXIII, No. 4, Oct.-Dec. 1972, pp. 401-02.

Anthony, Frank, "Friend of Minorities", *Citizen's Council*, New Delhi, 1969.

Bhave, Vinoba, "The Man", *Citizen's Council*, New Delhi, 1965.

Bose, Ashish, "Municipal Socialism", *Economic and Political Weekly*, Vol. VI, No.12, March 20, 1971.

Bose, Ashish, "Municipal Socialism", *Economic and Political Weekly*, Vol. VI, No. 12, March 20, 1971.

Charlesworth, Neil, "The Middle Peasant Thesis and The Roots of Rural Agitations in India, 1914-17", *The Journal of Peasant Studies*, 7, 1979-80.

Chaturvedi, Badrinath, "The Place of Individual in Indian Political Thought and Polity", in Imtiaz Ahmed, Partha Ghosh and Helmul Reifeld (ed.), Pluralism and Equality: Values in Indian Society and Politics (New Delhi: Sage Publications, 2000, p. 34).

Dalton, Dennis, "The Dandi Drama" in Peter Robb and David Taylor (ed.), *Rule Protest Identity: Aspects of Modern South Asia* (London: 1978).

Giri, V.V., "Architect of India", *The Indian Nation*, 15 December, 1974.

Gokhale, Balkrishna Govind, "Sardar Vallabhbhai Patel : The Party Organiser As A Political Leader", in Richard L. Park and Irene Tinker, (ed.), *Leadership and Political Institution in India* (Princeton: 1959).

Gough, Kathleen, "Indian Peasant Uprisings", *Economic and Political Weekly*, IX, August, 1974.

Hardiman, David, "The Roots of Rural Agitation in India, 1914-1947: A Reply to Charlesworth", *The Journal of Peasant Studies*, 8, July, 1982.

Iengar, H.V.R., "Sardar's Ways: Focus on Main Tasks", *The Indian Express*, 31 May, 1965.

Iengar, H.V.R., "On Working Together," *The Indian Express*, 18 September, 1969.

Iengar, H.V.R., "The Image of the Police", *The Indian Express*, 8 September, 1966.

Iengar, H.V.R., "Officials and Ministers", *The Indian Express*, 8 July, 1964.

Iengar, H.V.R., "Sardar Patel – A Man of Decision", *The Indian Express*, 7 May, 1964.

Iengar, H.V.R., "Making of Decisions by Government", *The Indian Express*, 4 February, 1964.

Iengar, H.V.R., "The Image of the Police", *The Indian Express*, 8 September, 1966.

Iengar, H.V.R., "Officials and Ministers", *The Indian Express*, 8 July, 1964.

Jagmohan, "The Ground Architect", *Hindustan Times*, 3 November, 2000.

Kamath, H.V., "Sardar Vallabhbhai Patel: Some Memories", *Bhavan's Journal*, 16 January, 1982.

Kelekar, Kaka, "Long Live Sardar", *Mangal Prabhat*, January, 1951.

Low, D.A., "Dominant Peasants: Intimations from Asia", *Flinders Asian Studies*, Lecture 12, June, 1981.

Mahajan, Meherchand, "Answer to Plebiscite Demands", *Bhavan's Journal*, 5 December, 1965.

Marwick, Dwain, "Political Decision Makers in Contrasting Milius" in Marwick (ed.), *Political Decision Makers, Recruitment and Performance* (Glencoe: Free Press, 1961).

Mavalankar, G.V., "Sardar Patel", *The Tribune*, 3 November, 1945.

Metcalf, Thomas, R., "Rural Society and British Rule in Nineteenth Century India", *Journal of Asian Studies*, XXXIX, 1 November 1979.

Mishra, Ranganath, "Why Do We Remember Sardar Patel Today", *Patel Memorial Lectures*, 13 October, 1995.

Morris Jones, W.H., "Parochialism in Political Thought", *Political Studies*, Vol. 20, No. 4, 1972, pp. 475-77.

Mukherjee, Mridula, "Peasant Resistance and Peasant Consciousness in Colonial India-Subaltern and Bengal", Part I and II, *Economic and Political Weekly*, 15 October, 1988.

Narayan, Jayaprakash, "Sardar Patel", *The Indian Nation*, 15 and 22 December, 1978.

Narayan, Jayaprakash, "Sardar Patel: A Reappraisal", *Bhavan's Journal*, 22 December, 1974.

Narayan, Jayaprakash, "Sardar's Immortal Legacy", *Swantra Jyoti*, 1973.

Palmer, Norman D., "Indian and Western Political Thought: Coalescence and Clash", *American Political Science Review*, Vol. 9, No. 3, September, 1955, p.761.

Patel Vallabhbhai, "When I was a Child", *Shankar's Weekly, Children's Special*, December, 1949.

Patel, H.M., "Sardar and the First Year of Independence", in *Sardar Patel: Collection of Sardar Patel Memorial Lectures* (Vallabh Vidyanagar: 1982).

Rajagopalchari, C., "The Good Administrator", in *Patel Memorial Lectures*, 1955-85 (New Delhi: Publication Division, 1990).

Ram, Jagajivan, "The Great Administrator", *The Statesman*, 31 October, 1950.

Shah, Ghanshyam, "Traditional Society and Political Mobilisations: The Experience of the Bordoli Satyagrha (1920-28)", Contributions to Indian Sociology, New Series, 1974.

Shanin, Teodor, "Peasantry as a Political Factor", *Sociological Review*. 14 January 1966.

Shankar, V., "India of Sardar's Dream and Reality" in *Sardar Patel: Collection of Sardar Patel Memorial Lectures* (Vallabh Vidyanagar, 1982).

Shankardass, Rani Dhavan, "Spokesman for the Peasantry: The Case of Vallabhbhai Patel and Bordoli", *Studies in History*, Vol. 2, No. 1, 1986.

Shankardass, Rani Dhavan, "Patelism Sans Gandhism: An Inadequate Alternative to Nehruvism, *Mainstream*, 9 January, 1988.

Shankardass, Rani Dhavan, "What we Lost In 1947", *Mainstream*, 26 January, 1988.

Spodek, Howard, "On the Origin of Gandhi's Political Methodology: The Heritage of Kathiawar and Gujarat", *Journal of Asian Studies*, XXX, 2 February, 1971.

Spodek, Howard, "Sardar Vallabhbhai Patel at 100", *Economic and Political Weekly*. Vol. X, No. 50, 13 December, 1975.

Vajpayee, Anil Kumar, "Sardar Patel and Pandit Nehru: A Comparative View", *Bharatiya Pragna*, Vol. 2, Number 10, October, 2000.

Wolf, Eric, "Peasant Rebellion" in Teodar Shanin (ed.), *Peasant Studies*, Select Readings (London: 1971).

Wood, John, R., "British Versus Princely Legacies and the Political Integration of Gujarat", *Journal of Asian Studies*. XLIV, 1 November, 1984.

Zakaria, Rafiq, "Was Partition a Historic Blunder"? *Hindustan Times*, 14 January, 2002.

Index

M

N

O

P

U

V

W

Y